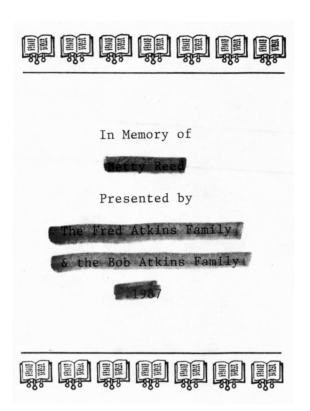

THIS BOOK BELONGS TO

_____

_____

_____

ABOVE: Fully jointed German Teddy Bears. ELI//Puppen und Spieltiere// Germany. Catalog Page, 1959.

LEFT: Fully jointed German Teddy Bears. ELI//Puppen und Spieltiere// Germany. Catalog page, 1959.

FRONT COVER

17in (43.2cm) tall very old mechanical Bruin-Teddy who pours from bottle and then lifts glass to drink. At the Teddy Bear Tree, White House Doll and Toy Museum, Hobby City, Anaheim, Ca. *Bea DeArmond Collection.*

IN OVAL: Early Ideal Teddy Bear in storage vault at Smithsonian, Museum of History and Technology, Washington, D.C. Note rounded ears and head, long nose, curved front paws, and long thick feet. *Photograph courtesy of Margaret Mandel.*

A Collector's History of the TEDDY BEAR

by Patricia N. Schoonmaker

Published by   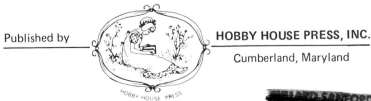   HOBBY HOUSE PRESS, INC.

Cumberland, Maryland

HOBBY HOUSE PRESS

Dedication

Written in the International Year of the Child, 1979, this book is affectionately dedicated to the children of the world and to the child in all of us.

TITLE PAGE DESCRIPTION

Comparative view of two early Steiff bears, 9½in. (24.9cm) and 10in. (25.4cm) tall, one with glass eyes and one with shoe-button eyes. Button in ear. Left: *Judy Johnson Collection.* Right: *Helen Sieverling Collection.*

© 1981 Hobby House Press, Inc.
Second Printing 1981
Third Printing 1983
Fourth Printing 1985, © Patricia N. Schoonmaker and John Schoonmaker.
Printed in the United States of America
ISBN: 0-87588-161-0

Table Of Contents

Acknowledgments

Teddy Bear collectors are the most sharing and generous people imaginable! When help was needed, one had only to ask to receive and usually much additional material was offered. Warm friendships have been formed, thanks to the Teddy Bears.

So many people were generously helpful in contributing to this book that one hesitates to compile a list of names for fear of inadvertently omitting someone. Each and every person who offered assistance is extended sincere thanks.

Without the permission of Harry J. Guckert of *Playthings* to publish original material from this trade magazine, the book would not have been nearly as definitive. Deep appreciation goes to his assistant, Priscilla Meyer, who was instrumental in assisting with the research.

Thanks are also extended to Lt. Col. T. R. Henderson, the Historian of **Good Bears of the World,** for allowing use of his article "Collecting Bears" as the Foreword and for the additional enriching material he furnished. Mr. Jim Ownby graciously granted permission to use material from *Bear Tracks* to tell the story of **Good Bears of the World.**

Dorothy S. Coleman, author of *The Collector's Encyclopedia of Dolls,* took time in her busy life to note Teddy Bear factories in *Toys and Novelties,* a trade magazine, while working on her own latest book. Mary Hillier from England sent some entries, adding an extra dimension which would not have been possible otherwise. Mr. A. Christian Revi, of *Spinning Wheel,* gave permission to reprint a rare catalog page on Teddy Bear spoons from his magazine.

One cannot adequately thank Loraine Burdick, fellow researcher and good friend, who bundled up her complete and extensive file on Teddy Bears for use in compiling this book. The premium offers, as well as many other sections of the book, would not have been nearly as complete without her help. Ruth Douglas loaned an enormous stack of vintage magazines to clip where necessary for photographing. This also contributed to the fascinating premium and advertising section.

Patricia Rowland, who responded to a plea for help in *Bear Tracks* magazine, the **Good Bears of the World** newsletter, has given help beyond measure. She had her bears photographed by Dale Smith and Tony Rankin and shared her priceless collection of Steiff catalogs, post cards and other Bearmobilia treasures. Susan Gaskill, also a Good Bear member, wrote lots of exciting bear news and sent photographs of some of her bears.

Helen Sieverling, a fellow doll collector, brought four large boxes of rare and valuable bears to be photographed and studied. She has given much support and further help as well.

Doll club members Jean Anderson, Naiadene Blackburn, Thelma Bouchey, Lola Escarcega, Jeanne Niswonger and Gerrie Voorhees loaned precious family photographs to be copied. Thelma Bouchey loaned the tapestry of Santa Claus with Teddy as well. Betty Brink, a former national United Federation of Doll Clubs President, sent her entire file of Teddy Bear items. Special permission was asked of Robert Tynes to reprint the article "Have You Ever Performed a Growlectomy" which first appeared in the Fall 1977 issue of *Doll News.* Parts of the article "Theodore Roosevelt, More Than A Teddy Bear" by Robert Zimmerman, from the Summer 1978 issue, is reprinted by permission of *Doll News* and the author.

A tremendous thank you goes to artist/writer Beverly Port, who has spread so much joy with her Teddy Bear articles in *Doll News, Bernice's Bambini* and elsewhere. Vivian and Jim Larson loaned the rare cartoon from *Judge* magazine, and sent considerable information about their outstanding collection.

Rich Rusnock sent rare paper dolls through the mail, as did Kay Bransky. Joyce Stafford, a NIADA artist, gave permission to use her original art work and so did Betty Grime. Betsy Slap sent a lot of paper doll data on bears.

Bea DeArmond opened cases in her museum to work mechanical bears and showed the wonders of the Teddy Bear Tree at the White House Doll and Toy Museum at Hobby City, Anaheim, California.

Mr. F. M. Gosling loaned a rare Teddy Bear factory photograph from his files, as well as rare Cracker Jack Bears card and a Teddy Bear Bread advertising booklet.

Judy Johnson, a Poppy Doll Club member, loaned her bears for study. Margaret Mandel telephoned long distance to see if bear photographs could still be accepted and sent more good information. A local collector who wishes to remain anonymous was most hospitable in allowing her outstanding collection to be photographed.

Bill Boyd allowed a selection from among his 500 spoons with bears on them to be photographed. Appreciation also goes to Elizabeth R. Copeland, Diana Downing, Rita Dubas, Frankie James, Jean Millen, Florence Mosseri, Fern Olson, Phyllis Roberts, Arline Roth, Audrey Anne Shuman, Elayne Shuman, Billie Tyrrell and Anita Wright.

To my husband, John Schoonmaker, who did so much of the photography and made countless trips to Camera Graphics with old catalogs from our own collection, many many thanks. To Virginia Ann Heyerdahl and Donna Felger for their patient and kindly editing efforts to make this a better book, go my sincere appreciation. And last of all, sincere thanks to the publisher, Gary R. Ruddell, for believing in this book.

Introduction

Since the beginning of my interest in collecting Teddy Bears and dolls, I have yearned to pour over the early pages of the American trade magazine, *Playthings.* The process of writing this book has enabled me to do so.

Some of the material has been touched upon in the past, at least in prose, but scarcely at all pictorially. I wondered if the dates later given by factories were correct, since the passage of time often clouds the memory. I longed to see for myself how the first bears looked, and to read the editorials of the day to better understand the phenomenal acceptance of the Teddy Bear into the world of toys.

The waiting was well worth the culmination; the material was fascinating. There has been a great need in the collecting world to identify more of the bears than has been possible in the past. There will be still further researching to do on Teddy Bears but the material in this book will bring collectors much nearer to the early true facts of the day, without myth or legend.

How To Use This Book

You may have only the year of your bear as a clue. Study the Advertising chapter since it is arranged chronologically. You may be able to find a similar, if not identical, bear. If you are fortunate enough to own one of the Teddy Bears in the Identification Aids chapter, you will find much more about his background there. Also study the Teddies chapter for a similar item which may have original tags or marks, noting the shape of the head, the length of the legs and other workmanship. Any photograph or sketch of an identified bear is a clue, if you **own** one of those particular specimens. They are recognizable. You will find a thorough study of the many types will make identification much easier. It is an adventure. Enjoy!

Foreword
Collecting Bears

The hobby of collecting models of bears is called arctophily. Lovers of bears are arctophiles and collectors of bear-like models--arctophilists. These words are derived from the Greek words "arktos," bear, and "philos," friend or lover, in the same way as Arctic and Arcadia (Bear Country) and the name Arthur (Bear Man).

Every model bear in a collection tells a story, and by association has links with people, places or things; especially a Teddy Bear. That is how a collection of bears grows. The bears are souvenirs as well as symbols of love, friendship, happiness and security.

Collecting bears in this way is a most enjoyable pastime. It appeals to the hunting instinct (without cruelty). Wherever you go you can look around for specimens. It is a great game that can be played anywhere, at anytime, and for as long as you like on each occasion. And you will find that every bear tells a different story. Therein lies their widespread interest.

As the collection grows it attracts the interest of like-minded people, who can then group together to form a local Teddy Bear Club. Quite a number of people in both the United States and the United Kingdom, as well as in the rest of Europe and elsewhere, have formed small dens around collections in this way. The members of the groups have great fun comparing notes and helping each other by sharing bear stories. Or organizing Teddy Bear picnics for children.

Once a collection becomes known, bears come to one from all directions on all sorts of occasions, just because they are souvenirs of so many different associations. In fact, they appear to multiply like rabbits.

There are no bears in Australia, but the Koala looks like a bear, so much so in fact that it is frequently referred to as a bear—the Australian tree-bear. Likewise in China, the Giant Panda which is the largest member of the raccoon family, is called the white bear. Accordingly, Koalas and Giant Pandas are included in the fold when it comes to collecting model bears. A model bear, especially a Teddy Bear, and more especially a friendly-looking soft and cuddly one, serves as a totem, that is, an outward symbol of an existing intimate unseen relationship. If it is a good model, or a good Teddy-Bear, it is a good totem or motif.

From this point of view the word "model" should be considered in both senses of its two meanings, namely as a three-dimensional imitation, generally in miniature, and also as a pattern of excellence. Only "model" models of the bear are worthy of being called "Good Bears of the World."

Historian GBW
Lt. Colonel T. R. Henderson
Edinburgh, Scotland

Lt. Col. Robert Henderson, with part of his collection. Photographed by W. G. Allan Inglis.

SHIRLEY TEMPLE . . . . 20th CENTURY-FOX PLAYER

Illustration 1. Shirley Temple and her large white Teddy Bear. *Arline Roth Collection.*

Color Illustration 3. A famous "Teddy" who modeled for the Lettie Lane paper doll series by Sheila Young. He was 71 years old in 1979. *Elizabeth Copeland Collection.* Niece of the artist. *Photograph by Elizabeth Copeland.*

Color Illustration 2. 14½ in. (36.9cm) blue mechanical bear with silk taffeta ribbon. Brown glass eyes with black pupils. Non-jointed head, metal box in torso with excelsior. Metal legs covered with long pile plush. Hand embroidered brown nose. Black claws on front paws. Bear walks, stops and growls, walks again. *Helen Sieverling Collection.*

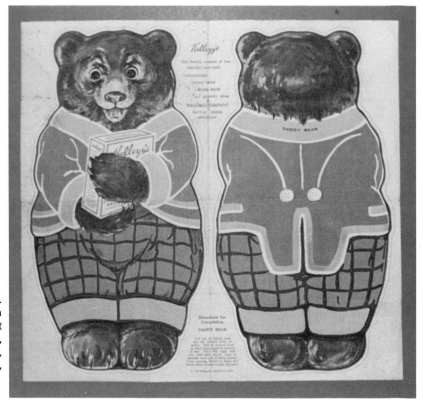

Color Illustration 4. 17 in. x 15½ in. (43.2cm x 39.4cm) uncut cloth premium, Kellogg's "Daddy Bear." Set also included Goldilocks, Mama Bear, and Johnny Bear. Copyrighted 1925, Kellogg Company, Battle Creek, Michigan.

2

Color Illustration 5.   5¾in x 9in (14.7cm x 22.9cm) box top of "TEDDY BEAR AND HIS FRIENDS." Set is Number 190 by Platt and Munk Co., Inc. The friends were pig, puppy, rabbit, kitten and monkey dolls. *Rich Rusnock Collection.*

Color Illustration 6. Woven tapestry of Santa Claus with Teddy Bear and rabbit, approximately 12 in. x 12 in. (30.5cm x 30.5cm). *Thelma Bouchey Collection.*

Color Illustration 7. Two of a series showing Teddy driving an automobile filled with dolls while small toys spill out into the snow. Second view shows Teddy guiding a toboggan, the "Xmas Limited." International Art Publishing Co., New York, Berlin, Printed in Germany.

Color Illustration 8.   "TEDDY BEAR AND HIS FRIENDS," set Number 190, Platt and Munk Co., Inc., publishers, Circa 1933. Teddy Bear models sailor suit. Extra costumes are Pilgrim costume (hat missing) and baseball suit. *Rich Rusnock Collection.*

Illustration 2. Marie O'Leary Anderson and her Teddy Bear. 1907.

Illustration 3. Gerrie Mangham Voorhies and her Teddy Bear. 1914.

Illustration 4. Emily Pesqueira, 18 months old, hugging her Teddy. 1940.

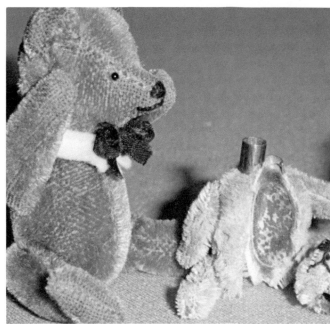

Color Illustration 10. 5¼ in. (13.4cm) miniature red brown bear, 3½ in. (8.9cm) opened compact bear, 5 in. (12.7cm) gold perfume bottle bear with head removed. *Helen Sieverling Collection.*

Color Illustration 9. 11 in. (27.9cm) gold Shuco German bear. Moving the tail causes this mechanical bear to nod yes or no. Tan German bear, fully jointed. Clear glass eyes with black pupils. Hand embroidered nose. Oblong metal tags on bottom feet read: "KERSA." *Helen Sieverling Collection.*

Color Illustration 11. 11½ in. (29.2cm) tall bear, light gold short plush. Brown glass eyes with dark pupils. Fully jointed. Peach tan felt pads. Black embroidered nose.

Color Illustration 12. 14½ in. (36.9cm) fully jointed white bear. Dark brown glass eyes with black pupils. Companion is rare black bear. Gold glass eyes with black pupils. Long pile wool plush fur. Claws are embroidered on the felt paws. *Helen Sieverling Collection.*

Color Illustration 13. 8½ in. (21.6cm) Father Christmas Bear, long coat-body of maroon blanket cloth. White plush face with black bead eyes and black embroidered nose. 3½ in. (8.9cm) lavender compact bear and 5 in. (12.7cm) gold perfume bottle bear plus choice miniature 5¼ in. (13.4cm) red brown bear with painted nose and beady eyes. *Helen Sieverling Collection.*

Color Illustration 14. 13 in. (33.0cm) Bruno Mfg. Co. Teddy Bear. Fully jointed. Hand embroidered pointed nose, humped back. Blue-gold woven label on right foot reads: "B. M. C." *Helen Sieverling Collection.*

Color Illustration 15. Very early Steiff (button in ear) cub "Teddy Baby." Clear glass eyes with black pupils. Long pile plush with sheared nose and feet. Brown embroidered claws. *Judy Johnson Collection.*

Color Illustration 16. 14½ in. (36.9cm) pale golden short pile plush bear. Button eyes and black embroidered nose. Hump on back. Front legs are 7 in. (17.8cm) long, rear legs 6½ in. (16.5cm) with tan felt pads.

Illustration 5. This shows two cubs, Sigismund and his sister, Brunetta, who have bent down the lowest branches of the plum tree. They thought they never tasted anything so delicious. Finally they are chased by a man and his dogs into the woods. *Plums,* a fable, 1879.

I. History Of The Teddy Bear
Prior To The Teddy Bear

Who claims credit for the Teddy Bear? There are many legitimate claimants, others whose claims might be somewhat dubious, plus still others who made few claims but could have done so. These include the artists and authors who helped bring about the birth of the Teddy Bear, many years prior to its actual inception, by their great fondness for sketching bears in all manner of fanciful adventures.

The Mike Indians in north central Arizona included in their deities the bear-god representing a mystic idea. This bear-god, an Indian in costume, danced in the annual rites and ceremonies of the tribe which probably date back to prehistoric times. Kachina-type dolls were made to symbolize this bear-god and these, in turn, were eventually given to the children of the tribe. Therefore, the Indian children were among the first to play with a "toy" bear.

Fierce mechanical bears were popular in the mid-1800s and later. The bear could be a formidable enemy with his great strength and ferociousness in the days when he roamed freely in the woods. At the same time a young cub possessed such appeal that the grown bear must have created great ambivalence in the mind of man who had to deal with him; we are often fascinated by that of which we are frightened. The bear as a subject has such magnetism that it is nearly uncomprehensible. There surely was a great urge on the part of many to tame this gigantic creature.

The talented Palmer Cox, more well-known for his Brownie creations, drew caricatures of bears for children's stories and used them as well to advertise Tarrant's Aperient Seltzer in 1887. The remedy was said to be "pleasant to the taste, readily taken by the smallest child or delicate invalid."

In 1888, manufacturers for Behr upright pianos illustrated their advertisements with three rollicking "upright" bears.

Included here is a copy of a trade card given with coffee by the Woolsen Spice Company in 1894. The fairy tale illustrated is that of "Rose Red and Snow White" gaily dancing with the great Bear. The story on the reverse side gives a clue to this yet unfulfilled yearning for a Teddy Bear:

> "In a cottage in the forest once lived two maidens with their mother, one so fair she was called Snow White--the other so rosey she was named Rose Red. One evening a Bear knocked at their door for shelter; every evening after that he came, and soon became their dear companion and playmate. Several times, in walking through the woods, the sisters met an ugly Dwarf, who was robbing the Bear of his treasures of jewels and gold; while talking with him up came the Bear, and with one blow he killed the Dwarf, and was transformed into a handsome prince, who had been enchanted by the Dwarf. He married Snow White, and his brother, Rose Red."

Fairy tales did not always come true in real life but gave great hope to those of simple lives and little opportunity. Yet the Bear becoming "the dear companion and playmate" of young children was to become a reality within a few more years with the creation of the Teddy Bear as we know him today.

Pettijohn's Breakfast Food conducted a large campaign for their product in 1889-1890 with "Bear in Mind, Our Trade Mark" printed on the back of a huge bear. These illustrated Bruins are nearly always standing, man-like, and were presented in a series of tableaux in assorted publications. These advertisements are collector's items in themselves.

" I find it good to regulate
The organs of both small and great.
It checks Sick Headache, and the woe
That sad Dyspeptics ever know.
Besides, 'tis pleasant to the taste
And none need gulp it down in haste.
The sparkling liquid quickly charms

The Infant in the Mother's arms.
While drooping age will strive to drain
Each drop the goblet does contain.
How seldom in our life we find
A Remedy and treat combined.
This Effervescent Seltzer fine
A blessing proves to me and mine."

Illustration 6. Advertisement for Tarrant's Seltzer Aperient, with artwork by Palmer Cox, famous for his Brownies. 1887.

Why do they wear those Medals?

Because they are the ONLY "Upright Behr's"!

Illustration 7. Advertisement for Behr upright pianos which had won awards at the World's Industrial and Cotton Centennial Exposition, New Orleans, Louisiana, 1888.

9

ABOVE: Color Illustration 18. A nursery rocker toy by Raphael Tuck. A double rocker set the toy in motion. From a boxed set of ten toys with verses by Norman Gale, this one reads: "At parties children should be neat, and not appear with muddy feet!"

LEFT: Color Illustration 17. 14 in. (35.6cm) standing "Teddy Baby" Steiff cub with button in ear. Pads were once peach with black claws. Original collar is clamped together with two Steiff buttons, and may have had a leash originally. Button in ear is twice as large as those on collar. *Judy Johnson Collection.*

Color Illustration 19. 11 in. (27.9cm) and 10½ in. (26.7cm) tall bears. Inexpensive examples at time of manufacture. Blown glass eyes on glass stem. Squeaker. Left: *Judy Johnson Collection.*

Color Illustration 20. Fully jointed. Brown glass eyes with dark pupil. Long pile plush, heavily stitched black yarn nose. Brown felt pads. Label on chest: "Hygienic Toys//Made in England by//Chad Valley Co. Ltd." Label on foot: "The Chad Valley Co, Ltd//By appointment//Toymakers to//H.M. The Queen."

Color Illustration 21. Unique teddy with composition (wood pulp) head. White satin bodice and blue print material. Circa World War II era.

Color Illustration 22. 10 in. (25.4cm) size early button in ear Steiff, short pile plush. Brown glass eyes with dark pupil. Tan-peach felt pads, squeaker. Fully jointed. Front legs are 5 in. (12.7cm), rear legs 4½ in. (11.5cm). Ribbon woven in metallic silver reads "Merry Christmas." *Judy Johnson Collection.*

Color Illustration 23. Pull toy of bear in muzzle on platform 9½ in. x 3¼ in. (24.2cm x 8.3cm). Bright gold mohair plush glued over a shaped model. Stands 6 in. (15.2cm) tall at shoulder. *Helen Sieverling Collection.*

11

One might think there was no such thing as a Bear Picnic before the writing of the well-renowned song. "There is nothing new under the sun" is the old saying. The discovery of an illustration from the "Children's Page" of the August 9, 1894, *The Youth's Companion,* conceived and executed by artist, D. Ericson, was amazing. Mother bear, in a fancy bonnet, hands out pie and cookies to eager youngsters. Many decades later, collectors would design similar scenes for exhibits or dioramas.

It is said there is no stopping an idea whose time has come. The Teddy Bear's era was soon to come to fruition and those concerned with this greatest staple toy of all time did not know how to evaluate his happening. Manufacturers who decided he was a fad and would surely soon die down, changed their minds and decided he was as strong as ever. They debated pro and con on his future popularity. But the Teddy Bear was to fill a basic need as simple as that for food. He made one brave, was a dear friend and companion, never-complaining and ever-faithful.

Preceding the Teddy Bears, the very first comic strip was that of "Little Bears and Tigers," created by James Swinnerton, first appearing in the *San Francisco Examiner* in 1892. When the eminent Marlon Perkins of the St. Louis Zoo and the television program "The Wild Kingdom" was asked what the single most popular animal was, he replied: "The bears."

Being a collector of Teddy Bears, along with antique dolls, I first wrote about them for the Souvenir Book of the United Federation of Doll Clubs in 1963. Later my husband and I were to do a slide program, "The Great Teddy Bear Saga," for a Regional Conference in California which was eventually repeated by request at a National Conference. When preparing this program we decided we would not include any actual bears or bear toys, only to discover that they were so intermeshed with the toy Teddies that it was impossible to separate them and still appreciate the full story. NOTE: A true Teddy Bear was usually jointed, cuddly and huggable. However, metal bear figures, mechanical bear toys, majolica china figures of bears and other items were referred to as Teddy Bears.

This dilemma of real bear or toy Teddy is illustrated on a divided-back post card of 1909. An erect Bruin mother and father stand looking at a seated Teddy with a worried mother saying to father, "Did we look like that?" This was meant in jest, but there was a certain amount of reconciling in people's minds the new lovable, harmless toy with the age-old fearsome live bear. Strangely enough, due to the immense popularity of Theodore Roosevelt, even bear objects which were strictly Bruin were dubbed "Teddy Bears." It appears collectors need some new language to differentiate items which are not actually Teddy Bears, and, in this book, these will be referred to as "Bruin-Teddies," rather than the true toy Teddy Bears.

From the collector's standpoint, the fascination of the Teddy Bear is an example of the never-ending variety of possibilities on a single theme. The workmanship of the Teddy Bear can be superbly elaborate and complicated, or amazingly simple. The quality of a Teddy Bear may be very high or sometimes even interestingly crude. They are never boring -- provided you are interested in Teddies in the first place!

Illustration 8. Free trade card, Woolson Spice Company, Toledo, Ohio, included in packages of Lion's Coffee. Story on back of card reads: "He [the Bear] soon became their dear companion and playmate." 1894.

Illustration 9A. From pre-Teddy days. Some of these illustrations ran in *Munsey's Magazine, The Delineator, American Monthly Review* and *Harper's Magazine.* A free book by L. Frank Baum of "Oz" fame was offered. 1899.

Children Love It.

Pettijohn's Breakfast Food
THE WHOLE OF THE WHEAT

Nurses Recommend It.

The happiness which springs from perfect health is alone ample reason why you should eat little meat in summer, and **Pettijohn's Breakfast Food,** which contains all the elements of nutrition, affords an easy, perfectly satisfactory and delicious substitute for meat. All of the wheat but the overcoat.

At all Grocers, in 2-lb. Packages.

Pettijohn's Breakfast Food
ALL THE WHEAT BUT THE OVERCOAT

NERVES AND MUSCLES.

Healthy nerves and strong, flexible muscles depend upon diet and exercise. The selection of food should be an intelligent process. A perfect food is one that contains protein, fat and starch in such a proportion as to give a properly balanced ration. Pettijohn's Breakfast Food meets these requirements perfectly.

FREE MOTHER GOOSE IN PROSE. FREE
By L. FRANK BAUM.

THE AMERICAN CEREAL CO., Monadnock Bldg., Chicago, Ill.

IT IS ASTONISHING

how careless some people are about their breakfast. It must be appetizing—no one is hungry for breakfast. It must carry us through the hardest part of the day. **Pettijohn's Breakfast Food** redeems a poor breakfast. Makes a variety of delicious dishes.

Send your name and address at once, and we will send you free, our beautifully illustrated Pettijohn Booklet. Address THE AMERICAN CEREAL CO., Dept. P., Chicago, Ill.

Illustration 9B. Pettijohn Advertisement showing Bear Cubs, nearer to Teddy, than the usual full grown rampant bear. (Compare shape of front legs to Steiff's "Teddy Baby.") 1900.

Illustration 10. Jeanne DuChateau Niswonger, age two.

Illustration 11. A photograph post card. 1907. *Fern Olson Collection.*

14.

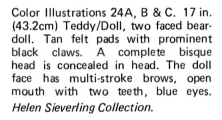

Color Illustrations 24A, B & C. 17 in. (43.2cm) Teddy/Doll, two faced bear-doll. Tan felt pads with prominent black claws. A complete bisque head is concealed in head. The doll face has multi-stroke brows, open mouth with two teeth, blue eyes. *Helen Sieverling Collection.*

Color Illustration 25. 3¼ in. (8.3cm) high German "scrap" figures. Circa 1908. *Loraine Burdick Collection.*

How It All Began

A PICNIC.

Illustration 12. Here is the "Teddy Bears Picnic" several years before the Teddy Bear was created. *The Youth's Companion,* 1894.

SEE "CHRISTMAS PICTURES" IN "OPEN LETTERS."
COLD SAUCE WITH THE CHRISTMAS PUDDING. BY F. S. CHURCH.

Illustration 13. Art work of F. S. Church showing a friendly, standing bear prior to the Teddy. 1894.

Beginnings can be complicated. But 1902 is definitely the earliest year possible for a true toy Teddy Bear to have appeared on the market. Many many versions of the origin of the Teddy Bear have been read with many facts repeated over and over again. Occasionally a writer seems to embellish the tale with tidbits of his own that do not seem to fit in with known history. Other errors are picked up and repeated from earlier writers with no basis in fact. It was decided to amass as much source material as possible and present it in this book to you, the reader, and allow you to make your own journey back through the years to 1902.

It was in this year that President Theodore Roosevelt traveled to Smedes, Mississippi, on November 10th, to settle a boundary dispute between Mississippi and Louisiana. In the ten days of hunting he did not shoot a single bear. Many accounts do not explain that the President was accompanied by an entourage including photographers and reporters. It was not **news** to have him end his sojourn without trophies. As they were about to leave, excited shouts of "Bear!" were heard outside the President's tent. He hurried out to discover a tiny cub tethered by a rope. Evidently those responsible were serious; here was the hunter's opportunity to finally "bag a bear." Roosevelt was contemptuous. He ordered the men to take it away, saying: "I draw the line. If I shot that little fellow I couldn't look my own boys in the face again."

Some accounts state that Clifford K. Berryman, the foremost political cartoonist of the day, was present in Mississippi and immediately drew the cartoon "Drawing the Line in Mississippi," which appeared in the *Washington Post.*

Mark Sullivan in Volume II of *Our Times* gives credit to Mr. Berryman for the Teddy Bear, saying:

> "The Teddy bear, beginning with Berryman's original cartoon, was repeated thousands of millions of times; in countless variations, pictorial and verbal, prose and verse; on the stage and in political debate; in satire or in humorous friendliness. Toy makers took advantage of its vogue; it became more common in the hands of children than the wooly lamb. For Republican conventions, and meetings associated with Roosevelt, the "Teddy Bear" became the standard decoration, more in evidence than the eagle, and only less usual than the Stars and Stripes."

In an article in *Good Old Days* magazine entitled "He Gave Us the Teddy Bear," by Wellington Brink, the author gives a personal account of events since he was a friend of Mr. Berryman's. Mr. Brink states that the artist could have made a million dollars had he chosen to sell his idea to a toy manufacturer. Instead, Mr. Berryman chose to use the little bear as a personal trademark. He cheerfully passed up the royalties he might have made, saying: "I have made thousands of children happy; that is enough for me."

Mr. Brink further states that the little bear made friends immediately. The morning after it first appeared in the paper, William E. Chandler, then President of the Spanish Claims Commission and a former senator from New Hampshire, called the artist to tell him that he and Senator Henry Cabot Lodge had laughed heartily at the little bear in the cartoon and hoped that Mr. Berryman would continue to draw him. Hundreds of letters poured in from many other sources offering congratulations to Mr. Berryman.

In a newspaper story of March 27, 1949, entitled "Teddy Bear Creator Still on Job at 80," essentially the same story is given regarding the 1902 bear cub, except that two men are said to have run up to the President with the cub on a rope. The story mentions that Berryman drew the pitiful little Bruin in such a way that the cartoon got a laugh from a stern New Englander, Senator Henry Cabot Lodge, and goes on to state that it was at Senator Lodge's

"The little bear strongly objected."

Illustration 14. Lifelike art work showing the fascinating family life of the bears. (Note the humps copied for early Teddy Bears.) *Chatterbox,* a magazine for children, 1899.

Illustration 15. Divided-back post card, by artist L. A. Davis, C. E. Bucklin and Company, card #54. This card points out the contrast of the familiar Bruin-Teddies and the newer toy Teddy Bears. 1909.

Illustration 16. Cartoon by Clifford K. Berryman. President Roosevelt refuses to shoot a helpless bear cub. November 10, 1902.

urging that Berryman continued to draw the little Bruin, forerunner of the actual Teddy toy. Hence the market for toy Teddy Bears flourished for years. The fact that Roosevelt decided he could not shoot the cub and face his sons afterwards is corroborated in this 1949 account.

Mr. Berryman, a Pulitzer Prize winner in 1944, was said to dislike publicity and chatted reluctantly about old times. When asked to name the subjects he found easiest to draw (he had been a cartoonist since the second Cleveland administration), Berryman picked up a pencil and in less than a minute roughly outlined the faces of Theodore Roosevelt, "Uncle" Joe Cannon, William Jennings Bryan and Franklin D. Roosevelt. Said not to be a caricaturist but a sketcher of true likenesses, the artist turned out the "spittin' images" of the quartet. "Teddy Roosevelt was the easiest with the goggles and teeth," he smiled.

Margaret Hutchings of England did a superb job of research on Teddy Bear origins in her *Book of the Teddy Bear.* She presented five cartoons by Mr. Berryman including one drawn for the artist's own father, never previously published. This depicts the President in full hunting garb, smiling and sitting with his arm around a smiling Bruin-Teddy Bear. This cartoon is even more appealing than the original 1902 effort since it symbolizes President Roosevelt as the defender of the underdog (or underbear?), the helpless or needy, which portrayal was so popular with the masses.

Another claimant as the originator of the Teddy Bear was Seymour Eaton, author of *The Roosevelt Bears* series of books. In 1943 his daughter, Jean Eaton Warren, wrote to *Life* magazine in reply to an article on wildlife in Australia in which mention had been made that the Teddy Bear was inspired by the koala.

She wrote: "I thought he might be interested to know that the teddy bear was named after "Teddy" Roosevelt. My father, the late Seymour Eaton, was the creator of this bear.

"During the Theodore Roosevelt administration he wrote a series of adventures in jingle form for children, called the *Adventures of the Roosevelt Bears.* The bears in these books resemble our toy bear of today. *Who's Who* gives my father the credit of creating the teddy bear, and I believe I am correct in stating that until these books were published, children did not have the bear as a toy."

The title of the first book by Seymour Eaton is *The Roosevelt Bears Their Travels and Adventures* published prior to Christmas, 1906. The works were copyrighted in 1905 since they originally appeared in the Sunday supple-

Illustration 17. Full page color Sunday supplement or "funny paper" of "The Roosevelt Bears Abroad." "Teddy B." and "Teddy G." "Meet the King of England." *The Sunday Oregonian,* Portland, 1907.

ments or comic sections of the newspaper. Included here is a 1909 illustration of one of these sheets, the original of which was in color, showing the bears meeting the King of England!

In reality "Teddy B." and "Teddy G." were not Teddy Bears by any stretch of the imagination. They were enormous Bruins, but were coming nearer to the Teddy Bear image due to their dispositions. They were friendly and approachable, which the real-life model certainly was not. Strangely enough, these storybook creatures would in turn inspire various toys which would classify as "Bruin-Teddies," by our own definition. Some of these items were advertised as "Teddy Bears" due to the great popularity of Theodore Roosevelt, and the great desire to be associated with him in the slightest manner.

Actually, the Seymour Eaton books have not received as much credit as perhaps they should have for the degree of influence they created. These books, which are highly cherished collector's items, will be dealt with in more detail in the chapter on books. Included here is one of the first advertisements for the first book.

Long forgotten in most accounts of the origin of the Teddy Bear is a story from *National Magazine,* the March, 1907, issue. A bright little girl was said to have written to the author to ask him to look up the origin of "Teddy Bears." The writer replied, stating that he could not give the data secured official countenance; he would repeat the story as he heard it. A man was said to have brought a pair of ten-week-old cubs to New York and exhibited them in Madison Square Garden. They were so young that they had to be fed every three or four hours so the fellow took them with him to his hotel room at night. When he overslept and did not give them their feeding one night, they made such noises that they awakened the other tenants in the hotel. The hotel clerk demanded to know what the uproar was all about. While the poor man was trying to warm the milk and quiet the cubs, he was ordered out of the hotel.

During a subsequent show, President Theodore Roosevelt is said to have taken a fancy to the cubs and finally bought them for his children. Later, when they became too large for pets, he presented them to the zoo in New York. They were the main attraction for all the children who knew them as "Teddy's Bears," and thus originated the name now applied.

To quote from the account of 1907:

"It took an alert German manufacturer [probably Steiff] to see the point of this little story; and when he saw it, he promptly began to make 'Teddy Bears,' rightly conjecturing that if the real bears had delighted the Roosevelt children, the reproductions would please children all over the country. Then the newspapers began to discuss the President's fondness for bear shooting; and thus the animals came into prominence, and the first thing we knew the Christmas market was flooded with bears of all sorts and sizes. 'Teddy Bears' came pouring in from Germany, and found their places in millions of homes, much to the joy of little ones. Where is the child who does not love to hug a furry bear; which not only satisfies the craving for a pet, but suggests to the infant mind stories about the President of the United States?"

Illustration 18. Advertisements for the first "Roosevelt Bears Book" for Christmas. "Teddy B." stands for black and brave, and "Teddy G." is gray and gay not bad and good Bears as has sometimes been reported. 1906.

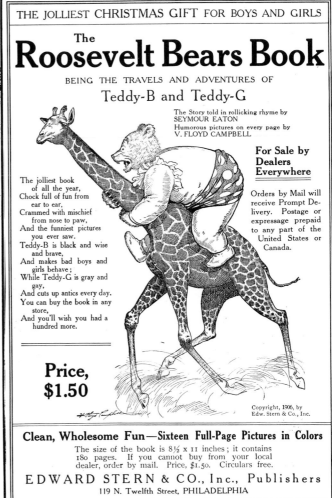

JUDGE'S PLATFORM: "STAND PAT. LEAVE WELL ENOUGH ALONE."

VOL. 52 NO. 1321   FEBRUARY 9, 1907   PRICE 10 CENTS

Judge

"DO I LOVE MY TEDDY BEARS?"

Illustration 19. Cover of *Judge* magazine. Satirical political cartoon by artist FLOHRI. February 9, 1907. *Vivian and Jim Larson Collection.*

The "Cracker Jack Bears" N°. 15.

Illustration 20. "Cracker Jack Bears" card #15. "Oh! Don't Shoot Mr. President. We're the Cracker Jack Bears," says the first bear. "Yes, we met you at the White House in Washington. Don't you remember?" pleads the second. 1907. *F. M. Gosling Collection.*

At first judgement, one might think the aforementioned series of events to be merely another myth, until one reads the legends on a #15 Cracker Jack Bears post card. Two large Bruins are speaking to the President from up in a tree. "Oh! Don't shoot Mr. President -- we're the Cracker Jack Bears," says one bear, while the second bear, looking below, says: "Yes, we met you at the White House in Washington, don't you remember?" The post card is dated 1907.

The Cracker Jack Bears are strongly reminiscent of the earlier Seymour Eaton Roosevelt Bears, actual Bruins with human powers of speech and actions. For more details on these intriguing characters, see the section on post cards.

The strongest claimant in America for the origin of the Teddy Bear is the Ideal Toy Corporation of New York. Mr. Benjamin Michtom, son of the late Russian-born Morris Michtom, founder of Ideal, wrote quite detailed explanations to Margaret Hutchings in 1964 when she was preparing her *Book of the Teddy Bear.* Benjamin Michtom repeated the tale of the Berryman cartoon in the *Washington Post.* He stated that his father had a few samples of bears made up and sent one to the President asking for permission to call

these bears "Teddy Bears." The President is said to have replied in longhand that he did not think his name would be worth much in the bear cub business, but Ideal was welcome to use it. Unfortunately neither the original letter nor a copy has been located.

In 1903 Butler Brothers, wholesalers, are said to have taken the entire output of Mr. Morris Michtom and guaranteed his credit with the mills. Mr. Michtom did not have a factory at this time, only a small confectioner's shop. Many articles have said that Mrs. Michtom stitched up a bear, put it in the window of the shop and when it was sold, replaced it with another. The time involved and cost necessary to make a profit would have been considerable. Her son, Benjamin, explained that his mother, who was deft with a needle, made *samples* for his father and that his father operated as an individual from 1903 to 1907. During that time he called his operation Ideal Novelty and Toy Company. In 1938 the name was simplified to Ideal Toy Corporation. Benjamin Michtom was two years old at the time of the birth of the Teddy Bear and said that these facts were related to him by his father.

20

Since the Teddy Bear became so closely associated with Theodore Roosevelt, those of the opposite political persuasion were reluctant to give Teddy Bears to their children at first. As a result, Sears and Roebuck Company advertised in 1907 that the Teddy Bears were not a fad or a campaign item, but something that had come to stay on merit alone. Little did the advertisers of that day realize how true this would prove to be!

The trade magazine *Playthings* was established in 1903 and the first Teddy Bear advertisement appears in May, 1906; this is an early date for Teddy Bears in America. It is said the craze began to build in 1905 with the introduction of Teddy Bears in the shops of the summer resorts along the New Jersey shore.

The following account is taken from *Playthings,* 1906:

The Plush Bear Craze

Over in Germany there is a little old woman commanding a company of more than two thousand workers whose busy fingers fly from early morning till late at night cutting out, stitching up and putting together plush bears for the American market. The people here, grownups as well as children, have apparently gone crazy over these bears. Years and years ago this woman designed a pattern for a bear which was so natural and appealed so to youngsters that she was called the mother of the bears. Then she had a tiny shop in her house and only a few young girls to help her. That was before the bear fad struck America. Now she has a factory that covers a whole square and the machinery and employees are worked week in and week out at high pressure because Young America must have his bears. As the orders pile in with every mail and cables arrive almost hourly the little old frau and her workers hold up their two thousand pairs of hands in consternation and wonder if every man, woman and child in America is sending for a whole family of bears.

They are not far wrong. The entire country is in the clutches, or rather the embrace, of the plush bear. His Majesty Bruin now reigns.

The bear rage started at the summer resorts along the Jersey shore, some say it was Atlantic City. At any rate, a nice, fat, winsome little brown bear sitting on a counter in a boardwalk shop attracted the eyes of a youngster, and nothing would do but mamma must stop and look at the lovely plush animal. Mamma liked the bear, too. He was an excellent pocket edition of those big cinnamon bears way up in Bronx Park, and the youngster remembered the fun he had had one day watching the bears lumber around the sides of the big iron enclosed pit and give each other love pats with their huge paws. He would have a bear pit, too. Only this little plush bear looked so clean that it would be a shame to get him all dirty and frowsy. The youngster took hold of the coveted plaything and his delight grew. Bruin had such a realistic little hump at the back of his neck, and, bully! he had a voice and his legs moved.

They were jointed and his solemn little pointed head would turn any way you wanted it to, and the soles of his feet, really the bottoms of his paws, were all soft and flat and velvety, and he had such dear little ears and beady black eyes. And the youngster remembered that the Bronx bears had mouths exactly like this one and even the expression of his face was like the best behaved and finest looking bear at the Park. Mamma must buy Bruin for him. He begged her to, and after a little conversation with the shopkeeper over the price, for the bear was rather an expensive plaything, she finally paid the price and the wistful and anxious eyes of her small son and heir fairly beamed with joy as he marched away hugging his prize just as proudly as a grown-up man or the President of the United States returning from a successful hunt.

That started the bear fad. Of course, every other little boy on the boardwalk had to have a bear. It was just the thing for a boy. Girls had dolls to play with and boys ought to have something like that when it was too hot for baseball or to play Indian in the park or shipwrecked sailors on the sand. They grew eloquent in convincing their mothers of their needs. And the man in the shop found his bear stock totally unequal to the sudden demands made upon it. Inside of a few hours every bear in the shop had been sold, tiny ones and big ones, for they come in several sizes from the length of your hand to the size of a well grown youngster. So the shopkeeper

telegraphed to New York for more, and these, too, went "like hot cakes." No sooner were the plush figures put in the window than the shop was swarming with ladies after bears.

Then other shops stocked up with them, and the big ones in New York found themselves overwhelmed with orders for Teddy bears. By this time Young America had christened them, appropriately, too. Isn't the President the hero of every boy who longs to grow big enough to hold a gun to shoot bears and some day do just the very same things that "Teddy" Roosevelt does? So Teddy the bears were named, and as Teddy they are known now the length and breadth of our country, as well as on the other side of the Atlantic.

Never in the history of Wall street was the country more at the mercy of bears than it is to-day. Stuffed plush Teddies are fairly rampant, and indications show prospects of a long and continued reign. Department stores are stocking up with them, and little out of the way shops have them for a while, but not for long, because as soon as the youthful hunters get on their tracks they swoop down and bring them to bay.

The mother of the bears, the little German frau, is almost at her wits' end to know what she is going to do. There is a fear that the supply of brown and white plush will give out, and then what would she do, for they wouldn't be as good if they were made of any other color. One New York store, the largest we have, has already sold over sixty thousand Teddies, and every week it gets hundreds of dozens, which are bought up at once.

But boys are not the only lovers of Teddy bears. By no means. Their little sisters like them, too. At first little girls looked at the new playthings with some trepidation. Bears and dolls are so very different. Dolls are always ladylike in their manners, but there is no counting on the actions of bears. But closer examination proved that they weren't so very different after all. They were jointed just like dolls, and their bodies were plump and round, and they had such dear, quaint little faces. They may have all been cut after the same pattern, but there was a different expression in the eyes and mouth and the whole face, in fact, of each Teddy. Instantly the baby sister decided she liked bears too.

However, the changeable young mother soon found that she could not count on being able to borrow Teddy from her brother, so with the wisdom of her sex she decided that the only thing to do was to have one all for her very own. And mamma's purse was drawn on for more Teddy's bears. Then, when the little sister got her new toy, she was undecided whether to choose a brown or a white bear. She felt lost, as though she were neglecting some of her motherly duties, with no dressing and undressing to do. One day the family was surprised to see the tiny daughter make her appearance accompanied by the inseparable Teddy dressed in a dainty white and blue sweater and with a skating cap to match perched jauntily over one of his ears.

In his new attire Teddy made an instantaneous hit. Wasn't it enough to worry over supplying bears without getting clothes for them? But bears had to be dressed. The people up at Bronx Park might let their bears run around the pit without any clothes on but their fur coats, but when a bear lives respectably in a fine house with people and goes out to walk and play in the park and on the avenue of course he has to be properly clothed. There were no two ways about it. So the toy man laid in a stock of Teddy bear sweaters, and Tam o'Shanters and skating caps, and the little girls were delighted, for their dollies' clothes weren't always a good fit for the bears. He had pink and white sets for the brown bears, "Teddie B," as he is called, and blue and white ones for the white bears, "Teddy G."

Then some one suggested that Teddy really needed work clothes, and the toy man had the most attractive little sets of blue overalls, with a bib in front and straps crossing over the shoulders and buttoning on the back of the overalls. With these go tiny white shirts, made with a turnover collar and tied nattily under Teddy's plush chin with a scarlet cravat. Naturally the boys thought this outfit intended just for their pets and the dainty sweaters for the girls, but little sisters like the whole wardrobe, though they usually omit the dangerous looking toy gun that goes with the hunting outfit. Across the bib of the overalls is embroidered the name of the bear, "Teddy G." or "Teddy B."

Illustration 21. *Playthings* magazine carried no Ideal advertising for Teddy Bears in 1906 or 1907. This half-page advertisement is the only one in the 1908 issue. Ideal claimed to be the "Largest Bear Manufacturers in the Country." Ideal's main distributor at this time was Butler Brothers. *Playthings*, 1908.

WATCHFUL WAITING
HOW CAN TEDDY "BEAR" IT?
COPYRIGHT BY HARRY BRETON 1908

Illustration 22. Political post card showing a large Teddy Bear with the symbolic "Big Stick", Rough Rider boots, pince-nez glasses, standing on a trunk labeled "T.R." 1908.

But the Teddy bear fad has not confined itself to children. Though it began with the youngsters, grown-ups have always shown a fondness for these little plush toys, with their attractive bodies and quaint features so full of expression. It did not take long for older people to fall under the enchanting spell of Teddies, and now the wonder is where is it going to end. Habitues of Central Park asked themselves this question the other day when they were confronted by the sight of a pretty young woman dressed in the height of fashion and speeding along with the utmost unconcern. She was driving her Columbia electric victoria and by her side was not a girl companion, nor a footman, nor even the accustomed pet bull terrier, but a small Teddy bear who sat up in solemn state. The girl looked perfectly unconscious that she was doing anything unusual or startling as she rolled past the throngs of pedestrians and threaded her way through the tangle of vehicles moving in a long procession. She instantly became the mark for every eye and the thought that flashed through the minds of those to whom the sight was a novelty was—has Teddy bear now usurped the place of the pet poodle?

There he sat, resting one front paw against the side of the victoria and nestling close to the warm motor coat of his mistress, while his beady eyes gazed straight ahead unflinchingly and without any undue pride. From time to time the girl bent forward to see how he was enjoying the drive, and she gave him an affectionate pat now and then as she spoke to him in a gentle voice. Some thought the bear might have belonged to a small brother or sister, but they were soon convinced of the realness of the fad among older people when, within a quarter of an hour, another automobile whizzed by with a Teddy bear occupying the seat in the tonneau heretofore held sacred to His Highness the pet dog. There was no denying the existence of the fad in dead earnest.

Summer visitors in a certain Paris hotel were accustomed to seeing one or two particularly beautiful French women come down to the restaurant with Teddy bear companions, who were given a place by the side of the lady, while the erstwhile favorite bat-eared French dog was nursing his feelings all alone up stairs. His poor little nose—what there is of it—is quite out of joint, and he is wondering how long his ridiculous rival will reign. There are no more pleasant walks in the park with his beautiful mistress. When she goes now she takes along Teddy, whether she is joined by the children or not.

"The next thing, I suppose, we will be hearing of Teddy bear bench shows, and every woman will be trying to buy blue ribbon bears, with pedigrees as long as your arm," said a man who had seen no less than half a score of pretty girls either driving or walking with their bear pets.

It is hardly necessary to state that there are now many concerns in America engaged in the manufacture of Teddy bears, and every one of these concerns is rushed to its utmost capacity. The demand is far greater than the supply, and firms that have long been engaged in other lines have put aside their regular work to devote all their time and energy in supplying the American public with these magnificent plush toys.

"All For Dear Bruin."

"Marie, is dear little Ivan ready for his drive?"

"Not quite, madame I didn't know whether madame wished him to wear his khaki uniform or one of his sweaters."

"His red sweater, Marie. Or, no; his little overalls to-day, I think; he is so cunning in those. And put on the pearl necklet I bought him yesterday."

So Ivan is garbed by the deft French maid, and presently, erect on the front seat of the carriage, with my lady in her exquisite gown sitting opposite, an irreproachable footman perched behind, an equally irreproachable coachman driving the prancing dock-tailed horses, Ivan takes the air. He betrays no vulgar interest in the sights they pass; his manner has all the impassivity of the real elect. For Ivan is not a boy, nor is he a dog. Ivan is, in fact, a toy bear, a fuzzy, jointed toy bear.

If the German toymaker who invented these new playthings for children had been told, when he put them on the market, that grown women would be making a fad of them, toting them around, he probably would have remarket, "Ach, Himmel! Nein!" Yet that is just what some of New York's wealthy women are doing.

"Do the fashionable women really buy these bears for themselves?" repeated a salesman in the toy bazaar of a Broadway shop, when the query was put to him. "Indeed they do. Mrs.___, who is well known in Newport, I believe (he mentioned a wealthy member of the summer colony there), bought several of them before she left here for the seaside and a whole wardrobe of the uniforms and things that come for them to wear. She always has a bear with her in her carriage or automobile.

A rich woman who lives in Cornwall-on-the-Hudson came in the other day and got a brown one for her little girl and a white one for herself. Oh, a great many buy them for themselves. Yes, and they buy jewelry for the bears, too, real jewelry. Absurd?" He smiled deprecatingly. "Oh, I don't know. Fashionable women, you know——"

He seemed to feel that that last unfinished sentence explained a lot of things.

But is it imagination to think that as the stalwart footman, bearing Ivan into the house in the wake of his mistress at the end of the drive, passes the liveried man at the door, his usually unexpressive wooden face is disarranged for an instant by a flicker of the left eyelid?

Another claimant to the origin of the Teddy Bear was the Steiff factory in Germany. The first toy Margarete Steiff made was an elephant, not a bear. His uniqueness was his softness and resiliency to touch. This elephant was made of felt from scraps of material used to make women's and children's clothing in her small shop. Up to this time, most little animal toys were made of china or wood. Actually this first elephant was used as a pincushion, not a toy.

MARGARETE STEIFF

Some thirty years ago, in Giengen, a town in Wurttemberg, southern Germany, a visitor could quickly find, by inquiring of any child, the modest little home of Fraulein Margarete Steiff, a young woman with a kindly heart, a perpetual smile and a wonderfully active mind, though an invalid and unable to take part in active amusements.

On any bright morning she could be seen in her chair in her little doorway with a group of children at her feet, listening intently to cheerful child stories from the lips of one who longed and yearned to be off with them on a mad romp down the street.

It was in her anxious desire to please her little friends and find new means for their enjoyment that she cast about her, and her inventive genius showed her a very harvest of play to be made up from scraps of felt—the waste pieces from a nearby large felt factory.

With deft fingers and a skilful mind these pieces of felt were rapidly turned into wondrous toy animals, and the fame of good Margarete Steiff spread rapidly among the children of Giengen and on to other towns.

With a none too large income for her own support, and with never a thought of the trying work, she turned nobly to her increasing task to meet the demands of a growing army of small admirers, and made animal gifts for them all as fast as her needle could ply and shears could cut.

Children, as all toy men know, are emphatic in their toy likes and dislikes, and are the arbiters of the fate of many a vast enterprise; but never was this more clearly delineated than in the case of Margarete Steiff, the play friend of the children of Giengen. Her praises were soon sung by the children all through southern Germany, and in time reached the sharp ears of the ever-watchful buyer of toys, seeking new playthings for his little customers.

Illustration 23. Artwork from *Pictorial Review* magazine showing Theodore Roosevelt as a Teddy Bear with a gun and a flag on a hunting expedition in Africa. Drawing dates from 1909.

Illustration 24. Unidentified Teddy Bear Factory, circa 1910. *Courtesy F. M. Gosling and Spinning Wheel magazine.*

Illustration 28. Unidentified Teddy Bear factory. Circa 1930.

Many of Margarete's younger years were spent learning to become a dressmaker. She owned Giengen's first sewing machine, which she had to work backwards because of her paralysis. In 1877, when she was still in her teens, she opened a shop specializing in women's and children's clothing. The material she used came from the Haenhle felt factory, which was owned by her mother's family. She did well and in the first year hired several other women to help with the output. About then Margarete wrote in her notes, "At this point the model of an elephant fell into my hands; felt was well-suited to copying it." The finest shearings were used for the stuffing. This little elephant first served as a pincushion. And so the world's first stuffed toy was born.

At first these were given as gifts to children who came to visit. But, as demand for them grew, Margarete's brother Fritz realized a business potential and carted a sackful off to the country fair. In a short time all were sold, and Margarete's hobby was put on a paying basis. From this point on (1880) to the year 1897 is the relatively typical of the growth of a small family business into a thriving industry.

In 1897, after completing his art studies in England and Germany, Margarete's nephew, Richard, joined the firm. While studying in Germany, he spent many hours sketching the playful brown bear cubs at Stuttgart's famous zoo. Working from these sketches, Richard designed a little toy bear, with moveable joints made of mohair plush (the first stuffed toy having moving joints). The first models were introduced in 1902 and found their way to America a year later, 1903.

The name "Teddy Bear" came out of a hunting incident involving the President. In 1902, the year Steiff made its first bear, Theodore Roosevelt traveled into the backwoods of Mississippi on a bear hunt. After several days in which no bears were sighted, the expedition's guide chased a little bear cub out of the brush and cleared the way for the President to get off his shot. Mr. Roosevelt refused and shooed little bruin back to his mother.

On this same expedition was the Washington Post's famous political cartoonist, Clifford Barryman, who was so moved by the President's gesture that his first cartoon upon returning to his drawing board was one showing the President refusing to shoot the cub. From that point on, in each cartoon Berryman did on the President, the little bear cub showed up, which Berryman named "Teddy's Bear."

Steiff's bear sales for the first few years were disappointing, but in 1906 an event took place in Washington, D.C., which put Steiff's factory on an overtime basis and boomed the prosperity of Giengen. This was the time of the Theodore Roosevelt administration and guests were invited to attend an affair to be held at the White House. As they came in they saw Steiff bears posed on the festive tables — dressed and equipped as hunters and fisherman — a theme chosen by the caterer because of the President's reception as an avid outdoorsman. When the illustrious Teddy admitted that even as a bear expert he couldn't name the breed, a guest spoke up and said, "Why, they're Teddy Bears, of course!"

The publicity attending this dubbing brought about a crush of orders for the suddenly fashionable Teddy Bear, and over one million were sold that year. The factory is still owned by the Steiff family and is headed by fortyish Hans-Otto Steiff, great grandnephew of Margarete.

THE TEDDY BEAR

There still comes the cry for more Teddy bears, and far from taking to the woods for their long winter nap, the charming little animals are dragged from their forest lair and roasted before the glowing fireplace. Roosevelt can't catch Bruin; so with quiet humor and great delight, his countless friends clamor for the downy bear, whose very expression is that of friendliness, honesty and of good-will—the Teddy bear.

A personal and careful inquiry in the trade circles, concerning the toy bear, shows a cheerful, and in most cases, an enthusiastic satisfaction in regard to the bear market. The many factories visited are working at white heat to gratify the demand, employing extra hands to turn out their product. The commission houses report a strong and steady trade, and the large department firms say, "Teddy is as popular as ever." To any one who is constantly in touch with a public idol like this, it is very often hard to account for the popularity of "that crazy bear," and very natural predictions of a sudden slump are offered. Now, it must be borne in mind that public demand, and timely, judicious encouragement of these demands (by advertising and clever exhibits) are the life of trade; and also, it must be borne in mind, that this public demand must be gratified. Trade successes are not a gamble; they are obtained by a careful study of public demands, and that study can be obtained through the trade journal, the organ of your business—the pulse of your trade.

A tour of the toy departments in the large dry goods houses in New York show tables heaped high with plush bears—bears of white and bears of brown: black-furred bruins, with real claws and auto goggles, beating drums and wheeling baby carriages; bears, bears everywhere, even wearing Columbia, Yale and Princeton jerseys and carrying footballs.

The approaching winter will find Teddy feted and dined by his many friends, treated to sleigh rides, taken on bob-sled parties, and once again taken into the Four Hundred. In song, game and story he has come to stay. The books and press sing his praises, the games keep the pace that is set, and the comic opera does the rest for Teddy.

Briefly, the Teddy bear is no longer a fad or a passing fancy. He is the children's darling. And, in the word of a successful wholesale man, the Teddy bear is "the goods."

Playthings, 1907.

Illustration 29. "Original Teddy Bear." Ideal dates this one and he appears to be the actual model at the Smithsonian. Note marking on foot. *Photograph courtesy The Ideal Toy Corporation.*

Illustration 30. Teddy Bear Festival on the centennial of the birth of Theodore Roosevelt donated by the Steiffs, was unveiled by a United States State Department representative. Jubilee Celebration of the Steiff Factory, 1953.

ABOVE: Illustration 32. Child models pose with Ideal's 75th anniversary bear and the original model. The older bear is not the same as the model given to the Smithsonian. 1978.

LEFT: Illustration 31. Ideal's 75th Anniversary prototype Teddy Bear such as shown in *Playthings,* February, 1978. The eyeglasses were said to be Theodore Roosevelt-type and the bear reputedly similar to the original model. Actually, there were various differences. Teddy was not jointed and had a lighter muzzle and different eyes and paws. 1978. *Photograph courtesy of The Ideal Toy Corporation.*

Illustration 33. Ideal's 75th Anniversary Teddy Bear. The separate tag of the prototype bear is now glued directly onto the plush and the Roosevelt-type glasses have been eliminated. 1978. *Photograph courtesy The Ideal Toy Corporation.*

II. Identification Aids

In actuality, one needs to study the entire book for best results in identifying Teddy Bears. There are clues and tips in each chapter. Yet, herein are gathered some of the more specific identifications. The Teddy Bear was such an unprecedented success that manufacturers tried to create other animals that would meet the same reception. These jointed toys were new and unique, and children loved them dearly.

The early advertisements did not say "Teddy Bear," but "Bruin" or simply "Bears." According to *Playthings* evidence, there was no such thing as a "Teddy Bear," so named, until 1906. The appeal of the toy with the soft, yielding body and moving joints was enough to carry itself. The plus factor of identifying this toy with Theodore Roosevelt as "Teddy's Bear" compounded its success with the public.

New versions were added to the cast of characters, Teddy Bear dolls, a Billikin with a Teddy body and a two-way Teddy which had a doll face on one end and a Teddy on the other. Scarcely any possibility was left untried. All of these creations are outstanding collectors items today.

Patent applied for.

Illustration 34.

The Aetna Bear (formerly the Keystone Bear).

"Made in seven sizes - - 1 to 7 (size numbers, not inches). Style and workmanship equal to the finest imported. See that Aetna is stamped on the foot of each bear. It means the best. Highest grade materials and workmanship. Geo. Borgfeldt & Co. Sole selling agents."
Playthings, 1906.

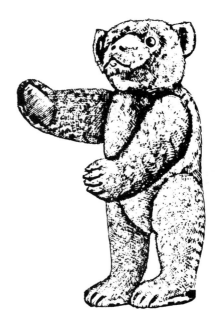

Illustration 35.

"This is Bruin's Day. The American line of jointed plush bears is the real thing. Polar Bears, Cinnamon Bears, Grizzly Bears."
Notice no mention yet of Teddy Bears. Baker and Bigler Co., New York. *Playthings,* 1906.

Illustration 36.

"BEARS" or "GOOD BEARS," (no mention yet of Teddy). "Best in the market, superior material and construction. Four sizes. Five colors: white, cinnamon, silver grey, brown, and black. A. S. Ferguson, New York. Sole Agents."
Playthings, 1906.

Shown by A. S. Ferguson & Co.

LEFT: Illustration 37. Plush Animals.

"The jointed plush bear is still the king of toy animals and as is usual the king has lords in waiting. The members of the bear king's family to date are the jointed rabbit and the jointed monkey—the latest addition. . .The Aetna Toy Animal Co. is responsible for the latest specimen we have seen in stuffed animals, and with their other animals, plush bears and rabbits, they will certainly need all the space recently acquired for manufacturing purposes during the coming year."

Playthings, 1906

PATENTED FEB. 19TH '07.

ABOVE: Illustration 38.

"When a certain manufacturer first thought of the idea of having Bruin's eyes lighted up by electricity it was hard to tell just how successful the experiement would prove, but, as the saying goes, "nothing ventured, nothing gained," he went ahead and had the thing perfected. Now Electric Bright Eye Teddy Bears are known and liked the country over. The manufacturers are desirous that buyers send in orders for daily shipments, so that when the bears are sold in the stores the batteries will be fresh. If orders are received for large quantities and the bears remain in stock for many weeks it will naturally result in the discovery of many weak batteries. This novelty will make a very desirable Christmas article and will be excellent for store or window decorations."

Playthings, 1907.

LEFT: Illustration 39. This enigmatic company name does not refer to "black skirts made rapidly" but to the "fast color" as dyes were not as perfected at this time. Steiff made an electric eye Teddy as well. *Playthings,* 1907.

"A decided novelty in the plush toy line is an Electric Bear, an illustration of which is given herewith. The eyes are tiny glass globes either white or pink, and the dry battery is placed in the body of the bear with the wires connecting the eyes and paw. When the right paw is squeezed the eyes light up, making a very pretty effect, and something that will be sure to please the little tots. The seam in the body can be opened and the battery renewed at a small cost. The bears are made in four sizes, 15, 18, 24 and 36 inches, and come in the most popular colors. Already this novelty is having an expansive sale and the good quality of the bears themselves is a strong point in their favor."

Playthings, 1907.

DOMESTIC TOYS

"It requires a pretty careful search of the market to locate anything radically new at this time of the year, but one excellent novelty has recently come to light. This is the Musical Teddy bear, shown in the accompanying illustration, and it is made of brown or white plush, in five sizes — 10, 12, 14, 16 and 18 inches—to retail at a reasonable figure. Musical Teddy appeals directly to that instinct of childhood which prompts children to follow the organ-grinder and his monkey. Possessing all the charm of a Teddy bear, perfectly constructed of soft, silky bear skin, and having the added fascination of furnishing beautiful music whenever his master wishes it, this new arrival in the toy world is an ideal playmate for children of all ages. Best of all, it is an American-made toy, equipped with concealed music-box imported from Germany, which any child can play by means of the little crank on Teddy's back. This novelty promises to be an excellent holiday item."

Playthings, 1907.

LEFT: Illustration 41B. Ladies *Home Journal,* December, 1906.

RIGHT: Illustration 42. Strauss Musical Teddy.

"Made in brown or white plush, in five sizes - - 10, 12, 14, 16, and 18 inches. American made toy with imported German music box played by turning crank in the back."

Playthings, 1907.

Illustration 40A. Article in *Playthings* calls this item "Tumbling Teddy Cub." This new style bear has a heavy weight concealed in his "innards." Turns somersaults, will stand on his head. This attractive bear came in cinnamon or white, packed in a box, and retailed for $1.25. Mrs. G. C. Gillespie, Manufacturer and Patentee, New York. Shown by E. I. Horsman. *Playthings.* 1907.

Jointed Animals

"The domestic lines of stuffed toys are growing more and more complete all the time and about the newest things in this line are the two dogs. The savage-looking bulldog is supposed to represent "Tige," the faithful friend of Buster Brown, and the dachshund is about the most natural looking toy of them all.

One of the latest novelties brought out is a small-jointed bear, jet black, with sparkling eyes of rhinestones, and the effect is quite striking." (Standard Novelty Mfg. Co.)

Playthings, 1907.

"Here he is, the Great American Bear. He is made of plush, and has all the joints found in Bruin himself. He is made in five different colors, just like the real bears, and can be had in a great number of different sizes. He is warranted harmless and gentle, and is a great favorite with the children. The demand for bears is something astonishing just now, so that buyers who want to get a good stock should place orders at once. They sell all the year round; at least, they are selling in retail stores just now faster than they can be obtained, and if the demand increases in anything like the usual proportion at Christmas time it will be a most fortunate buyer who will be able to get all he can sell."

Playthings, 1907.

"Every little child is probably familiar with the lovely old story entitled "The Three Bears," and anything which pertains to the story will therefore interest the young ones. A concern which was about the first to offer "Teddy Bears" for sale in New York City has just brought out a splendid novelty, "The Three Bears," being a box containing "Big Bear," "Middle Size Bear," "Tiny Bear," and "Goldy Locks," the sweet little girl of the story. The bears are made of plush just like the regular Bruins, and are all dressed in fascinating costumes, while the little girl is very tastefully dressed likewise. This toy will appeal very strongly to the little boys and girls, especially if they have recently heard the story. As a Holiday article it should command heavy sales."

Playthings, 1907.

THE AMERICAN DOLL AND TOY MFG. CO.

47-49 WEST 13th ST.   (Tel. 2449 Chelsea)   **NEW YORK**

MANUFACTURERS OF

"CAN'T BREAK 'EM"
Patented Dolls
AND
The Celebrated
"WHITE HOUSE"
TEDDY BEARS

Agents for the "White House" Teddies

BAKER & BIGLER CO.
77 Bleecker Street   **New York**

Illustration 43.

"The celebrated 'White House' Teddy Bear with voice, ribbon, and bell. The only American made Bears that are fully the equal of the Imported. Bought by discriminating buyers."

Playthings, 1907.

Illustration 44.

Harman Mfg. Co., New York City.

"Well made Teddy Bears. All our bears have imported voices and are made from the very best bear skin cloth. We have no large jobbing house as a distributor, as they don't distribute for pastime. You buy from the manufacturer. 'NUF SED.'"

Playthings, 1907.

TEDDY BEARS	
Made from our new Light Brown	
or White Plush	
10 in.,	$6.50 per doz.
12 in.,	9.00 "
14 in.,	12.00 "
15 in.,	15.00 "
18 in.,	18.00 "
22 in.,	24.00 "
26 in.,	30.00 "
30 in.,	40.00 "
36 in.,	60.00 "

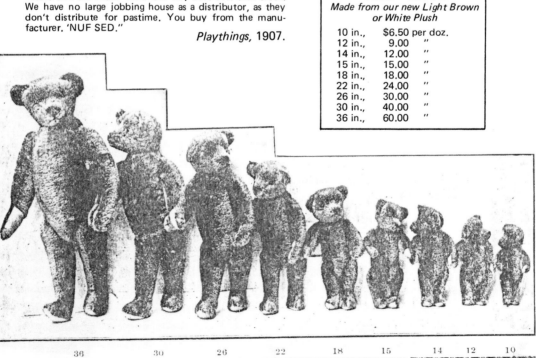

36   30   26   22   18   15   14   12   10

Illustration 45.

Dreamland Doll Co., Detroit, Michigan.
"A full line of Teddy Bears with realistic voices.
Also the maker of the original 'Natural Face' rag dolls."

NET PRICES

No.	Length	Dozen	With nursery outfit	No.	Length	Dozen	With nursery outfit
1	10 in.	$7.50	$9.00	4	16 in.	$18.00	$20.00
2	12 "	10.00	12.00	5	18 "	22.00	24.00
3	14 "	13.50	15.00	6	20 "	28.00	30.00

These bears are made of the finest bear cloth, with construction and workmanship of the very best. We invite comparison of these bears even with imported goods. Cinnamon or White. If you are interested in Teddy Bears we would be pleased to send you samples at quantity prices.

Two of the dolls were: "Sandy Andy" 13 in. (33cm) doll and bear combined, and "Teddy Turnover" doll and bear combined. (See Teddy Bear dolls.) *Playthings,* 1907.

Illustration 46.

The original imported Teddy Bears, E. I. Horsman, New York.

Number	Length	Price per dozen
1 B—5317 Cinnamon	9 inches	$7.50
1 W—5317 White	9 "	7.50
2 B—5322 Cinnamon	12 "	12.00
2 W—5322 White	12 "	12.00
2½ B—5325 Cinnamon	14 "	18.00
2½ W—5325 White	14 "	18.00
3 B—5328 Cinnamon	16 "	24.00
3 W—5328 White	16 "	24.00
4 B—5335 Cinnamon	18 "	36.00
4 W—5335 White	18 "	36.00
5 B—5343 Cinnamon	24 "	54.00
5 W—5343 White	24 "	54.00
6 B—5350 Cinnamon	30 "	72.00
6 W—5350 White	30 "	72.00

COLORS—WHITE AND CINNAMON
Shipments constantly arriving. Prices from stock.

	Length	Per Doz.		Length	Per Doz.
5317	10-inch	$7.50	5335	18-inch	$36.00
5322	12-inch	12.00	5343	24-inch	60.00
5325	14-inch	18.00	5350	30-inch	72.00
5328	16-inch	24.00	5380	46-inch	126.00

Special attention is called to the following big sellers:
8-inch, No. 75, Imported White Bear, with red
  jacket, with voice, per dozen $4.00
10-inch, No. 100, Imported Steiff White Bear,
  with red jacket, with voice 8.50
12-inch, No. 200, Imported Steiff White Bear,
  with red jacket, with voice 13.50

Playthings, 1907.

Illustration 47.

Hahn and Amberg (Makers of Suit Cases, Traveling Bags, Leather Goods) - - New York. Some advertisements in 1907 do not yet say "Teddy Bear."

"BEARS, the very finest silk plush, cinnamon or white, only imported voices. Perfectly shaped, hardest cork stuffed. Bears go direct from our factory to your store.

Playthings, 1907.

Shown by the E. I. Horsman Co.

Illustration 48. Hecla Bears.
"Equal to the imported. Don't Worry over the uncertainty of obtaining imported bears. Save 25%. Made of imported plush, have voices, and perfectly formed." E. L. Horsman Co.

Playthings, 1907.

THE NEW "HECLA" TEDDY BEARS.

"It is hard to find in the history of the toy business a parallel to the craze for Teddy Bears, which, starting nearly two years ago, grew in unexpected proportions, and last fall fairly swept the trade off its feet."

"Undoubtedly the fine material, good modeling and handsome finish of the imported bears made in Germany by Mrs. Steiff has a great deal to do with the remarkable vogue of this toy, and it was not surprising that domestic manufacturers found it difficult to meet the public's educated demands last fall with domestic bears."

"So far as being on the decrease, there is every evidence that the demand for Teddy Bears this coming fall is going to exceed that of last fall, and in the face of this prospect those posted in resources of the foreign bear manufacturers say there is no chance that a quarter of the demand will be supplied with imported bears."

"It is then "up" to the domestic manufacturer to meet the situation, and this he seems to have done if one can judge by the "Hecla" Teddy Bears which have just been placed upon the market, and which are illustrated in the cut shown below. These bears have been manufactured of imported plush of fine quality, the heads and bodies of all sizes have been skillfully modeled, they have been provided with voice and are put together by skilled workmen who have had experience in the German workshops. Altogether, it takes an expert eye to tell these bears from the imported product, and this being so, they should go a long way toward filling the wants of dealers needing a high grade article and who are having trouble in having their import orders filled."

Playthings, 1907.

ABOVE: Illustration 49.

Aetna Bear.

"Domestic teddy bear novelty made of best bear cloth so far as the head, paws, and feet are concerned. The body is cloth in several colors, blended harmoniously. A fancy wide collar is fastened around the neck and the edges are pinked. Surmounting the whole is a dunce cap trimmed with gold tinsel."

Playthings, 1907.

LEFT: Illustration 50.

Miller Mfg. Co.
Advertised "BEARS" in 1906. By 1907 it was "Teddy Bears."

"Fully equal to the imported, finest workmanship, best materials." Made in new cinnamon, white and black, with voices. Made: The Uncle Sam Bear, The Antiseptic Bear and the Miller Bear.

Number	Size	Per Doz.
1	12 in.	$9.50
2	15 in.	14.50
3	16¼ in.	18.00
4	18 in.	20.00
5	22 in.	24.50
6	26 in.	41.50
7	30 in.	58.50

Playthings, 1907.

A Group of
B. M. C. Playmates

LEFT: Illustration 51. Bruin Manufacturing Company, New York. Selling Agent: The Strobel and Wilkin Company, New York.
"Trademark: BMC. Look for the label, every piece carries our trademark in gold letters. The only featherweight line on the market. BMC stamped on the foot."

Playthings, 1907.

ABOVE: Illustration 52. Columbia Teddy Bear Manufacturers, New York.
"Our bears all have voices and are made of imported plush. Due to the increased demand for our stuffed animals, we have been compeled to seek larger quarters. We make the famous "Laughing Teddy Bear". We are making a special 7 inch Teddy Bear with voice to retail for twenty-five cents."

Playthings, 1907.

RIGHT: Illustration 53. This is the very first time that bears were called Teddy Bears, actually "Teddy's Bears." E. I. Horsman. *Playthings,* September, 1906.

35

ABOVE LEFT: Illustration 54. Notice that these importers had available this great selection in size. There was even an amazing 46 in. (116.8cm) bear. It seems not as many of these larger specimens survived as did the smaller versions due to the difficulty of storing them. *Playthings,* 1907.

ABOVE RIGHT: Illustration 55. Steiff Bears. As yet the expression "Teddy Bears" has not come into common usage. *Playthings,* 1906.

LEFT: Illustration 56.   Self-Whistling Teddy Bears. Trade mark: "That's All." Full page advertisement with Teddy shown as a portrait, as though the Strauss Mfg. Company were photographers. Also made the Musical Teddy Bear. *Playthings,* 1907.

LEFT: Illustration 57. The Dreamland Doll Company made two-in-one 13 in. (33cm) dolls, Sandy-Andy and Teddy Turnover. Rare. *Playthings,* 1907.

BELOW: Illustration 58. The Clown Bear.
"Made of the best bear cloth and with the cloth body in various attractive combinations of colors."
The Aetna Toy Animal Co. New York. Geo. Borgfeldt & Co., Distributors. *Playthings,* 1907.

Redrawn by Matthew Dillon.

Redrawn by Matthew Dillon.

Illustration 59. Havana Novelty Co., New York City.
"Into the limelight comes the Teddy Doll. The demand has exceeded our expectations. Bodies of finest imported plush. We import the heads direct from Europe. They are very handsome, lifelike, and unbreakable. May be had in white and cinnamon at $12, $15, $18, and $21 a doz."

Playthings, 1907.

Illustration 60.
"A comparatively new novelty [there may have been some in 1906] shown herewith is meeting with tremendous favor wherever shown. It is called the "Teddy Doll", because the body is made of a fine imported plush on the same order as the "Teddy Bears". It is jointed at the arms and legs. The head is unbreakable and is imported direct from Europe by the manufacturers. Inasmuch as the supply of heads is limited, and also on account of the scarcity of the fine plush used, it looks as if the mfgs. would not be able to supply the demand."

Playthings, 1907.

As early as 1907 the importing house of George C. Poirier announced that they had brought over a complete line of Margarete Steiff plush toys, including in all over 100 completely different numbers. All of the animals were represented along with clowns and comical figures.

Announcements on the Musical Teddy Bear stated that one squeezed his diaphragm gently in and out and the musical attachment gave out a pleasing melody. A 14 in. (35.6cm) bear of this sort sold for $12 per dozen.

George Borgfeldt and Company, distributors for Steiff in 1908, announced special drives in Teddy Bears. They also announced exclusive control of the novelty ten-cent "Big Stick" horn. To quote: "It is a good noisemaker, and is perfectly applicable to the season, as everyone knows that the retiring President is bound to make himself known and heard at stated intervals during the next few years, and then a few more." They also reported splendid business in Indian suits, which had recently become so popular with the boys. (This accounts for the appearance of Teddy Bears and Teddy Paper Dolls in Indian suits.)

"The Art Novelty Co. are making a specialty of the Teddy Bear for fall and winter trade. They have chosen it from all the other stuffed toys and have decided to make their leader of the same high quality which was maintained throughout last season. Knowing that the craze, as such, for Teddy Bears has died out, the Art Novelty Co. still recognize the hold which this little toy has upon the hearts of the little people everywhere, and are prepared to meet the season's demand."
Playthings, 1908.

"The Art Novelty Co. claims to be the first on the market and also the originators of the patriotic red, white and blue Teddy Bear made in these three colors of fur. He comes in all the popular sizes and needs only to be retailed at two or three nickels higher, to yield the dealer the same liberal profit that comes from the regular bear. The bear market is reported by this firm to be growing stronger with each passing week, and they are looking forward to a strong holiday trade."
Playthings, 1908.

"Three new Teddy dolls are now ready for the trade. There is no real point of difference between the new numbers and the old, and this splendid little doll could not undergo any change of construction which would render it more attractive and bewitching than it always has been, but three of her sisters have been fitted out by the cleverest of doll tailors and the result has been almost a new character. All of these three sisters are wrapped warmly in brown bear skin with close fitting hood. One, with dark hair so deep and rich that it is almost purple, has laughing eyes of deep blue, delicately tinted red footwear, and straps of gold crossing each other and passing over either shoulder."

"The other two charmers, either one of which might easily be Queen of the land of the Northern Lights, have that exquisite combination of golden hair and dark eyes, with peach complexion. Their costumes harmonize accordingly, and they are worthy of all the good things which are said of them."
Playthings, 1908.

HOW ABOUT TEDDY?
"The general opinion as to the immediate future of Teddy bears in this section of the country seems to be that this line is about due to drop from its position as a craze to the more normal and lasting plane of a good-selling staple. But this opinion is by no means unanimous, for several authorities in the toy trade spurn this idea of "stapleness," and say most emphatically that another great big season is at hand which sould equal the last at least. January is rather early for prognostications, but early as it is there are several orders on record for a larger quantity than the same houses used last year. Consequently, it seems fair to assume that it will be a big year for Teddy and stuffed animals in general, and that buyers will order pretty well up to their last season's mark."
Playthings, 1908.

" 'The Laughing Teddy Bear' is the latest of the toy bear family to make its bid for juvenile popularity. It is stuffed, covered, shaped and voiced in exactly the same fashion as are other Teddy bears, with this attractive addition—two rows of shinning white teeth, carefully modeled after the teeth of the live bears, gleam between the little animals' jaws, and literally grin from "ear to ear," from which fact the new stuffed toy gets his name."
Playthings, 1908.

"The Columbia Teddy Bear Manufacturers, makers of the Laughing Teddy Bear, report that this new bear, who shows his teeth, is being well received throughout the trade."
Playthings, 1908.

"Something brand new and good comes to us at this season, in the way of an American-made Teddy rabbit for Easter and general use. The color is a full, rich shade of deep steel gray, a gray that just faintly suggests a tinge of purple. It is a "warm" gray, taken from a pet rabbit that has not before been used in the stuffed animal, and one that is bound to become widely popular with the young-sters."

"Blended with the steel gray, this Teddy rabbit has the soles of his feet and the inner parts of his ear tinted with a delicate shade of pinkish red. A tiny colored ribbon and bell is fastened around the rabbit's neck."
Playthings, 1908.

"Hahn & Amberg are making a new and attractive line of Teddy dolls, made of silk plush, in eight colors, with bisque sleeping head and long, flowing hair. Joseph L. Amberg is now touring the West with this line among others, and reports a very satisfactory business."
Playthings, 1908.

My Teddy Doll

Illustration 61. Hahn and Amberg, New York.
"The novelty sensation of 1908 Our new H. AND A. TEDDY DOLLS Made of silk plush in 8 colors."

12 inch, with voice,	$6.75 per dozen		
13½ " " "	9.00 "		
15 " " "	13.50 "		Made of Silk
18 " " "	18.00 "		Plush, in 8 colors

Playthings, 1908.

Art Novelty Co., New York City.

"For over three years we have been working exclusively for the two largest Broadway houses. We have decided to GO IT ALONE this season, and sell direct to you, giving you the benefit of their profits. You have bought our goods time and time again through these houses. Our bears are exact reproductions of the famous imported Steiff bear. Highest grade mohair made in this country and the best imported voices."

HERE ARE OUR PRICES			
	Per Doz.		Per Doz.
10 in.,	$5.50	18 in.,	$18.00
12 "	8.50	20 "	22.00
14 "	11.00	24 "	30.00
16 "	15.00	30 "	42.00
	36 in., $60.00		

Playthings, 1908.

ANIMAL TOYS GOOD.

"There being a very, very wide interest in the trade as to the future or fate of the Teddy bear, we have gathered together as many facts as we could on the subject, and will endeavor to present the situation as nearly correct as possible. On every hand we hear the same question: "What do you think of Teddy bears for 1908?" and it is not a difficult one to answer. It must be admitted that the so-called craze for them has entirely subsided, that is, as far as women carrying them around is concerned; but as for being "dead," we think that extremely absurd. The Teddy bear, as well as the whole family of jointed animals, will unquestionably be staple sellers for many years to come. The child has become altogether too fond of the soft pets to turn them down, and the parents consider them excellent playthings for their youngsters. Not long ago, when bears held absolute sway in toyland, it was next to impossible to get enough to supply the demand. Then a rival was introduced in the shape of an ugly appearing bulldog, which had a splendid run, and is still immensely popular. After this there were all sorts of followers, each one coming in for a large share of favor. Cats, monkeys, elephants, etc., all being made of the same material as the bears. During the early part of this month we visited from ten to fifteen factories, and found in every one the same work going on—that of making up sample lines for 1908, the lines including a very wide range of subjects. Most of these makers were very enthusiastic over the prospects. Reports from retailers in nearly every section of the country are to the effect that little or no stock was carried over; therefore it would seem as though these merchants would be compelled to place orders immediately, unless they contemplate closing their toy department for the year, which is not a very likely thing. Last August, when manufacturers were working night and day to keep up with the demand, one of the factories in this city was photographed, and we show it herewith. This shows only one-half of the shop, but gives a pretty good idea of the extent to which the industry has grown. The picture shows Teddy bears, bulldogs, St. Bernard dogs, cats, etc. Last year [1907] the public wanted Teddy bears, but many of them wanted only the very best. Now that the American make has improved so wonderfully there is no reason why the demand should not be large enough to keep most of the factories busy. In Europe we hear that 2,000 hands are employed in a single factory, in addition to several other smaller factories; and surely, with our increased facilities and improved methods, we ought to be able to keep many factories at work, where only about from ten to fifty hands are employed in each. The popularity of Teddy bears is causing trouble in the furniture business, for while the plush of the bear is by no means identical with the plush used for upholstering, the same machine is used for making both. The enormous demand for bearskin plush during the past two years has kept these machines so busy that comparatively little furniture plush has been turned out. Consequently the latter material is scarce and high, the price having advanced almost 30 per cent. What is called fur cloth of all kinds has become higher because of Teddy bears. Plush and felt rabbits will probably have a large sale for the Easter trade. We are strongly of the opinion that any toy in the shape of an animal will have a good sale in 1908."

Playthings, 1908.

Redrawn by Matthew Dillon.
Illustration 62. Harman Mfg. Co. Esquimo Doll--made in all colors to retail at twenty-five cents.

ESQUIMO DOLLS
Made in all Colors

8 inch,	$2.25 Doz.
9 "	4.50 "
	Moving Eyes
10 inch,	$6.00 Doz.
12 "	8.00 "
14 "	10.50 "

Playthings, 1908.

Unfortunately *Playthings* did not include an illustration every time a Teddy Bear was mentioned. For those fortunate enough to own a "Teddy Bear, Traveler" or a "Yankee Doodle Teddy Bear" the following will aid in authenticating and dating the bear.

"Teddy Bear, Traveler, has reached New York. He comes in a well-made traveling case, and his clothes are neatly folded and packed in the opposite box cover. Teddy has several changes of raiment, and ought to travel all over the States right into the hearts of his little friends."

Playthings, 1908.

"September's offering to the bear market is "The Yankee Doodle Teddy Bear." Gay and resplendent in his patriotic fur coat of red, white and blue, he should beat a quick-step march into the hearts of all good little citizens who love their flag, their country and their Teddy. Children of an older growth swear by their Teddy bears, and the red, white and blue comedies of Cohan, and it is just as logical that the little fellows should fall in love with this purely fantastical red, white and blue Teddy bear. As a contrast to the regular bears, and as a decorative toy, his success is certain; and as a strong seller, his chances for success bear all the earmarks of previous patriotic successes. The body has two each of red and white stripes running up and down; the legs and arms are blue, and the head is white, with red ears. This "Yankee Doodle" bear is a bold stroke, and is worth every consideration and trial."

Playthings, 1908.

Redrawn by Matthew Dillon.

Illustration 63. Hahn and Amberg, New York.
"Have you seen the distinctive novelty of 1908 - - The Teddy or Eskimo doll?[Note: they were considered the same thing.] You know what popularity the teddy bear attained. Here is a Plaything that is similar to the bear but different, in that it is a doll - - the toy that will always endure. With removable hood, disk joints and steel pins, and imported voice, it is almost indestructible and will outlast a dozen dolls. With sleeping eyes, blonde or brunette."

Playthings, 1908.

TEDDY DOLLS

8 inch Celluloid Face Teddy Doll, made in 5 colors, silk plush	$2.25 doz.
10 " " " " " " " "	4.25 doz.
12 " Bisque Head, Sleeping Teddy Dolls, 7 colors, silk plush	6.75 doz.
13½ " " " " " " " "	9.00 doz.
15 " " " " " " " "	13.50 doz.
18 " " " " " " " "	18.00 doz.
22 " " " " " " " "	27.00 doz.

Also French Teddy Doll in Cinnamon only, with Gloves and Shoes.

12 inch	$8.50 doz.	15 inch	$15.00 doz.
13½ inch	12.00 doz.	18 inch	19.50 doz.

Hahn and Amberg, *Playthings,* 1908.

THE DELINEATOR.

Illustration 64. Advertisment similar to those previously shown on Page 15, Illustrations 11A & 11B. *The Delineator.*

A SHORT CUT
to a thoroughly satisfying breakfast and to improved health--**Pettijohn's Breakfast Food.**
It is not mushy when properly cooked; richest in protein and phosphates. All of the wheat but the overcoat. Can be made into a variety of dainty dishes.
Send your name and address at once, and we will send you free, our beautifully illustrated Pettijohn Booklet.   Address THE AMERICAN CEREAL CO., Dept. P, Chicago, Ill.

Illustration 65. Inside view of early Teddy Bear and other animals being readied for the market.

III. Needle & Thread
Costumes Ready Made

The rage for commercially made Teddy clothing was in full force in 1908. Samstag & Hilder Brothers, Importers and Manufacturers, advertised a full assortment of dressed and undressed bears, both foreign and domestic. A large photograph in *Playthings* depicted an orchestra of bears playing horns and drums while a group of bears dance in pairs. They are costumed in elaborate sailor suits, fancy trimmed jackets and skirts.

As early as 1906 Kahn and Mossbacher manufacturers of clothing for bears and dolls, stated that they had enlarged their facilities three times within the season due to the great popularity of bears and their clothing. "Everybody everywhere wants the Great Bear Twins, Teddy B. and Teddy G. Dress up the bears with the K&M outfits."

Kahn and Mossbacher Teddy Bear clothing included sweaters, overalls, blouses, Rough Rider uniform, Baseball uniform, hats, and more. Play costumes or dress up costumes for children were fairly new in this period. The "Uncle Remus" trademark line included Indian, Rough Rider, Cowboy, Policeman, playsuits and accessories. These in turn inspired the various outfits for Teddy Bears, which would then be depicted in post cards, storybooks and paper dolls.

The plush material with which to sew the bears was widely advertised in *Playthings*. Tingue Manufacturing Company in Seymour, Connecticut, was said to be the largest manufacturer in the country. They made claim to being the real home of the Teddy Bear since they were using a crop of 4000 Angora goats per week to manufacture the bears' outer covering. Some of the colors were white, cinnamon and gray.

John and James Dobson called themselves "Leading Mfgs. of BEARSKIN and all other fur effects" with mills in Falls of Schuylkill, Philadelphia, Pennsylvania.

Still another competitor was Salts Textile Manufacturing Company, New York, who advertised, "Teddy Best Yet." "In all things there are GOOD, BETTER, AND BEST. If you want in Teddy Bears and other stuffed animals results equal or superior to the best imported article, Salts Fur is what you want."

Even the yarn for Teddy's nose was a matter of concern. It seems some of it was so coarse that it looked bad, or so fine that it was difficult to work with. In 1907 *Playthings* announced that one manufacturer had produced a yarn said to be exactly right, to fill this need. All kinds of yarns and threads in different colors were made available.

Fortunate indeed was the child who received the ready-made sweaters and caps, Rough Rider suit, automobile coat or other garments especially designed for a Teddy Bear. The bear alone was considered expensive in 1906-09 so any of the original bear clothing that has survived will be collectors' treasures indeed. No doubt some of these creations have been mistaken for doll clothing in the past, but will be recognized now and restored to their true intention.

A speech was made by TEDDY–B,
Who told the boys and girls that he
Believed in fun and honest strife,
And manly sport and strenuous life.
And things which made for stronger will,
And helped weak boys to climb a hill.

81

Illustration 66. Teddy clown suit from *The Roosevelt Bears, Their Travels and Adventures* by Seymour Eaton. 1906.

Illustration 67. Rubberized automobile coat for a Teddy Bear. The automobile goggles are made of metal and leather and came in six different colors at ten cents per pair. *Playthings,* 1907.

"Reg. U. S. Pat. Office."

Illustration 68.

"The Popular Bears, Teddy B. and Teddy G. Dressed in K. and M. Outfits. The demand grows larger every day." Kahn and Mossbacher, New York.

Playthings, 1907.

"D. W. Shoyer & Co. are making a very handsome line of knitted Sweaters, Toques, etc. for the popular "Teddy Bear". They also make a line of Jackets, Sweaters, Toques, etc. for Dolls.

The remarkable popularity of the jointed plush bear has resulted in the production of complete outfits for these interesting animals. A wide-awake manufacturer has brought out a line of these goods, consisting of sweaters, overalls, dresses, hats, caps, slumber robes and numberless other things. The sweaters have embroidered letters across the chest, reading "Teddy B." and "Teddy G." This feature is protected by copyright. The idea is an exceedingly clever one, and should prove an attractive feature for window displays as well as on the toy counters."

Playthings, 1906.

Illustration 69.

"Everything for Teddy B. and Teddy G. and all other Members of the Bear Family. There has never been anything like the Bear craze; old folk, middle age people all take delight in the new fad." Kahn & Mossbacher, New York.

Playthings, 1906.

Illustration 70. Knitted sweaters and toques available in six sizes and two colors; white with pink or blue trimming. Manufactured by D. W. Shoyer and Co., New York. *Playthings,* 1907.

COLLEGE BEARS.

"Teddy bears are now blossoming out in college colors, and the shop windows are full of Yale, Princeton and other varieties. They have an alluring appearance, with their little sweaters and caps, all done in the popular colors."

Playthings, 1907.

Shown by A. S. Ferguson & Co.

Illustration 71.

"It has been decreed that the bear of fashion must be dressed up in some sort of rig, and everybody is now familiar with those smart looking sweaters, coats, etc. Realizing the demand for bear accessories an enterprising firm has brought out a splendid line of boots made to fit any size bear or cat. They are made of black, red or tan leather, with green or red velvet tops, and are very dressy in appearance. The red boots with green tops are most popular of all. These boots can be had separately or they can be had on the "Uncle Remus" animals, as desired. If a merchant wants to make his stock of bears move a trifle faster it might be a good plan to slip a pair of these pretty boots on each one, and besides this, they will help to brighten up the window or counter. Being a novelty they will cause people to stop and examine, then perhaps purchase. In order to make Bruin's wardrobe complete it must contain boots as well as other articles."

Playthings, 1907.

"Dolls are not the only ones that require clothing, for shortly after Teddy bears began to be so popular they demanded wearing apparel. Sweaters, overalls, coats and hats were turned out in large quantities to meet the demand. To-day the bear can have his choice of suit—a fireman's, soldier's, sailor's, janitor's, policeman's and many other varieties."

Playthings, 1908.

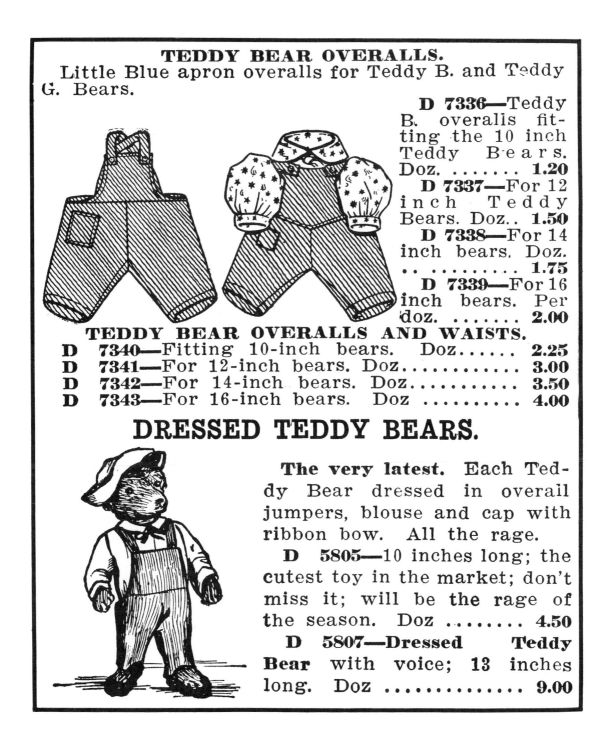

TEDDY BEAR OVERALLS.

Little Blue apron overalls for Teddy B. and Teddy G. Bears.

D 7336—Teddy B. overalls fitting the 10 inch Teddy Bears. Doz. **1.20**

D 7337—For 12 inch Teddy Bears. Doz.. **1.50**

D 7338—For 14 inch bears. Doz. **1.75**

D 7339—For 16 inch bears. Per doz. **2.00**

TEDDY BEAR OVERALLS AND WAISTS.

D 7340—Fitting 10-inch bears. Doz...... **2.25**
D 7341—For 12-inch bears. Doz............ **3.00**
D 7342—For 14-inch bears. Doz............ **3.50**
D 7343—For 16-inch bears. Doz **4.00**

DRESSED TEDDY BEARS.

The very latest. Each Teddy Bear dressed in overall jumpers, blouse and cap with ribbon bow. All the rage.

D 5805—10 inches long; the cutest toy in the market; don't miss it; will be the rage of the season. Doz **4.50**

D 5807—Dressed Teddy Bear with voice; 13 inches long. Doz **9.00**

Illustration 72. G. Sommers catalog #184, 1907.

43

THE THREE BEAR
FAMILY

Illustration 73.
"Best quality Father Bear, Mother Bear and Baby Bear of soft plush, all most becomingly dressed and terribly surprised because -- but you may buy the story book with the group of all three, all for $15.75. Baby Bear, 8¼", $3.50; Mother Bear 12½", $4.75; Father Bear 14", $6.75; storybook, $.75."

F.A.O. Schwarz Christmas catalog, 1932.

BEAR TROUSSEAU

Illustration 74.
"Bear Trousseau--This nice, soft stuffed, tan plush bear with a voice appears first in green flannel trousers with blue top, a red jacket and white collar and tie and wearing spectacles. Then in a red, white and blue clown suit trimmed with yellow balls, and the peaked cap and white ruff. Gingham dress with blue apron and white blouse and a gingham kerchief round the head. Light blue flannel jacket trim with yellow and cut tasseled cap. Bear 9" EXCLUSIVE $5.00."

F.A.O. Schwarz Christmas catalog, 1932.

No. 21/267 — Bearkin Trousseau —
Not all bears are as attractive, playful or as fortunate as this one. He
comes with his various outfits in a
blue leatherette suitcase which
measures 8 x 12 x 3 inches. His
brown plush 8 inch body with high
squeaky voice may be dressed
Tyrolian—short pants and jacket,
pointed cap with feather—or Ski
outfitted in his red felt ski blouse,
pants and cap—even a Scottish
touch can be added with tartan
kilt, red velvet blouse, glengarry
cap, sporran and red shoes—of
course the blue suit with apron
is for general use. OUR OWN
DESIGN $7.50

Illustration 75. F.A.O. Schwarz Christmas catalog, 1936.

Illustration 76. Italian Teddy
Bears. Cost $24.95 each,
1955.

WE'RE LOOKING for HOMES ·· *Know of Any?*

We All Have Strong Voices

Our Heads Turn

79¢ Smallest Size

Plush-Covered Throughout

These Bears Can All Be Undressed

We can be jolly or sympathetic and we're wonderfully comforting when the light's been turned out for the night. Our coats are bright orange felt with black collars; we wear white pleated shirts, black felt trousers, sporty ties and jaunty bright colored felt caps. Clothes have snap fasteners, we're easily dressed and undressed. Our fur is fine brown plush—we're correctly stuffed.

Our legs and arms have inside joints. Shiny glass eyes. Noses, mouths and nails on our paws are embroidered in black. Strong voices.

10½ in. tall.	14 in. tall.	16½ in. tall.
48 C 3170	48 C 3171	48 C 3172
Ship. wt. 8 oz. . . . . . . .79¢	Ship. wt. 12 oz. $1.25	Ship. wt. 1 lb. 8 oz. . . .$1.69

Illustration 77. Montgomery Ward catalog #115, 1931.

STUFFED ANIMALS

This assortment consists of 6 styles, 3 bears and 3 cats, as illustrated. Head made of long pile plush with glass eyes. Beautifully dressed in appropriate colors with hats to match costumes. Self standing. Height 22 inches. Come assorted only. Packed 6 to carton, we do not break cartons.

No. 71/10. Per Assortment of 6 . . . .$10.00

Illustration 78. Circa 1940.

46

COWBOY BEAR

Fine silky plush head in assorted colors. Has glass eyes, embroidered nose and mouth, stuffed duvetine cloth body and composition feet. Self-standing. Dressed like a cowboy in assorted colored leatherette chaps and vest. Fitted with felt 10 gallon hat and neckerchief. Height 14 inches. Each packed in box.

No. 8D00. Sample Each.......**$0.80**
Per Dozen **8.00**

Illustration 80. Circa 1940.

This Wooly Plush Bear Has a Snappy 5-Piece Outfit

Little tots love these soft cuddly bears and love their tricky outfits! The bears have a wooly, fine brown plush covering, glass eyes, and embroidered noses, mouths, and paws. Correctly stuffed—arms and legs with inside joints. And their suits, which can be taken off, are as cute as can be—black felt trousers, sporty ties, and white pleated shirts, topped with bright orange felt coats with black collars, and bright felt caps.

10½ in. tall.	*14 in. tall.*	*16½ in. tall.*
48 T 3170	**48 T 3171**	**48 T 3172**
Ship. wt., 8 oz...... **69¢**	Ship. wt., 12 oz.... **$1.00**	Ship. wt., 1½ lbs.. **$1.45**

CBA
KSD *Montgomery Ward & Co.* ★

Illustration 79. 10½ in. (26.7cm), 14 in. (35.6cm) or 16½ in. (42cm) bears with black trousers and bright orange felt coat with black collar and bright felt cap. Montgomery Ward catalog, 1932.

Our New Boy Bear

Isn't he cute? Your bear family will not be complete without him. Imagine the fun in dressing and undressing him, for his cloth sport shirt has real buttons. Has natural looking glass eyes, tie, cloth cap and colored trousers. Bear made of short pile plush and is 14 inches tall. Squeaker voice. Shipping wt., 1¼ lbs.
49N4325
$1.49

Illustration 81. "Boy Bear" of short pile plush, 14 in. (35.6cm), with squeaker. Sears, Roebuck and Co. catalog, 1928.

Illustration 82.

"Not all bears are as attractive, playful or as fortunate as this one. He comes with his various outfits in a leatherette suitcase which measures 8x12". His brown plush 8" body with high squeaky voice is ski outfitted in red felt ski blouse, pants and cap or Tyrolian short pants and jacket, pointed cap with feather--even a Scottish touch is included with tartan kilt, red velvet blouse, glengarry cap, sporran and red shoes--of course the blue suit with apron is for general use. Our own design. $7.50."

F.A.O. Schwarz Christmas catalog, 1938.

Bearkin, Trousseau

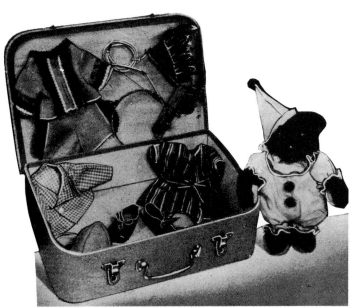

Bearkin Trousseau

Illustration 83. Bearkin Trousseau.

"A cute little 8" brown plush bear with an astonishing assortment of clothes. He is dressed in a white clown suit adorned with red pompoms, red bandana handkerchief and ten-gallon hat; and last but not least is his full feathered Indian Chief suit, all packed in an 8x13" suitcase. $7.50."

F.A.O. Schwarz Christmas catalog, 1941.

RIGHT: Illustration 84.

"Tyrolian Bearkin, Dressed in the Tyrol's best, he measures 8" high from the top of his green cap with feather, to the bottom of his brown shoes. His brown plush body is well dressed with a gray felt coat with felt trimmings and his brown trousers are belted in the true Tyrolian style. Our own creation — $2.75."

LEFT:

"Scotch Bearkin-Scotland's best! He measures 8" tall from the top of his plaid cap to the soles of his red leather shoes. His brown plush body is fittingly dressed with a red jacket, plaid kilts, sporran and all. Our own design. $2.50."

F.A.O. Schwarz Christmas catalog, 1938.

Scotch Bearkin   Tyrolian Bearkin

BEARKIN AND HIS TROUSSEAU

"BEARKIN" AND HIS TROUSSEAU

No. 21/239 – Look at "bearkin" this time all ready for his big jump in full ski costume—bright felt ski-suit and beret, bright plaid scarf, leatherette shoes, and wooden skiis in hand that buckle on very easily. His ski poles are there too, and a most complete trousseau nicely packed in his fine strong blue leatherette suitcase that he fits right into. There's a Scotch costume, including tartan kilt, red velvet blouse, glengarry cap, spooran and red patent shoes, also a blue playsuit with apron, blue felt overalls and striped shirt and a pair of pajamas. "Bearkin" stands 9" tall, of soft light tan wooly plush and he has a high squeaky voice. Suitcase, 12" x 8" x 3½". **Our own design** . . . . &7.50

ABOVE: Illustration 85. F.A.O. Schwarz Christmas catalog, 1935.

Illustration 86. Ski Teddy.
   "This darling teddy is all set on his skis. He's softest fuzzy plush dressed in felt ski suit and beret and on his feet, leatherette ski shoes with wooden skis that buckle on and off. His scarf is bright plaid and he carries the very necessary ski poles. He has a voice too. Stands 8½" tall - - $3.00."
   F.A.O. Schwarz catalog, 1935.

SKI TEDDY

To-Be-Sewn

"Rough Rider."   *"Little Farmer."*   *Clown Suit.*

"Rough Rider."   *"Little Farmer."*   *Clown Suit.*

"Rough Rider."

Clown.

"Rough Rider."

308—Set of Clothes for Boy-Doll or Teddy-Bear: consisting of a "Rough Rider," Clown, and "Little Farmer" Suit.

THE "Rough Rider" suit consists of trousers and jacket and a hat having a sectional crown and a rolled brim. The body and trousers of the "clown" suit are in one, and a cap completes the outfit. Overalls and a blouse comprise the "little farmer" suit.

Set 308 is in 5 sizes, from 12 to 28 inches in height. For 20 inches, the "Rough Rider" suit requires ⅝ yard of Khaki or denim 36 inches wide; the "clown" suit, ⅝ yard of muslin 36 inches wide; the "farmer" suit, ⅜ yard of denim 36 inches wide for overalls, and ½ yard of percale 27 inches wide for blouse. Price, 10 cents.

Illustration 87. Pattern #308 came in five sizes, from 12 in. (30.5cm) to 28 in. (71.1cm) in height. *The Delineator,* December, 1906.

Illustration 88. Suit for a Chubby Teddy Bear. *Needlecraft* magazine, November, 1938.

Illustration 89. Premium offered for a 7½ in. (19cm) bear, thimble, needles and thread, workbox and trunk. *The Youth Companion,* October 21, 1909.

Suit for a chubby Teddy Bear.

Chubby, the bear, is about twelve inches tall, ten inches around waist. His outfit uses navy knitting yarn for the trousers, scarlet for the sweater, navy and scarlet for cap, green for mittens and scarf, brown for bookbag; a No. 3 crochet-hook, and a pair each of No. 1 and No. 2 knitting-needles.

CHUBBY'S TROUSERS—The stitch gauge is 7 stitches, 11 rows to the inch.

With navy yarn and No. 2 needles, cast on 40 st. K across and p back, increasing 1 st at each end of every k row until there are 50 st on the needle. Then decrease 1 st at each side every ½ inch until there are 40 st on the needle. Bind off. Make 2 pieces alike. Fold. Sew up legs from cast-on st to the row where decrease began. Sew both pieces together making seams down the front and back. Make a row of d c around top, hem legs. With red yarn and tapestry needle, work a stripe in back-stitch down each side of trousers. Suspenders: Crochet 8-inch ch. Work d c in each loop. Make two of these, and sew ends to each side of the front and back of trousers, crossing in the back.

CHUBBY'S SWEATER—With red yarn and No. 2 needles, cast on 36 st. K 2 and p 2 for 1 inch. K across and p back for 3 inches.

K 2 and p 2 for 1 inch. Bind off loosely. Front and back alike. Sew shoulder seams for ½ inch on each side. Sleeve: Pick up or cast on 40 st. K across and p back, decreasing 1 st at each side every ¼ inch 6 times, 28 st on needle. K 2, p 2 for 1 inch. Bind off and sew seams. Pocket: Cast on 9 st, k across and p back for 1 inch. Sew pocket in place.

BEAR'S CAP—With navy yarn and No. 2 needles cast on 64 st. K 2 and p 2 for 1 inch. 1st decrease: K every 7th and 8th st together across the row. Tie in red, start stripe of 2 rows red, 4 rows navy. (Decrease every ½ inch, 5 decrease rows in all.) 2d decrease: K the 6th and 7th st together across row. 3d decrease: K the 5th and 6th st together across row. 4th decrease: K the 4th and 5th st together across row. 5th decrease: K the 3d and 4th st together; 16 st left. Gather together. Sew up seam, matching stripes. Wind yarn over a one-inch cardboard strip, tie the top, clip the ends for a tassel.

CHUBBY'S SCHOOL BAG—(A little girl might use this for a purse.) With brown yarn and No. 2 needles, cast on 17 st. K in seed st, like scarf, for 5 inches. Then k 2 together at each end of every row until all st are off. Crochet a loop for button. Sew up sides. Crochet an 11-inch ch and fasten in place.

Needlecraft magazine, November, 1938.

No. 936—Teddy Bear's Overalls and Bathing Suit
Pattern cut in one size, for a 15-inch bear

No. 837—Toy Bear
15 inches high

No. 940—Teddy Bear's Pajamas and Bathing Suit
Pattern cut in one size, for a 15-inch bear

Illustration 90. Doll and Animal Patterns.

"The dolls and animals illustrated on this page make just the best sort of an inexpensive Christmas present for the little people in the family. The patterns cost but ten cents apiece and they are extremely simple to put together."
Woman's Home Companion, 1908.

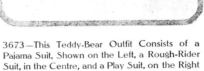

3673—This Teddy-Bear Outfit Consists of a Pajama Suit, Shown on the Left, a Rough-Rider Suit, in the Centre, and a Play Suit, on the Right

3673   3673

EVEN the crossest Teddy Bear would be pleased if he found this nice set of clothes in his Christmas stocking! The Rough-Rider suit would be pretty made of tan linen or chambray, with pockets, lapels and cuffs trimmed with red and tiny brass buttons. The play suit could have overalls of blue gingham or chambray with a gay red-and-white striped shirt. Teddy's sleeping garment—the pajama suit—may be of any light-colored chambray or outing flannel with white braid trimmings. Patterns (No. 3673) for this outfit, consisting of three complete suits, come in three sizes to fit 12, 16 and 20 inch bears.

Illustration 91. Pattern #3673 consisting of a pajama suit, rough-rider suit and a play suit. For 12 in. (30.5cm), 16 in. (40.6cm) and 20 in. (50.8cm) bears. Fifteen cents per set. *Ladies' Home Journal,* December, 1907.

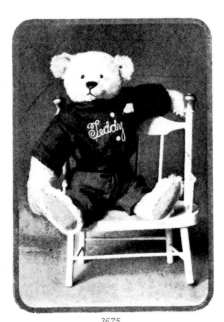

3675—Three Suits for Teddy Bear: on the Left is Shown a Fireman's Suit, in the Centre, a Sailor Suit, and on the Right, a Clown Suit

3675   3675

ABOVE, on the left, the Teddy Bear is ready for work in his fireman's suit. Red flannelette would be a good choice for the blouse, and blue gingham for the trousers. In the central illustration Teddy is dressed as a "jolly sailor boy." Any dark-blue cotton or woolen fabric may be used for this with trimmings of white soutache braid. The rollicking bear on the right is ready for a romp in his clown suit. This could be made of any bright-colored or dotted material. Patterns (No. 3675) for this outfit, consisting of three complete suits, come in three sizes to fit 12, 16 and 20 inch bears.

Patterns for the sets of doll clothes and Teddy-Bear clothes illustrated on this page can be supplied on receipt of their price, fifteen cents for each number, post-free. The amount of material required for the different-sizes is printed on the pattern envelopes. Order from your nearest dealer in patterns, or by mail, giving number of pattern and the size required, and inclosing the price to the Pattern Bureau, The Ladies' Home Journal, Philadelphia.

Illustration 92. Pattern #3675 for a fireman's suit, a sailor suit, and a clown suit. Fifteen cents per pattern set. *Ladies' Home Journal,* December, 1907.

"Teddy Bear" in Overalls

FIG. 2. TEDDY BEAR KNITTED SUIT

ABOVE: Illustration 93. Teddy Bear suit for an 18 in. (45.7cm) bear. *Knitting* magazine, April, 1908.

LEFT: Illustration 94. Good view of early Teddy Bear used to illustrate the story in "The Doll's Dressmaker" column. Notice the extra long arms with curved shape. *The Delineator,* April, 1907.

TEDDY BEAR SUIT

This suit is for a Teddy bear eighteen inches in length.

SWEATER. *Materials.*—Two skeins of red German-town and two fine bone needles. Cast on **44** stitches (sts) for the front and rib 1½ inches by knit (k) 2, purl (p) 2. Knit 17 ridges plain (pl). Cast off 6 sts, work to the end of the row and in next row cast off 6 for the other side. Knit, narrowing 1 each side in every alternate ridge until 26 sts are left. Knit 4 ridges plain. Then widen each side in every ridge until you have 36 sts on the needle, k 13, slip these 13 sts on a cord, cast off 10 for the neck, and on the 13 sts left work 5 ridges, widening 1 at the shoulder and narrowing 1 at the neck in each ridge. Cast off. Take up the other 13 sts and finish in the same manner.

For the back, cast on 32 sts, and rib same as the front, work 17 ridges. Cast off 2 under each arm and shape the arm's eye, and shoulder same as the front.

For the sleeve, cast on 32 sts, and rib 1 inch. Make 6 ridges plain, then work 13 ridges, widening each side in every 3d or 4th ridge until there are 40 sts on the needle. Cast off 3 sts under the arm, then work back and forth, narrowing each side in every row until 6 sts are left on the needle. Cast off. Sew up the sweater under the arms, one shoulder and under sides of the sleeves. Sew in the sleeves, placing the seam a little in front of the seam under the arms. Take up stitches around the neck, and rib 1 inch. Cast off loosely.

TROUSERS. *Materials.*—Two skeins of zephyr Germantown and four coarse steel needles.

Cast on 72 sts and rib 1 inch pl. Knit about 1 inch pl without widening. Then in every 4th row widen after every 10th st. Knit in this manner until there are 100 sts on the needles. Divide the sts evenly for the legs. Slip 50 sts on a cord. Cast on 8 sts, between the legs to form a gusset. Work round and round on the 58 sts, narrowing 2 in every alternate round for the gusset, until the 8 sts are all narrowed off. Knit 1½ inches plain, then k a round by narrowing every alternate st. On the remaining sts

rib ¾ of an inch and cast off. Take up the other 50 sts, 8 on the 8 cast on, and finish same as the first leg. The trousers slip on easily, and the ribbed top keeps them up under the sweater.

CAP.—The cap is made of the red wool.

Cast on 60 sts on 3 needles, rib 1 inch. Then k pl 1 inch. Knit, narrowing every 7th st until 21 sts are left. Then narrow at end of each needle until all the sts are narrowed off. Turn up the ribbed portion over a strip of buckram to keep it stiff, and fasten.

With a crochet-hook take up 20 sts at the edge, and work back and forth in single crochet (s c) to form the peak, narrow 1 each side in every row, until about 8 sts are left. Make a row of slip stitches all around the peak. Attach a rubber cord to the cap to keep it in place on the head. Children can easily be taught to knit these simple garments and it can be made very fascinating employment for them on rainy days, for every little girl is always very proud if she can make the garments for her doll. This sweater could also be used for a doll of any size by calculating the extra number of stitches required. Children's fingers can also be easily guided to knit the tiny cap, which, like the sweater, can be enlarged for a doll. Neither pattern should be enlarged enough for a child, but full directions for making all kinds of knitted garments for children as well as for men and women, will be found in the new "Priscilla Knitting Book."

Knitting magazine, April, 1908.

"Jacketed Teddy bears, in sweater jackets, jumpers and all manner of colored worsted and linen clothing make a strong appeal to all owners of Teddy bears. They add color and attractiveness to the bear, and, besides, can be secured at satisfactory rates. Last year these costumed bears were unusually popular with the little tots, and 1908's innovations bid to keep up the good work."

Playthings, 1908.

"The Story of a Jenny Wren Club - - sixth meeting:

"The fact is our little dressmakers had become little tailors for the day. Their first task was making overalls for the bears. They cut them of blue gingham, as being nearest to the regulation denim, and ever so much easier to sew. When the garments were ready to be tried on, I don't think the Teddy bears enjoyed being fitted. They were too polite, to be sure, to show this in their faces; they stayed as sweet and appealing as ever. But each held his forepaws very stiffly, as if in silent self-defense, as they had a most surprising way of squirming their shaggy little selves right out of your hands, just when you least expected it. Finally after much coaxing and petting and make-believe scolding, the awkward little fellows allowed the awkward little tailors to push their clumsy hind-legs into the overalls; after that they stood still long enough to have the trouser legs turned up to the right length, or rather right "shortness", as Winnie called it. Any one could see how delighted the fat cubs were when the fitting was over, for they tumbled back into the box very quickly, and there hugged and clawed one another with great gusto.

"When all finished, they put the overalls on the Teddies, making them look very businesslike indeed. And I believe the fuzzy little creatures knew how well they looked, for they cocked their funny heads to one side and looked as if they would wink wickedly the very next minute.

"The above Teddies and a group of dolls which had been dressed by the Jenny Wren Club members all went into a large box which was mailed to the "Children of the Willow Street Mission School" for an Easter gift. Each doll or bear had a bag of candies tied to one arm."

"The Doll's Dressmaker" column, *The Delineator*, April, 1907.

TEDDY BEAR

DESIGN NO. 438

Illustration 95. Crochet pattern for bear. *Seattle Post Intelligencer*, 1940s.

Illustration 96. Cloth bear by O. C. Grinnell, Jr., New York. *Playthings*, 1906.

Playthings

RIGHT: Illustration 97. Art Fabric Mills Bear to-be-sewn. *New Idea Woman* magazine, 1906.

BELOW: Illustration 98. Muslin sheet which came inside Strobel & Wilkin Co. envelope (see Illustration 97) for making cloth Bruin-Teddy. Note collar with "Teddy Bear" in center nameplate. Color printing was out of synchronization on bottom half of cloth. Copyright 1906, O. C. Grinnell, Jr., New York.

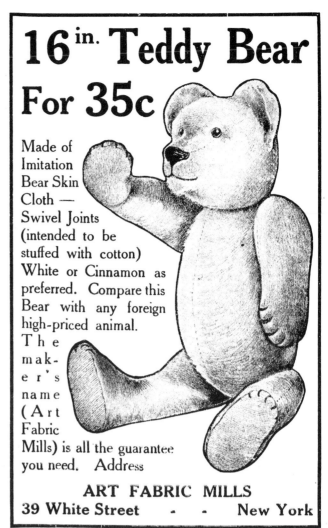

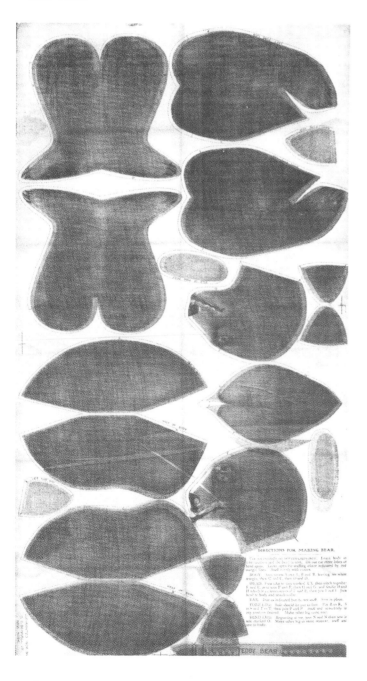

Illustration 99. 20 in. (50.8cm) "Ted the Hunter," in four colors, on muslin. To be cut, and sewn together and stuffed. Clothes were included. Sold for twenty-five cents. The Pictorial Review Company, New York. 1909.

"If TEDDY BEAR could be vain he surely would have been long before this, for he is the most popular, soft, fuzzy little bear you can possibly think of. It doesn't matter at all to him that he often has nothing but commonplace shoe buttons for eyes, and that his skin isn't real fur, but is just made of material that can be bought by the yard. And why should it, when Teddy Bear was a success from his very first appearance?

All last summer he was seen at the most fashionable summer resorts, and frequently displayed a wardrobe fit for a real and very fashionable little girl. Even in the public dining-rooms of the big hotels and restaurants Teddy is often seen occupying a place of honor. To say that he has put the nose out of joint of many a bewitching French doll, is really to express it mildly. The funny little bear toy is hugged and loved by more little folks in this big land than you can count.

As a Christmas present Teddy Bear could not possibly have a rival. The fact that in the shops he is expensive makes it all the better news to the WOMAN'S HOME COMPANION subscribers that any one of them can easily make a Teddy Bear by following carefully our toy bear pattern, which costs but ten cents. Brown and white are the favorite colors for this cute little bear, and any of the following materials will make him most attractive—plush, bearcloth, coarse velour, eiderdown, astrakhan cloth, or even flannel.

Preparing for Christmas each year when there are many little folks in the family and but little money to spend, often means many a big heartache for the mother who makes the Christmas. It was especially for this good mother that this page of homemade Christmas presents was planned.

Though Teddy Bear is far and away the most loved toy animal at present, yet, all animals, and especially dogs, are sure to please children."

Woman's Home Companion, December, 1906.

4137. A TEDDY BEAR AND RAG DOLL,
2 sizes, 14 and 18 inches; Price 10 cents.
For the bear 14 inches long, ⅝ of a yard of bear-skin-cloth 44 inches wide and a piece of kid 6 x 9 inches are needed, and the same size doll requires ⅝ of a yard of 36-inch-wide material.

Illustration 101. Pattern to make 14 in. (35.6cm) or 18 in. (45.7cm) bear from fabric called "bear-skin-cloth." *Ladies' World* magazine, February, 1907.

No. 837—Toy Bear

Pattern cut in one size—bear 15 inches high. Quantity of material required for making this bear, half a yard of material thirty-six inches wide, with a small piece of chamois or leather eight inches square for paws, and two buttons for eyes

Illustration 100. *Woman's Home Companion,* December, 1906.

Illustration 102. Cinnamon or white bears to sew, in six sizes. *The Ladies' World* magazine, April, 1907.

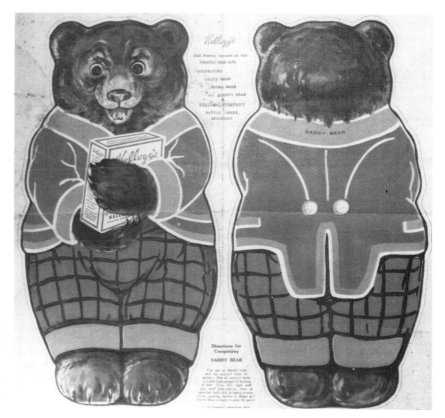

Illustration 103. 14 in. (35.6cm) "Daddy Bear," from Kellogg's Doll Family. He wears a red jacket with yellow trim, green trousers with navy stripes and yellow cuffs. Included in the series were "Mama Bear," "Johnny Bear" and "Goldilocks." The 1926 "Daddy Bear" version had red and yellow striped trousers and a blue jacket. 1925.

HOW TO GET THE PATTERN

A pattern is all ready to be mailed to you for 15 cents in stamps, cash or money order; it is printed full size in green ink on a strong pattern paper, and full directions for making Little Bear come with each pattern.

The Editor of the
Children's Page
8 Arlington Street,
Boston, Mass.

All he needed was a cap and some trousers and a pink checked pocket handkerchief to make him sort of dressed up

Illustration 104. "Little Bear" was featured in illustrated children's stories of the day. "The Children's Page," *The Youth's Companion,* December, 1926.

6464

The Jungle Animals

THE Teddy Bear was one of the most wonderfully popular toys ever offered to children. It is most realistic when made of plush; ⅞ of a yard 27 inches wide are required to make the 16-inch size. The pattern No. is 6464, and it is cut 12, 16 and 20 inches high.

Illustration 105. *The Ladies' World* magazine, December, 1913.

The following article from *Playthings* magazine notes the scarcity of the plush material used to make Teddy Bears:

"On another page we print an article relative to the popularity of the Teddy bear. We think that this matter is one which should receive very careful attention from buyers, particularly those located throughout the western section of the country. At the present time orders from the Pacific coast are coming in in such large quantities and with such urgent requests for immediate shipment as to practically swamp the manufacturers. The plush from which the bears are made is now a very scarce article on this market, and it is practically impossible to increase the output of the factories during the present season. It was hardly expected by the manufacturers of plush that the increase in the demand for this fabric in the toy trade would amount to anything like what it has now reached. The looms for making this plush are very expensive, and the output from a loom is necessarily limited. As far as the East is concerned, especially those houses which place import orders early in the season, deliveries are being made in a satisfactory manner, and we believe that in most cases the supply will be fairly adequate. Late buyers will find it difficult to get the goods.

A very noticeable feature of the plush animal business at the present time is the great shortage of plush, and on that account quite a number of the smaller factories have been forced to shut down during the past month. These concerns, possibly only a few of them after all, did not look far enough ahead, and purchased only sufficient material for immediate use. consequently they are now visiting some of the larger concerns in the hope of securing a few pieces of the precious "stuff," but they cannot get it even at top notch prices. One large manufacturer of bears took the writer through the loft above his factory the other day and showed him upwards of 200 pieces of plush which were purchased last December for fear of just such a shortage. The cloak trade will soon be over, however, and then plush will be plentiful, but the loss of a few weeks in the height of the season is a thing not to be desired. Next in importance to the scarcity of plush comes the report that voices or "squawkers" are difficult to get. Most of the larger bear manufacturers placed import orders for large amounts of these goods, but deliveries have been awfully slow. A few concerns made their own voices for a while, but it was too much trouble and too expensive, and then a few firms started in the voice business exclusively, but they could not make them cheap enough. All the different animals such as bull dogs, cats, etc., are now being equipped with voices, and it takes an enormous quantity to supply the demand. Judging from the looks of the various summer resorts there has been nothing but an increase in the demand for Teddy Bears, and people seem to go just as wild over them as ever. About the newest thing in this line is a jet black bear with extra long hair, a red nose, and real claws instead of the soft imitation ones. No, Teddy Bears are not dead, as many were inclined to think they would be, and you are just as safe in buying them to-day as you ever were."

Playthings, 1907.

TEDDY BEAR

14 Inches High When Made Up.

Price 10 Cents.

Lithographed in natural colors on Cloth. Ready to cut out and stuff.

- **EASY TO MAKE** -

Full Instructions Inside.

The Strobel & Wilken Co.

DISTRIBUTERS.

New York.

Illustration 106. Brown manila envelope contained muslin sheet to make a cloth "Teddy Bear", actually a Bruin-Teddy.

Illustration 107. "The Roosevelt Bears," about 10 in. (25.4cm) tall in a seated pose, gray-brown in color. Sheet is 16 in. (40.6cm) x 18 in. (45.7cm). This pattern is adapted from the Bruin-Teddies of the Eaton storybooks. *Playthings,* 1907.

Shown by Selchow & Righter.

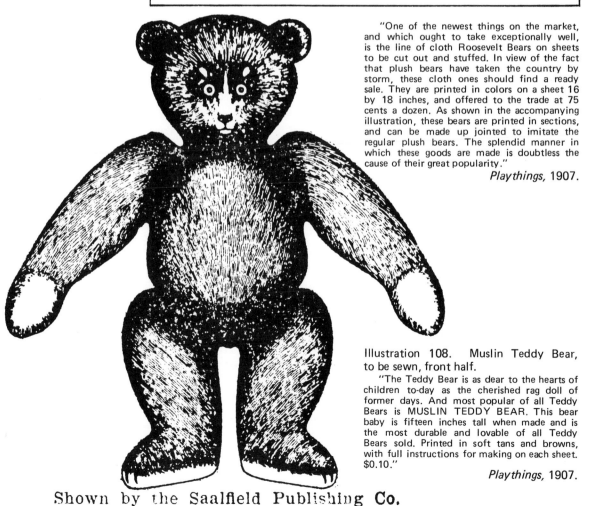

"One of the newest things on the market, and which ought to take exceptionally well, is the line of cloth Roosevelt Bears on sheets to be cut out and stuffed. In view of the fact that plush bears have taken the country by storm, these cloth ones should find a ready sale. They are printed in colors on a sheet 16 by 18 inches, and offered to the trade at 75 cents a dozen. As shown in the accompanying illustration, these bears are printed in sections, and can be made up jointed to imitate the regular plush bears. The splendid manner in which these goods are made is doubtless the cause of their great popularity."

Playthings, 1907.

Illustration 108. Muslin Teddy Bear, to be sewn, front half.

"The Teddy Bear is as dear to the hearts of children to-day as the cherished rag doll of former days. And most popular of all Teddy Bears is MUSLIN TEDDY BEAR. This bear baby is fifteen inches tall when made and is the most durable and lovable of all Teddy Bears sold. Printed in soft tans and browns, with full instructions for making on each sheet. $0.10."

Playthings, 1907.

Shown by the Saalfield Publishing Co.

Collingbourne's   1916

Illustration 109. Flossie, Baby Teddy and Pussy, ready to cut out, sew and stuff. Pattern is entitled "Collingbourne's Happy Family." Doll's name is "Flossie" and the bear's name is "Collingbourne's Mascot." See *Playthings by the Yard* by Frances Walker and Margaret Whitton for actual uncut sheets. *Collingbourne's* magazine, 1916.

Illustration 110.

"Cuddly Toy Teddy. For the tiny tots on your Christmas list here's a cuddly toy Teddy that they'll love at first sight. Crocheted in loop stitch eyes are beads or buttons, Pattern 20¢."

Seattle Post Intelligencer, October 6, 1950.

See Illustration 116 on page 62 for made-up example.

Illustration 111. "The Deltor" pattern showing technique of making a Teddy Bear. *Needle-Art,* Autumn, 1925.

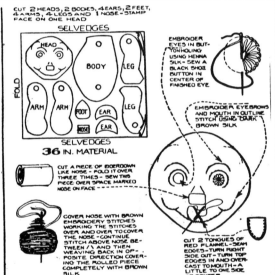

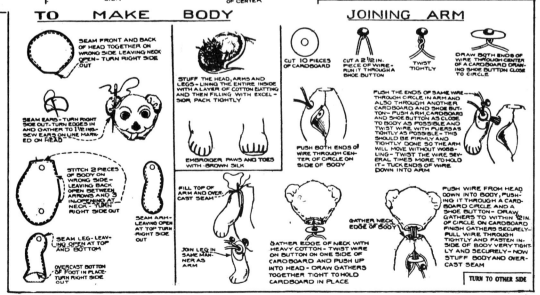

60

Illustration 112. *Home Circle* magazine, October, 1930.

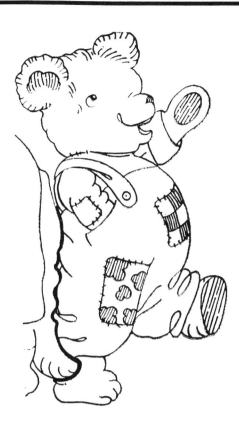

K2003

K2003, Teddy Bear, so dear to the heart of every child. He was stamped on tan, outlined in brown. His eyes, nose and bottoms of his paws were in black. His trousers in green, with a blue patch on his left leg and a red patch on his right leg. These patches are worked semi-solid or if desired, one can applique a piece of print in any bright color, on these patches. They are not furnished with the stamped toys. His suspender in white is effective by sewing a white or black pants button, in place. The lining of his mouth is done in red.

Illustration 113. Simplicity Pattern #8223 for a handmade Paddington Bear. 1977.

Illustration 114.

" 'Little Slipskin', 8½" tall, with zipper in his back. Body of muslin, slip cover of terry cloth. Removable bib and overalls. #3047 Illustrated directions 35¢."
Woman's Home Companion, November, 1938.

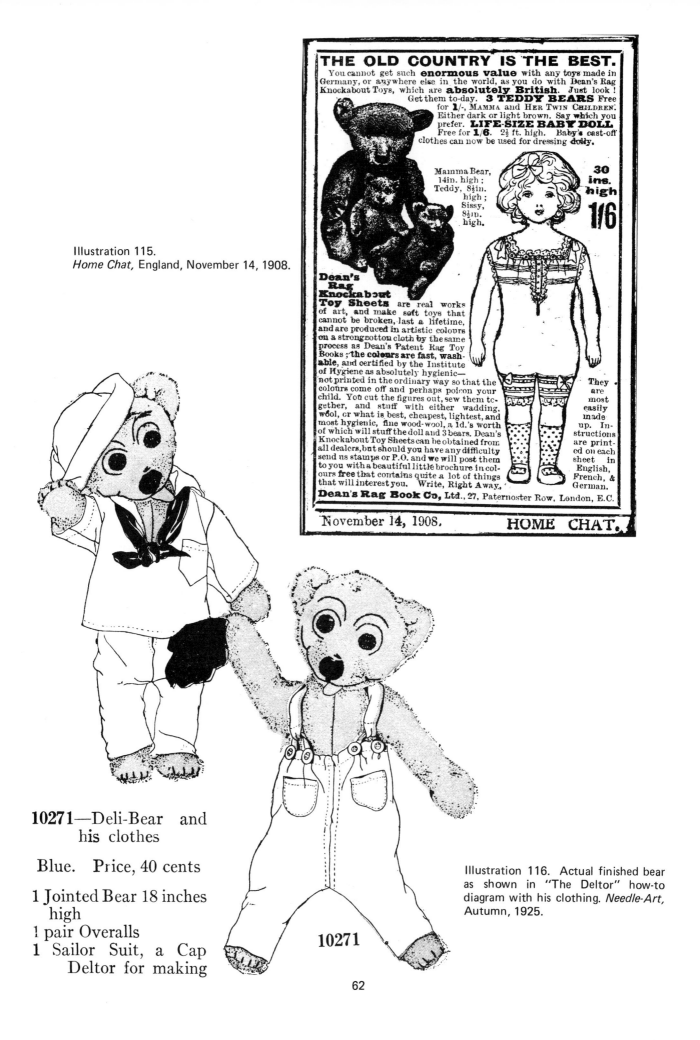

Illustration 115.
Home Chat, England, November 14, 1908.

10271—Deli-Bear and his clothes

Blue.   Price, 40 cents

1 Jointed Bear 18 inches high
1 pair Overalls
1 Sailor Suit, a Cap Deltor for making

10271

Illustration 116. Actual finished bear as shown in "The Deltor" how-to diagram with his clothing. *Needle-Art,* Autumn, 1925.

Illustration 117. "Quilty Cub," #3016. Plaid shirt, blue breeches, all materials included. Sold for forty cents. *Woman's Home Companion,* December, 1937.

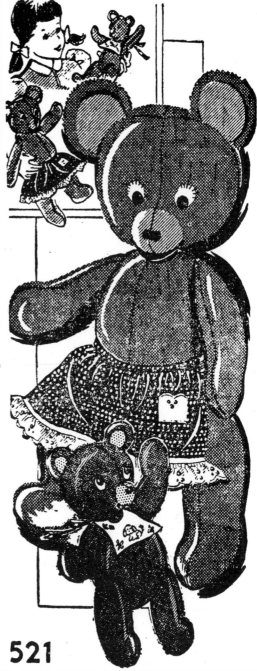

Mother and Baby Bear

By CAROL CURTIS

Made of felt—brown with light tan felt for the noses and ears, a dash of red felt for the tongues —the fat, chubby mama bear and the little baby bear are easy-to-make toys to delight the very young! Mother bears wears a polka dot apron, baby bear has a tiny scrap of print cotton bib. All cutting pieces on pattern chart, stuffing, finishing directions. Mother bear is 13 inches tall, baby is just 6 inches.

Send 25c for the mother and baby bear toys (pattern No. 521) your name, address, pattern number to Carol Curtis, 652 Mission St., San Francisco.

521

Illustration 118. *Seattle Post Intelligencer,* November 12, 1953.

Illustration 119. Goldilocks and the Three Bears pattern, 39 cents. Father Bear is 12 in. (30.5cm); Mother Bear is 10½ in. (36.7cm) tall. Father Bear has yellow and black plaid jacket. There was a second version issued wherein Father's jacket was blue and yellow, with other color variances as well. 1960s.

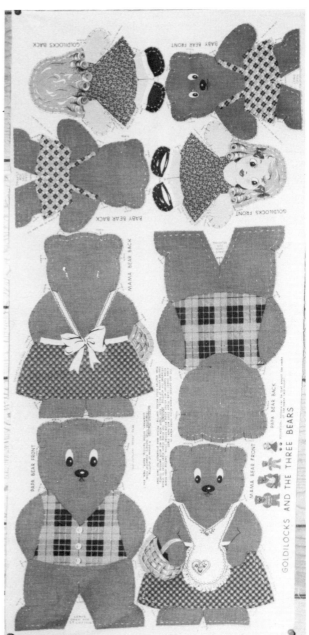

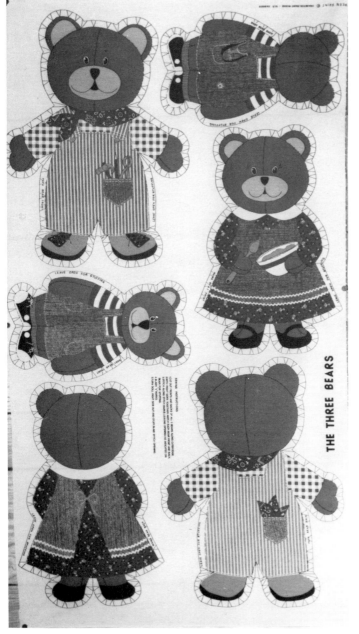

Illustration 120. Cranston Print Works, V.I.P. Fabrics, circa 1977.

RIGHT: Illustration 121. "Stitchin Time Doll." One of Hallmark's "BOSUN BEARS".

"Sew me, stuff me, love me! A learn-to-sew activity for children 8 and up. Needle, thread and stuffing not included. 13 x 7" finished doll $3.50."
Hallmark Cards, Inc., Kansas City No., 64141, 1979.

BELOW: Illustration 122. A Teddy on cloth; #5828 Wurzburg's Needlecraft Novelties, Grand Rapids, Michigan. Green and black checkered trousers, red buttons and patch on pants. Circa late 1930s or early 1940s.

ABOVE: Illustration 123. Large 32 in. (81.3cm) x 36 in. (91.4cm) bear piece on heavy twill material, with flannelette-type reverse surface. Shades of brown with red tongue, inner ear, paw pads. Black eyes and nose. Circa 1950s.

RIGHT: Illustration 124. A brown manila envelope contained directions for Art Fabric Mills Bear, including wooden buttons and brads and shoe-button eyes.

Illustration 125. Art Fabric Mills Bear, cinnamon-colored material, to be cut and sewn.

TEDDY
JOINTED
BEAR

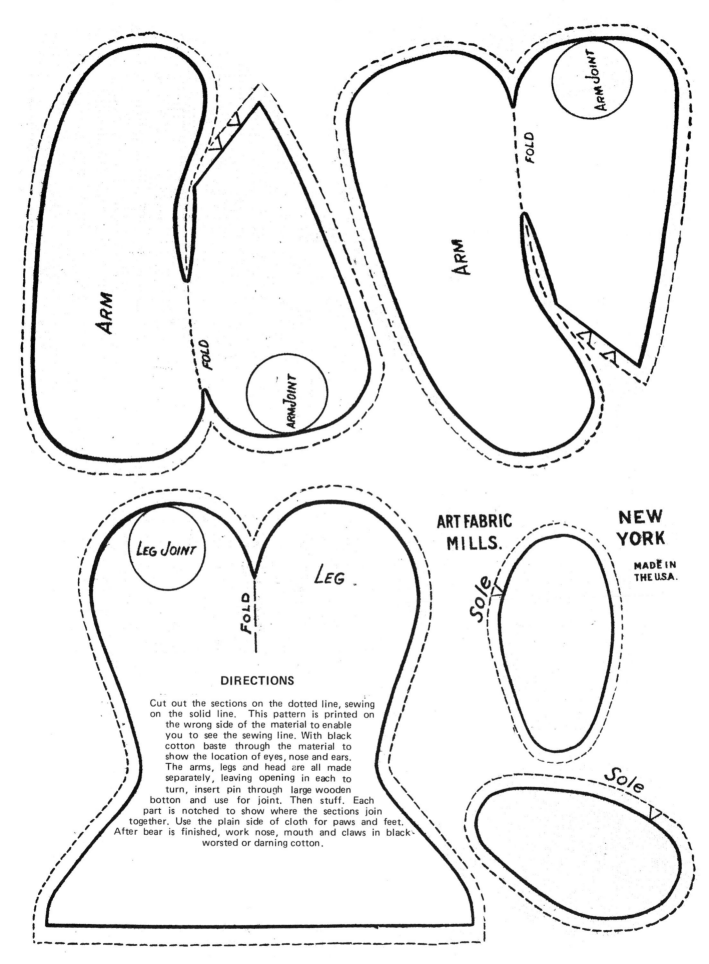

ARM

ARM

ARM JOINT

ARM JOINT

FOLD

FOLD

LEG JOINT

LEG

FOLD

ART FABRIC MILLS.

NEW YORK

MADE IN THE U.S.A.

Sole

Sole

DIRECTIONS

Cut out the sections on the dotted line, sewing on the solid line. This pattern is printed on the wrong side of the material to enable you to see the sewing line. With black cotton baste through the material to show the location of eyes, nose and ears. The arms, legs and head are all made separately, leaving opening in each to turn, insert pin through large wooden botton and use for joint. Then stuff. Each part is notched to show where the sections join together. Use the plain side of cloth for paws and feet. After bear is finished, work nose, mouth and claws in black worsted or darning cotton.

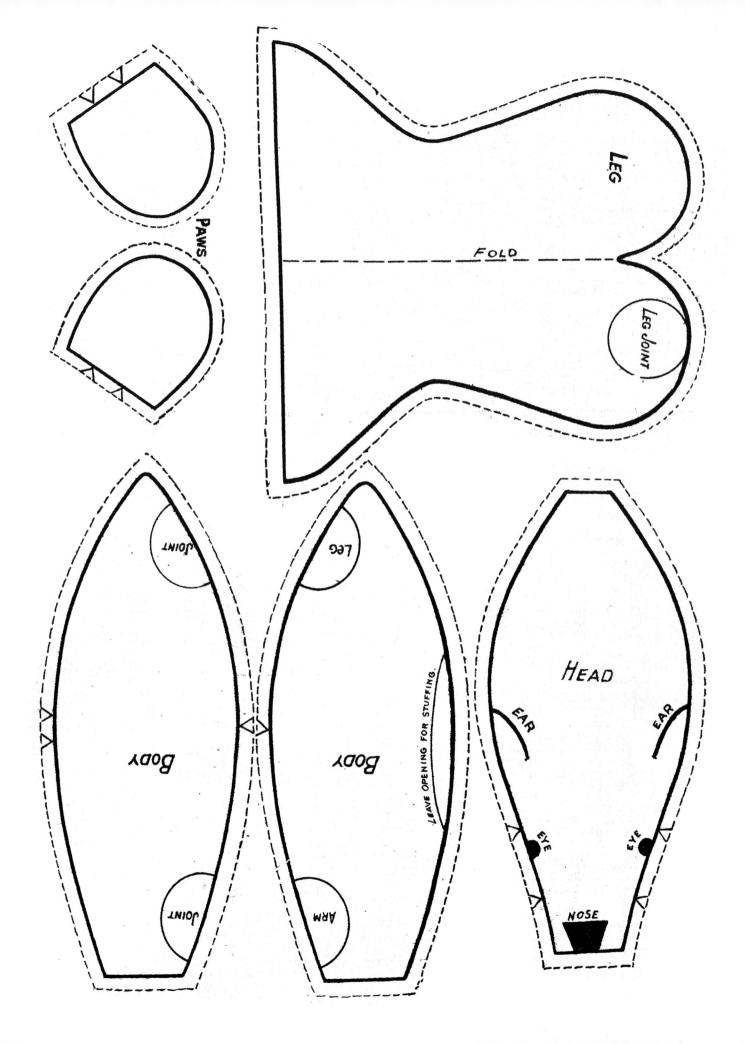

PAWS

LEG

FOLD

LEG JOINT

JOINT

LEG

LEAVE OPENING FOR STUFFING.

BODY

BODY

HEAD

EAR

EAR

JOINT

ARM

EYE

EYE

NOSE

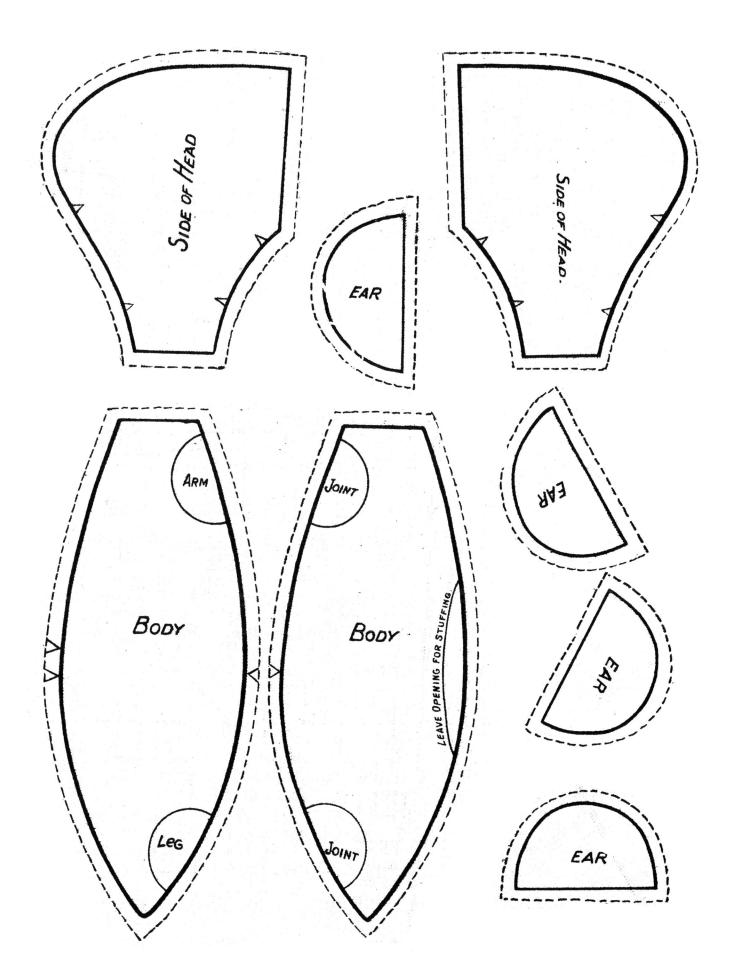

Bear-In-Style

So great was the influence of the new toy Teddy Bear that scarcely any aspect of life was left untouched by him. Teddy Bear coats of soft mohair with Teddy buttons were soon available, as well as hats and muffs. Small aprons were appliqued with Teddy designs to the great joy of the young recipients. It was even very chic for a child modeling a new garment to be holding a Teddy Bear, long after the years of the fad.

Illustration 126. Artist's rendition of Teddy wearing polka-dot clown suit first shown in *The Roosevelt Bears* book. Pattern #308. *The Delineator,* December, 1906.

Illustration 127. Designs That Make Fashion - - Applique Frocks for Kiddies #12684. Stories told in applique for children's clothing. Teddies are still very fashionable in styles. *Pictorial Review,* November, 1922.

9669, *with Open Neck and Puff Sleeves.*

ABOVE: Illustration 128. The Teddy "in style" and the highly desired toy of the day. Art work by Maude Humphrey. *The Delineator,* December, 1906.

9744

With Whole Back, and Belt.

With Bishop Sleeves and Cuffs.

ABOVE: Illustration 129. Stylish child cuddles Teddy Bear dressed in Rough Rider suit. Art work by Maude Humphrey. *The Delineator,* December, 1906.

8499

LEFT: Illustration 130. Boy and bear-in-style. *The American Woman* magazine, 1917.

71

Illustration 131. "Holiday Frocks for Little Girls. Lingerie frocks are de rigueur for little girls for dress, even in mid-winter." This dress could be made for $1.73. (Teddy Bear was "de rigueur" in style also.) *The Delineator,* December, 1907.

BOTTOM RIGHT: Illustration 133. It is still very chic to have Teddy in fashion illustrations. *The Delineator,* April, 1919.

31L5—Bungalow Apron. Fastens on shoulders. Ready-made, stamped for Embroidery. Buttonhole the "Teddy Bear Pockets" to apron with red, use black for eyes, nose and claws. *Colors: Blue, Pink, or Green. Sizes: 2 to 4 yrs.* Postpaid........ **$1.00**

Illustration 132. Knickerbocker Mail Order Co., Inc., catalog, New York. Circa 1914.

Rompers 1585

72

BABIES' COATS.

B 7229X.   B 7230X.

B 7229X—Infants' bearskin coats; smaller in size than sold by the regular cloak houses; a special line made to fit small children from 1 to 5 years old; a much needed line of sizes; made double breasted with 4 large, fancy pearl buttons; deep sailor collar; fastened with hooks and eyes; made of best quality white Salt's bearskin; just the thing for young babies. Each **2.25**

B 7230X—Same quality coat exactly as described above, but made of the whirl or caricule pattern bearskin; pure white; trimmed with 4 fancy pearl buttons; fine satin lining; good pointed sailor collar; fastened with hooks and eyes; sizes 1 to 4. Ea. **3.85**

RIGHT: Illustration 134. Bearskin coats were "the rage" even for babies. G. Sommers wholesale catalog #184, 1907.

B 3463X.   B 3440X.

B 3463X—**Black bear coat;** made of finest quality curly or whirl bear skin; lined throughout with baby blue French mercerized satine; made double breasted with fancy buttons; deep combination turn-down or storm collar; roll back cuff sleeves; black bear skin coats are very popular this season, as they do not soil nor show wear; every merchant can do a large business in these coats; sizes 2, 3, 4, 5 and 6. Each **4.50**

B 3440X—**Northwestern Coat.** Made of the extra heavy, long silky Salt's bear skin cloth; full length children's coat with 7 in. rolling round cape collar, trimmed with 5 small white fur animal heads, set on silk ring crochet ornaments; wide sleeves with deep turn-back cuffs; double breasted front with 6 large fancy pearl buttons; lined throughout with mercerized satine; sizes 2, 3, 4, 5 and 6. Ea. .. **4.50**

LEFT: Illustration 135. Teddy Bears coats, one with five Teddy heads on silk ring crochet ornaments. G. Sommers wholesale catalog #184, St. Paul, 1907.

INFANTS' CLOAKS.

B 3437X—**"Teddy Bear" Coat.** Salt's white silk bear skin coat; regulation length with coat collar and plain sleeves; lined throughout with silkoline; 3 fancy pearl buttons; large size coat of the popular selling cream white bear skin; sizes 2, 3, 4, 5, and 6. Each **2.25**

B 3444BX—**Blue Teddy Bear Coat.** Same coat as above described in dark navy blue; made of Salt's silk bear skin cloth with linings to match; coat collar; 3 gold Teddy Bear buttons; sizes 2, 3, 4, 5 and 6. Ea. **2.25**

B 3444RX—**Red Teddy Bear Coat.** Same coat as above described in solid rich red bear skin, with linings to match, and with 3 gold Teddy Bear buttons in front; sizes 2, 3, 4, 5 and 6. Ea. **2.25**

RIGHT: Illustration 136. White, blue, or red Teddy Bear coats with gold Teddy Bear buttons. The same Salt's manufacturer who advertised plush fabric for Teddy Bears. G. Sommers wholesale catalog #184, 1907.

73

Shirt-Waist 1053
of white linen

Kimono 1021
of cashmere, with bands

Flowered Japanese crêpe
Kimono 1021

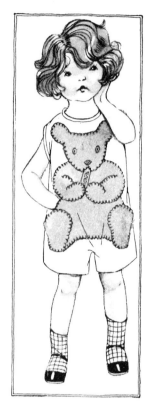

3652 Romper
3 sizes, 2-6

No. 3652, CHILD'S TEDDY
BEAR ROMPER; with spe-
cial embroidery design. Size
4 requires 1¼ yards of 32-
inch material, ½ yard of
32-inch contrasting.

Illustration 138. *McCall's*
magazine, 1924.

ABOVE: Illustration 137. Teddy was the object of affection
and admiration of all ages. *The Delineator,* April, 1907.

RIGHT: Illustration 139. Embroidery designs for children's clothing.
Two dancing bears, a large Teddy
head and bear on all fours serve as
designs. *Pictorial Review,* 1922.

Design 12685

IV. Advertising

There is no greater path to the understanding of an era, or event than that of reading the actual language of the period. The name of the game in *Playthings,* a trade magazine, was salesmanship. Everyone spoke in superlatives, hoping to create the highest opinion for his product.

Yet even after thorough reading of all of this material, the basic truths are apparent. The success of the Teddy Bear was overwhelming. The original popularity was not so much due to President Roosevelt, but to the uniqueness of the toy. The soft and silky mohair plush had not been used to any extent before, and earlier animals were not fully jointed. Some specimens had been made with soft outer coverings but the inner core was hard and unyielding.

The combination of the basic appeal of the bear animal, the yielding quality of the stuffing and the concealed joints was an unbeatable combination. The Teddy Bear was originally conceived as a bear-doll by Steiff intended for a boy child and named "Friend Petz." This apparently was never picked up by American advertisers. No one had any idea of the immense popularity and demand that would follow. Things moved more slowly in the days of no radio or television. Therefore, it was not until 1905-1906 that the American demand began to increase. The first advertisement of jointed bears in *Playthings* appeared in May, 1906, entitled "This is Bruin's Day." By December, 1906 the first mention of the name "Teddy" appears in an advertisement by Horsman.

The Americans began their struggle to compete with the superior imported products of the Steiff firm. If Americans used imported bearskin, or as much as used imported voices in domestic bears, this was a point to feature in their advertising. They hired German workers to come to America and divulge any manufacturing secrets they could. Steiff often mentioned that it was a simple matter for anyone to rip apart one of their specimens for a pattern, but this did not cause them any concern. They felt the finished product would not be the same.

Stobel and Wilken, importers and distributors of dolls and bears, advertised in 1907:

> "We have secured control of a new line of Teddy Bears manufactured here by experts formerly connected with a well-known foreign maker. The goods turned out by this American factory are fully equal to, and in fact cannot be distinguished from, the best imported article."

"Hahn and Amberg, doll and toy manufacturers in New York City, advertised in 1907:

> "We also manufacture very largely a line of golden, cinnamon and white Teddy Bears, made of imported plush and perfectly formed. This article is today virtually taking the place of the doll, and never since it was first introduced has the sale been so large as at the present time. It is practical, durable, and (unlike the doll) unbreakable. Every child wants one. Follow the advice of Oliver Cromwell and 'strike while the iron is hot.' Buy them now."

Illustration 140. Steiff Teddy Bear from 1903; photograph from 1978 Steiff catalog.

Illustration 141. Teddy Bears, Steinfeld Bros., 620 Broadway, New York.

"We carry a complete line of 'TEDDY BEARS' in stock. Made of Bear skin, colors White or Cinnamon, all having voices."

PRICES AS FOLLOWS:

Sizes 8 inch.,	$4.80 per doz. net	Sizes 18 inch.,	$18.00 per doz. net
" 10 "	7.00 " "	" 20 "	21.00 " "
" 12 "	9.00 " "	" 24 "	24.00 " "
" 14 "	12.00 " "	" 30 "	42.00 " "
" 16 "	15.00 " "		

Terms: Strictly 2% 10 days or net 30 days, F.O.B. New York City.

WE GUARANTEE SATISFACTION.

Playthings, 1907.

Illustration 142. The Uncle Remus Line, patented.

    "Don't monkey with our teddy bear patent. The United States Patent Office has granted to the manufacturer of the Uncle Remus line of Teddy Bears, Monkeys, Bunnies, Elephants, Cats, etc. a patent on the improved method originated by him. The patent refers to attaching the eyes in Teddy Bears and other stuffed animals, insuring PERMANENT UNIFORMITY in expression and shaping of the head. Those manufacturers who have copied this method are hereby warned to discontinue the use of same at once."

Playthings, 1907.

TEDDY BEARS

As good as the best. Our bears will sell on sight, because they are well made and look like the imported. Place orders early.

B. EPSTEIN, 724 BROADWAY, NEW YORK

Illustrations 143 & 144. *Playthings*, 1907.

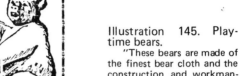

TEDDY BEARS

BUY DIRECT FROM THE MANUFACTURERS

PRICES THE LOWEST
LARGEST SIZES
WORKMANSHIP THE BEST

SEND FOR OUR CATALOG
ALWAYS SOMETHING NEW

WHITESON CO., Mfrs., 240 E. Madison St., Chicago, Ill.

Illustration 145. Play-time bears.

"These bears are made of the finest bear cloth and the construction and workmanship are of the very best. THE ROUECH-BOWDEN CO. DETROIT, MICH. New York Office, 777 Broadway."

Playthings, 1907.

Illustration 146.

"We invite comparison with the best imported lines. The ROUECH-BOWDEN CO., DETROIT, MICHIGAN. Showrooms: New York and San Francisco."

Playthings, 1907.

THE ANTISEPTIC
(Copyright Applied for)

BEAR

A New Departure Insuring the Utmost Cleanliness

Made in Seven Sizes   Two Colors

CINNAMON   WHITE

Be Sure to Ask for the Antiseptic

CAREFULLY INSPECTED BEFORE SHIPMENT

PROMT DELIVERIES

MILLER MFG. CO.

126 Maiden Lane   New York City

Illustration 147. The Antiseptic Bear, Miller Mfg. Co., New York City. *Playthings*, 1907.

D 5422—Performing Bear. Represents a black bear on hind legs with muzzle and cane; press the bulb and the bear runs along on his hind legs. Per doz 2.00

D 4922—The Bear Drummer; representing a big brown bear beating a bass drum. Doz. . . 4.40

Illustrations 148 & 149. G. Sommers catalog, 1907.

TEDDY BEAR ON WHEELS.

D 5412X—Regular brown plush Teddy Bear with turning head, riding a wooden tricycle with iron wheels; can be pulled along the floor by a child; about 11 inches high; ⅓ doz. in box. Ea. .... **.66**

THE PERFORMING BEARS.

Very handsome lifelike mechanical toys. The bears are made of real fur with rich glossy coats.

D 5414X.   D 5416X.   **D 5418X.**

D 5414X—Bear on rings. Couple of upright poles 14½ inches high on a wooden platform 5x6½ inches; the bear is hanging by a pair of rings; when wound up with key clockwork mechanism makes him swing rapidly; will attract all the neighborhood when running in a show case or window. Ea. ....**.85**

D 5416X—Represents wooden parallel bars; wooden platform 4x10 inches; when wound up the bear swings back and forward and does curious stunts. Ea. ....**.85**

D 5418X—Performing Bear with real black fur; wound up by key; swings on pair of upright ladders in very comical lifelike manner; stands on wooden platform 5¼x6½ inches; 14 inches high; makes a pretty show piece as well as toy. Ea. **.95**

Illustration 150. G. Sommers catalog, 1907.

March, 1908

Isn't He a Dear?

This is the cutest little Teddy Bear you ever saw. His legs, his arms, and his head all move, and you can twist him into so many funny positions that he will keep you laughing by the hour. When you squeeze him he cries. You will love him the minute you see him.

Given as a special premium to any boy or girl who will send us only four new subscriptions to The Modern Priscilla at 50 cents each.

Illustration 151. *The Modern Priscilla* magazine, 1908.

TEDDY BEARS ON WHEELS.

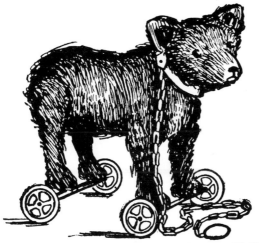

D 5809—Brown Plush Teddy Bear; turning head; leather collar; running on four strong iron wheels; 9 inches long; about 7 inches high, a new and popular toy. Doz **8.50**

M 5811X—Large Teddy Bear on heavy iron wheels; turning head; heavy leather collar and buckle; long nickeled steel chain for pulling along the floor. Ea.. **1.50**

MAMMOTH TOY BEARS For show pieces or toys. See cut above.

Heavy brown plush Teddy Bears on extra weight iron platform and wheels; to use in place of hobby horse; heavy leather dog collar; long nickeled steel chain.

D 5813X—This bear stands about 21½ inches high; his body is 27 inches long. Ea **7.50**

P. S. Cut of the Teddy Bear on wheels No. 5809 will show how this fine toy looks, only this is much larger.

Illustration 152. G. Sommers catalog, 1907.

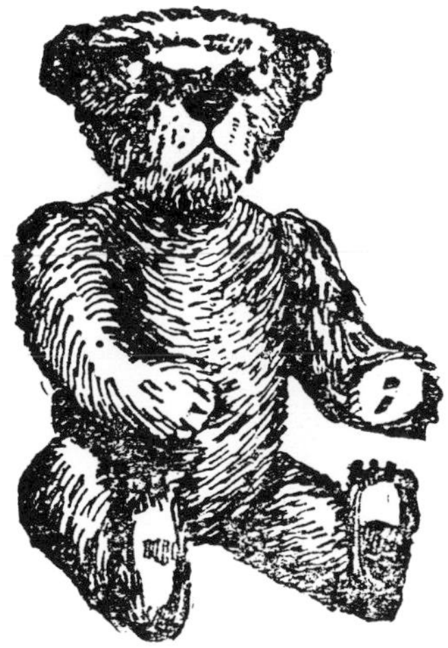

TEDDY BEAR FREE
12 Inches Tall.

Teddy Bear is a fine specimen of his kind, made of Shaggy Cinnamon Plush and 12 inches tall. His head, his arms and his legs are jointed on to the body so that they can all be turned in any direction. And you should see him shake his head and hear him grunt when you hit him in the stomach! Teddy is all the rage in the cities. The children carry him to school and even the grown-up ladies carry him with them when they go out for a walk or ride, or to the theatre. The more costly Teddys sell as high as $25.00 each. We have picked out this one for you on account of his good size, his jointed head, arms and legs, his cute grunt and his fine cinnamon color. We will send him to you free by mail if you will sell for us only five of our fine tinted 16-inch centerpieces at 25 cents each. They are hand tinted on Irish Linen finish Ulster cloth, and every lady wants one. We send centerpieces free. When you have sold them send us the $1.25 and we will send Teddy Bear to you at once. This is a fine Teddy for a very little effort and is sure to please you. Send to

F. R. BIRD CO., Dept. 222, 291 Congress St., Boston, Mass.

Illustration 153. *Comfort* magazine, 1907.

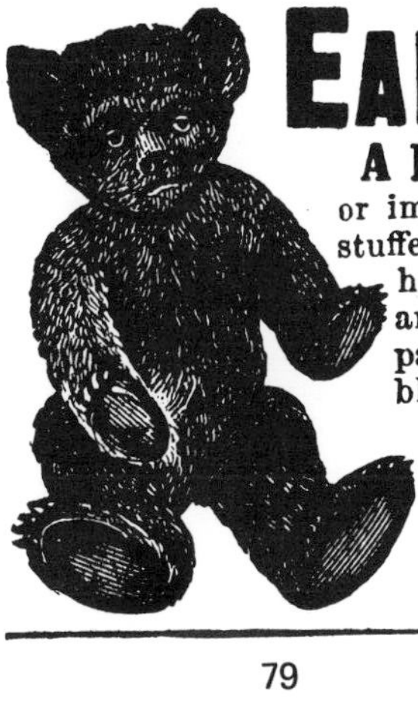

EARN A TEDDY BEAR
A REAL TEDDY BEAR—NOT A PATTERN

or imitation, a foot high, made of fine **Silky Fur Cloth** stuffed with cotton, making him soft, fluffy and durable. His head and legs are movable, his cunning face is life-like and appealing. Every one loves him. Free for selling 20 packages of Royal Sheet Bluing at 10c each. Order the bluing to-day. When sold send us the $2.00 and we will send you the **Teddy Bear made up complete,** just as described same day we receive the money. Your money back if he isn't the dearest little fellow you ever saw. Write to-day, Teddy is waiting for you.

ROYAL BLUING CO., DEPT. 211, CHICAGO

Illustration 154. *The Delineator,* magazine, 1907.

No. 406.—Imported Teddy Bear.

Teddy Bears are so popular that any little boy or girl who does not own one now-a-days is quite out of the fashion. With little girls they largely take the place of dolls as playthings, or are used in connection with dolls, and for little boys they are the greatest playthings ever invented. And so, as every little boy and girl in these days must have a Teddy Bear, we have thought that our offer of one of them as a premium will be appreciated by a large number of parents. This bear is imported from Germany, and is made of dark brown bear cloth, woolly and shaggy. He is eleven inches long, and his legs and head revolve, so that he may be made to assume all sorts of amusing attitudes. He sits down, stands up or walks on all four paws as the owner elects, and is a genuine contortionist in his ability to manipulate the various members of his body.

When his sides are pressed he emits a well-defined squeal. Altogether he is a most amusing little animal, and any little boy or girl who gets him on Christmas morning or at any other time will be provided with hours of solid fun. He is too large for the little one's stocking, but will make a good appearance when suspended at its side, and nothing that Santa Claus is likely to leave behind him when making his rounds on Christmas Eve will meet with a more enthusiastic reception. If Santa Claus doesn't take the hint it will be no fault of ours. We will send the Teddy Bear above described by mail post-paid as a premium to any one sending us a club of **Three** subscribers to THE PEOPLE'S HOME JOURNAL for sixteen months at 35 cents each, or for **Six** subscribers for sixteen months at 25 cents each, provided we receive the club on or before November 1st, 1909. After that date this premium will be given for the same number of subscriptions, but said subscriptions will then be for one year only.

Illustration 155. *People's Home Journal* magazine, 1907.

Illustration 156. Fully jointed Teddy Bear with voice, in cinnamon or white color; stands 12 in. (30.5cm) tall; complete with collar and leader; priced at $1.00. (For comparison, a jointed-body doll 23 in. (58.4cm) tall with fully-jointed arms and legs, good quality bisque head with moving eyes and pearly teeth, and sewn wig was also $1.00.) Featured on cover of the Christmas Gifts catalog #44A for Siegel Cooper Company, New York, 1907.

HAS A VOICE

ALMOST LIKE A LIVE BEAR

The Teddy Bear I want to give you is a big one, nearly a foot high. He is made of real, genuine bearskin cloth of the finest quality. His eyes, nose, mouth and skin are so natural he looks like a real, live bear. His arms, legs and head are movable, so you can make him do just what you want.

I have had several thousand of these real Teddy Bears made especially for me, to GIVE AWAY to the children of this country.

I know you will like him, because my own little girl has such fun with her Teddy, as she calls him, and that is why I want to give every one of you one of these Teddy Bears free. They are the LATEST NOVELTY TOY for children and are named after our own PRESIDENT "TEDDY" ROOSEVELT. because he is so fond of bears. PRESIDENT ROOSEVELT HIMSELF PRAISES THE TEDDY BEARS.

Remember, you can get the bear absolutely free. All I want you to do in return is to give me a few minutes of your time. Read my offer in the lower left-hand corner which tells you all about it.

Illustration 157. P. J. Allen, New York, December, 1907.

1914

Illustration 158. Steiff Catalog, 1914.

DOROTHY WITH HER TEDDY BEAR AND DOLL

Illustration 159. *Mother's Magazine,* December, 1907.

TEDDY BEARS

"HARMLESS PLAYFELLOWS"

The country has gone wild over TEDDY BEARS

Everywhere the little white and brown bears are contributing to the keen pleasure of the children with their droll antics and poses. They are substantially made, have movable joints which enable them to assume the scores of comical poses, and in their white and brown plush coats, are natural and lifelike to the last degree.

Price $1.50, $2.00, $3.00 and $4.00

ent prepaid direct from factory on

Get Your Teddy Bear

direct from the importer. Our jointed

Teddy Bears are the very best quality and we can save you money. Teddy Bears have been a wonderfully popular novelty with children. Will you let us send one for **your's?** The bears come in three colors, white, cinnamon or brown, in these sizes:
12 inch, $1.50; 14 inch, $2.00; 16 inch, $2.50; 18 inch, $3.00; 20 inch, $3.75; 22 inch, $4.75; 24 inch, $5.25.

Money order or postage stamps accepted. Orders received right away will be promptly filled.

ELMER MFG. CO., 1
(Established 20 years)

"We present herewith . . . a very wise looking bear, but you will consider him much wiser when you learn that he can talk. The Talking Bear is what they call him, and he should make friends with the children very readily. Outwardly he is just the same as any other plush bear, being made in all sizes and in various colors, but inwardly he is an entirely different proposition, for he is so constructed that he will grunt when tilted the least bit to one side, and such a natural grunt, too. It is more like a deep growl and will fascinate the youngsters. Each one of these new bears has a chain attached to his nose (which does not appear in the illustration), making him very similar to those which perform in the streets. They can be retailed at popular prices."
Playthings, 1907.

Illustrations 160A, 160B & 161. All from *The Delineator* magazine, December, 1907.

BIG 14 in. TEDDY BEAR
and Santa Claus House both for $1.00
Every boy and girl crazy over them. He squeaks when you squeeze him, has movable head, arms, and legs, and makes no end of fun. Just what you want for a Christmas gift.
G. H. W. BATES CO., Box 1540, Boston, Mass.

LITTLE FOLKS'

TEDDY BEAR FREE!

This is **just the nicest, funniest Teddy Bear you could possibly imagine,** and we are giving it away FREE! It is a **large-sized, life-like, genuine imported fuzzy, brown Teddy Bear —ONE OF THE REAL TEDDY BEARS** that people have fairly **gone crazy over.** Shining black eyes, a comical, movable head, and movable arms and legs. You can put Teddy Bear into all sorts of laughable positions. This Teddy Bear stands nearly one-half yard high, and is **really a talking bear besides,** for when you squeeze him Teddy gives a squeak that makes him funnier than ever. **You can get him easily,** for we give him for selling only 24 packages of Bluine at 10 cents a package. When sold return our **$2.40** and **we will send you this full-sized Teddy Bear just as promised.** Write today Address BLUINE MFG. CO., **36** Mill St., Concord Junction, Mass.

Illustration 162. *Little Folks* magazine, December, 1907.

Illustration 163.

"There are lots of Teddy Bears. In fact, 'the woods are full of them.' But there is only one Whistling Teddy Bear, and here he is. *Spare Moments* is the first and only magazine to offer a Self Whistling Teddy Bear. He is different from others—he does something. Stand him on his head and he whistles; restore him to an upright position and he whistles again. Why buy a dumb Teddy Bear when you can get one who has such a life-like, roguish look as that shown in the above photograph, and who stands up, sits down and whistles. In fact, he's as near like a live bear as a Teddy Bear can be made, and every boy or girl will go wild over him at sight. He is really a fine fellow—much better than a doll, and just the right size to carry in your arms. He is the most cunning and enjoyable Teddy Bear you ever saw.

We will send one of these Self Whistling Teddy Bears, carefully packed and postage paid, to any one who will send us four new yearly subscribers to *Spare Moments* at 50 cents each."

Spare Moments magazine, November, 1907.

A SHIPLOAD OF TEDDY BEARS.

"Teddy bears by the thousand, wee little fellows, larger ones and fuzzy monsters as big as a man, are the cargo of the steamship Macedonia, which arrived at Boston from Antwerp on the 4th of this month. Captain Porath said:

'Over in Germany the children don't take well to Teddy as a pet. Our girls love to make dresses for their dollies. It teaches them to sew and to be motherly, but you Americans are a strenuous people, you know.' "

Playthings, 1907.

PREMIUM No. 619

Eleven=Inch Teddy Bear for Children

Given Free for a Club of Only Two Yearly Subscribers at Fifty Cents Each, or Four at Thirty-five Cents Each ✄

Teddy Bears have become so popular during the past year that any little boy or girl who does not own one now-a-days is quite out of the fashion. With little girls they largely take the place of dolls as playthings, or are used in connection with dolls, and for little boys they are the greatest playthings ever invented. And as every little boy and girl in these days must have a Teddy Bear, we have thought that our offer of one of them as a premium will be appreciated by a large number of parents. This bear is made of dark brown bear cloth, woolly and shaggy. He is eleven inches long, and his legs and head revolve, so that he may be made to assume all sorts of amusing attitudes. He sits down, stands up or walks on all four paws as the owner elects, and is a genuine contortionist in his ability to manipulate the various members of his body. When his stomach is pressed he emits a well-defined squeal. Altogether he is a most amusing little animal, and any little boy or girl who gets him on Christmas morning or at any other time will be provided with hours of solid fun for a long time to come. He is too large for the little one's stocking, but will make a good appearance when suspended at its side, and nothing that Santa Claus is likely to leave behind him when making his rounds on Christmas Eve will meet with a more enthusiastic reception. If Santa Claus doesn't take the hint it will be no fault of ours. We will send the Teddy Bear above described by mail postpaid, also THE LADIES' WORLD for one year, upon receipt of **Eighty-five Cents;** or we will give the Teddy Bear *free* to any one sending us a club of **Two** subscribers for one year at 50 cents each, or **Four** subscribers at 35 cents each. Or we will send the Teddy Bear postpaid, without subscription to the magazine, upon receipt of 50 cents.

Illustration 164. *The Ladies: World* magazine, December 1908.

Illustration 165. *Playthings,* 1908.

Illustration 166. Left to right: Grandma Bear with cap and spectacles, speaks to Baby Bear when squeezed; 10 in. (25.4cm) Baby Bear; Old Growling Bear; Comical Cat; Clown Bear, dressed in regular clown costume with cap and bells; Grandpa Bear, wearing overcoat and hat. *The Modern Priscilla* magazine, 1908.

Just Look at the Teddy Bears!

Austrian-American Toy Novelty Mfg. Co., New York City.

"Manufacturers of all kinds of Animal Toys. We have been manufacturing this line of Toys for the past 16 years at Vienna, Austria, and are now ready to supply the trade with our line of goods, at prices that will meet the European market, saving the inconvenience of placing import orders.

The leading lines of stuffed animal toys made of real skins, hand painted velvet, felt and imitation furs. Our line is similar to that made in Germany and Austria."

Playthings, 1908.

Illustration 167. Butler Brothers wholesale catalog, 1908.

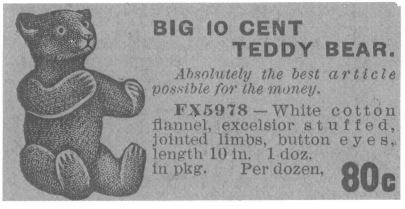

OUR GREAT "TEDDY BEAR" DEPARTMENT.

TEDDY BEARS.

Brown plush bears. All have swiveled legs so that they can be made to sit, stand and put in all kinds of positions. The biggest selling article of the day.

D 5781—Nearly 8 inches long, a Teddy bear to retail for 10 or 15c.; 1 doz. in pkg. Doz.................................98

D 5783—25c. Teddy bear with turning head; swiveled legs; about 9 inches long; 1 doz. Doz.............................2.25

D 5785—50c. Teddy Bear with voice; 11½ inches long; 1 doz. in pkg. Doz...4.00

D 5787—Large brown Teddy Bear with voice; turning head and sitting body; movable legs; ½ doz. in pkg. Doz...........6.00

D 5789—15-inch large Teddy Bear with voice; ½ doz. in pkg. Doz...8.50

THE ORIGINAL TEDDY BEARS.

Genuine Imported Teddy Bears with voices. Made by Margaret Steiff.

"The biggest craze that every struck the land."

A new line of stuffed bears; soft, silky imitation fur; leather padded feet; limbs and head are fastened with turning metal plates and can be twisted in all kinds of directions; bodies so flexible that they take any attitude; come assorted, cinnamon, brown and pure white.

D 5791—Genuine imported Teddy Bears, 10 inches. Per doz.........................8.50

D 5793—12½ inches. Imported Bears. Doz...12.00

D 5795—Imported Teddy Bears, 13½ inches. Doz...................................18.00

D 5797X—Big Roosevelt Bear. 15½ inches long; heavy body; will make a good show piece. Ea..2.00

D 5799X—Big Imported Teddy Bear; 20½ inches, big body. Each.....................3.50

D 5801X—Teddy Bear show piece. A mammoth bear show piece; 24 inches long; extra large body, Each..5.00

D 5803X—Our largest Teddy Bear show piece; 28 inches long; mammoth size; in every respect. Each..6.90

Illustration 168. G. Sommers catalog, 1907.

84

2 TEDDY BEARS and whole Play Suit GIVEN

The cutest and best two Teddy Bears ever given away. Any little boy or girl will hug them with delight and never tire of them as playmates. These are **imported bears** and of **best make. Their heads, arms and legs** can be moved into all sorts of comical positions. They keep their shape and their furry appearance in spite of the roughest handling. Send your name and address for 24 pieces of jewelry to sell at 10 cents each. When sold, send us the $2.40 and we will send both bears without delay. **As an extra premium we give a Play Suit and College Hat for the Bears.**

COLUMBIA NOVELTY CO.
Dept. 147   East Boston, Mass.

Illustration 169. *Mother's Magazine,* February, 1908.

Big Doll and Teddy Bear GIVEN AWAY

Girls—Do you want a great Big Beauty Doll and a Genuine Teddy Bear Free? Dolly has a genuine bisque head, hands and feet and a strong, well-made body. She can move her arms and legs, turn her head and go to sleep (eyes close automatically when you lay her down). She has large, expressive eyes, pearly teeth, rosy cheeks, natural golden curls. Dolly is completely dressed from head to foot in silks and laces.

Teddy Bear is the Cutest Fellow You Ever Saw. He is fat and shaggy; has movable head, arms and legs, so that he can stand up or sit down. In whatever position you put him he is so comical that you cannot help laughing at him.

Girls, if You Want This Handsome Big Dressed Doll, just as described, and the Teddy Bear, just write us and we will send you at once 18 Jeweled Lucky Star Scarf Pins to sell at 10c each. You can easily sell them all the same day you get them. When sold send us the money ($1.80) and **the same day** that we receive it we will forward both the Big Doll and the Teddy Bear. Write now to **AMERICAN DOLL CO.   Dept. 140   Attleboro, Mass.**

Illustration 170. *The Delineator,* magazine December, 1907.

85

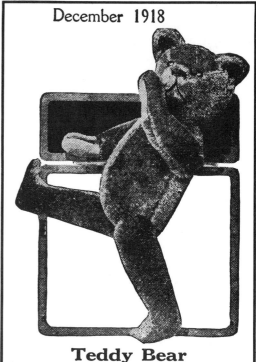
ABOVE LEFT: Illustration 171. Butler Brothers wholesale catalog, 1908; a close-out bargain.

ABOVE RIGHT: Illustration 172. *The American Woman* magazine, December, 1918.

RIGHT: Illustration 173. *Ladies' World* magazine, March, 1908.

86

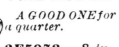

Illustration 174. Butler Brothers catalog, 1910.

Illustration 175. A special close-out stock offered in Butler Brothers wholesale catalog, 1908.

No. 18K23366 The latest idea in bears. This family consists of one bear measuring 7¾ inches in height and two 4½ inches. The large bear is cinnamon color and the smaller are cinnamon and white. Are made of prepared cotton on strong wire, the arms and legs being movable so that the bears will assume any position desired. These bears are practically indestructible, and no matter how roughly used by the children they can always be put back into their original shape. This is the first time that any one has been enabled to sell three bears at the astonishing low price of 25 cents. Come put up in neat box.

25c

Price the entire family 3 for.....

If by mail, postage extra, 6 cents

If you desire the larger stuffed bears with imported bear-skin plush, refer to Nos. 18K23358 to 18K23364.

MECHANICAL TUMBLING PLUSH ANIMALS.

Good models, regulation Teddy bear plush, wound by turning arms, when laid on table turns somersaults.

2F5992, Teddy Bear—9 in. ¼ doz. in box.
Doz. **$4.00**
2F5993, Cat—9 in. ¼ doz. in box...Doz. **$4.25**
2F5990, Teddy Bear—10½ in. 1 in box.
Each, **72c**

LEFT: Illustration 176. Sears, Roebuck and Co. catalog, 1908.

ABOVE: Illustration 177. Butler Brothers catalog, 1910.

THE TUMBLING TEDDY BEAR

I am the merriest, newest and best member of the Teddy Bear family. I will do all sorts of funny tricks, can turn somersaults down an ironing board, stand on my head, hind feet, front feet, or all fours. If you throw me right, I will turn in the air and land on my feet. ¶ I need no winding and cannot get out of order. In fact I can take the worst pounding a Teddy Bear ever got and still be ready for fun. My extremely amusing antics have made me the most marvelous success of any toy of modern times. ¶ I am made of the best material in white, brown and tan.

Every Child Wants Me. Get Me Early for a Merry Christmas.

Send $2.00 to **G. C. GILLESPIE**
Mail Order Office, 132 Nassau St., New York City

Illustration 178. Mechanical Teddy Bears, *Ladies' Home Journal* magazine, December, 1909.

Real Plush TEDDY BEAR **FREE**

Genuine real golden plush Teddy Bear, with head, arms and legs that move around, and funny face. Stands up, sits down, and has a funny squeak. One of the nicest Teddy Bears ever given away. Given for selling only 12 packages Bluine at 10 cents each.

BLUINE MFG,, CO., 838 Mill St., **Concord Junction, Mass.**

Illustration 179. December, 1915.

FAMOUS "BILLIKEN" DOLL.

A *"luck-bringer"* for your doll department. Still popular will never go out of favor with the little ones.

1F4903—13 in., well modeled chubby white or pink velvet body, jointed shoulders and hips, unbreakable head, painted features, ribbon bow at neck. ½ doz. in box.

Doz. **$8.50**

Illustration 180. Butler Brothers catalog, 1910.

TEDDY BEAR "MAMMA" DOLLS.

Says "Mamma" automatically when laid down. When shaken cries naturally. *You can sell any number of these.*

1F4726—13 in., soft stuffed, jointed limbs, well modeled long plush body, peak hood, felt hands and feet, celluloid face, painted features and hair. 1 in box. Each, **75c**

1F4727—16¼ in., as 1F4726. Each, **$1.10**

NOVELTY TEDDY BEAR DOLLS.

1F4871—8½ in., well modeled, soft stuffed sitting body, jointed limbs, covered with mohair plush, turning head with hood, celluloid face painted features and hair, voice. ½ doz. in box, asstd. colors. Doz. **$2.25**

1F4872—12½ in., felt hands and feet, muff as 1F4871. ½ doz. in box, asstd. gray, white, blue, etc...Doz. **$4.25**

1F4871   1F4872

Illustration 181 & 182. Butler Brothers catalog, 1910.

FINEST QUALITY PET ANIMAL TOYS

FINEST QUALITY PLUSH TEDDY BEARS.

Plush Bears are not a fad, but are actually more popular than ever before. No toy brought out in recent years will hold the interest of the child so well as the bear, besides giving most splendid service, as they are almost indestructible. The quality we offer is of celebrated German manufacture, the best that money can buy. Beautiful long silk plush, perfectly featured body, very true to life, full jointed, allowing the bear to assume countless comical positions. All sizes are fitted with the very latest improved automatic growling voice, which requires no pushing or pressing to operate. The bear growls when the body is tilted forward. All fitted with glass eyes. Comes in natural cinnamon color only. Priced according to size and proportion as given below.

No.	Height	Shipping weight	Price
No. 49K825	Height, 10 inches.	Shipping weight, 10 ounces.	Price..........$0.63
No. 49K826	Height, 12 inches.	Shipping weight, 16 ounces.	Price........... .97
No. 49K827	Height, 14 inches.	Shipping weight, 18 ounces.	Price........... 1.38
No. 49K828	Height, 16 inches.	Shipping weight, 24 ounces.	Price........... 1.77
No. 49K829	Height, 18 inches.	Shipping weight, 30 ounces.	Price........... 2.35
No. 49K846	Height, 20 inches.	Shipping weight, 34 ounces.	Price........... 2.75

Illustration 183. Sears, Roebuck and Co. catalog, 1912.

CINNAMON PLUSH BEARS.

The pick of products of domestic bear manufacturers.

Fine models, long pile brown plush soft stuffed, turning head, glass eyes, jointed limbs, chamois palms and soles, **voice.** 1 in box.

F3600—14 in	Each,	$0	55
F3601—16 "	"		72
F3602—18 "	"		84
F3603—20 "	"		95
F3604—22 "	"	1	10

F3493 —"Crying Cub." 12 in., brown, ribbon collar, double bellows crying voice. ⅓ doz. in box....Doz. **$4.20**

BROWN PLUSH BEARS ON WHEELS.

Strongly made, fine models, brown plush covered, nose rings with long chain leash, wheels connected by metal bars.

F3510—Length 8 in., ht. 5⅛. ½ doz. in pkg......................Doz. **$2.25**

POPULAR PRICED TEDDY BEARS.

F3491   F3492

F3491—7½ in., soft stuffed brown cotton plush, jointed limbs, button eyes, leatherette collar. 1 doz. in box......................Doz. **92c**

F3492 — Turning Heads. 9 in., brown, with voice, soft stuffed, long "Teddy Bear" plush, jointed limbs, felt soles, glass eyes. ½ doz. in box. Doz. **$2.15**

F3495—17¾ in., ribbon collar, **automatic deep growl.** 2 brown, 1 white. ¼ doz. in pkg....Doz. **$8.75**

F3509—Length 10 in., ht. 7⅛, long pile plush, metal muzzle. ⅓ doz. in pkg...................Doz. **$4.50**

Illustration 184. Butler Brothers catalog, 1914.

Plush Teddy Bear.

Given to any Companion subscriber for one new subscription and 15 cents extra, postage included. Price $1.00, post=paid.

This Teddy Bear is made of the finest quality cinnamon - colored plush, has jointed neck and legs, and stands 10 inches high, which is the popular size. It is a handsome little animal, too. Soft and comfortable to the touch, and will make the children a delightful bed companion. If desired, the Bear can be dressed in a variety of ways. It can also be thrown about, and is not easily injured. It is not necessary to create a demand for the Bear, for its fame has already reached every section of our land.

Illustration 185. *Youth's Companion* magazine, October 21, 1909.

"Electro" Teddy Bear
The Latest Toy Novelty
4L5580

The latest sensation of the season in the novelty toy line. A Teddy Bear that's different! It has eyes that shine—real electric eyes—that sparkle or grow dim as you want them. Also a good, strong bark that will please the children. No toy on the market will give the children more pleasure of amusement. Best of all, our price puts this excellent child's toy within the reach of all. A regular four dollar toy that we are selling at only $2.25.

Our "Electro" Teddy Bear measures 20 inches in length and has electric bulbs for eyes. By simply pressing a button in the stomach the eyes are made to flash. The battery supplying the current is good for 6,000 flashes, and in addition we give an extra battery with each bear. When the old battery is exhausted, the new one may be inserted by simply opening the seam in the back of the bear, detaching the two wires from top of old battery, inserting new one and attaching wires to it. The bear may then be sewed up and Teddy is alive again. Additional batteries may be purchased in any electrical supply house, or we can supply them at price shown below.

This bear is both instructive and amusing and will appeal to grown-ups as well as the children. Supplied in gray or cinnamon. The identical bear is being sold for $4.00. Our price is.................$2.25
Weight, 48 oz.

Illustration 186. Montgomery Ward catalog, 1914.

Growling Bear

When you roll this playful bear over on his back, he growls — "Grrr-grrr." He is mounted on four wheels, so you may pull him along the floor by the chain. Imitation leather muzzle. Papier-mache body, covered with soft imitation bearskin in dark color. Length, 8¾ inches. **Imported.** Shipping weight, 1¾ pounds.

48 C 3276.....................**98¢**

98¢

Illustration 187. Montgomery Ward catalog, 1922.

Plush Teddy Bear

4L5702—Price, 98c
Shipping weight, 1 lb.

Teddy Bear on Wheels. Plush covered. Metal wheels on feet. Has leather muzzle. Halter, buckle and leading chain. Bright, glass eyes. Well stuffed body. Height, 7¼ inches. Length, 10 inches.

Illustration 188. Montgomery ward catalog, 1914.

TOY ANIMALS

TEDDY BEARS WITH VOICE.

F3492

F3945

F3492—9 in., fine model, long plush, turning head, glass eyes, jointed limbs, voice. ½ doz. box. ....Doz. **$2.20**

F3495 — 16 in., long plush, jointed limbs, turning head, well modeled, automatic growl, 3 in pkg., 2 cinnamon, 1 white.
Each, **75c**

Push ALL THE YEAR Toys

Illustration 189. Butler Brothers catalog, May, 1913.

GENUINE IMPORTED

TEDDY BEAR.

Big 11 in. size, attractively put up.

F5981— 11 in., made of best long plush, soft stuffed, jointed head, arms and legs. Can be placed in most any position. Felt palms and soles, each with voice. Brown or white, Each in white glazed box.

Each, **69c**

Illustration 190. Butler Brothers wholesale catalog, 1908; a special stock close-out.

F5478 — **Teddy bear,** 8½ in. high, plush body, glass eyes, stitched features, jointed arms and legs, wound with arms, tumbling action. 1 in box.
Each, **95c**

F5481 — **Teddy bear,** 9¾ in. high, plush head and hands, glass eyes, stitched features, felt trousers, coat and hat, metal body, walks for-forwards and backwards, turns in circle, moving head and arms, foot levers adjust action, automatic stop in back, with winding key. ½ doz. in box.
Doz. **$18.00**

Illustration 191. Imported mechanical toys, Butler Brothers catalog, Fall 1923.

POPULAR NOVELTY DOLL.

F 4767 – "Teddy Doll." 24¾ in., unbreakable composition head, painted features, soft stuffed bodies, jointed limbs, turning head, felt hands and feet, blue, red or gray baby lamb cloth covered body and coat effect, patent leather belt with glove-button clasp, white baby lamb cloth collar and toque. 1 in box. Each 98 c

LEFT: Illustration 192. Butler Brothers catalog, 1910.

ABOVE: Illustration 193. *Ladies' Home Journal,* 1914.

Illustration 194. Sears, Roebuck and Co. catalog, 1908.

The EFFANBEE Teddy Bears and stuffed toys are made in sizes and qualities retailing as low as **35c.** each. Some of them growl, others squeak, some have electric eyes, and all are true to life in every particular.

21

Paint Will Not Come Off

Illustration 195. Dolls//Ancient and Modern//Fleischaker & Baum catalog, 1915.

PREMIUM No. 879
The Popular Teddy Bear for Children

Given Free for a Club of Only Two Yearly Subscriptions at 50 Cents Each, or Four at 35 Cents Each

Teddy Bears seem to hold their own; they are just as popular as ever with the little folks. Hence we feel that this Premium List would not be complete without an offer of one. This bear is manufactured especially for us, of dark brown bear cloth, woolly and shaggy. He is eleven inches long, and his legs and head revolve, so that he may be made to assume all sorts of amusing attitudes. He sits down, stands up or walks on all four paws as the owner elects, and is a genuine contortionist in his ability to manipulate the various members of his body. When his sides are pressed he emits a well-defined squeal. Altogether he is a most amusing little animal, and any little boy or girl who gets him on Christmas morning, or at any other time, will be provided with hours of solid fun for a long time to come. Nothing that Santa Claus is likely to leave behind him when making his rounds on Christmas Eve will meet with a more enthusiastic reception. We guarantee this premium to prove satisfactory. If upon its arrival it does not please the recipient, send it back and we will cheerfully refund the money paid us. Our policy is to endeavor to please and satisfy every customer in every transaction occurring between us. We will send the above described Teddy Bear by mail post-paid, also THE PEOPLE'S HOME JOURNAL for one year, upon receipt of **Eighty-five Cents**; or we will give the Teddy Bear *free* to any one sending us a club of **Two** subscriptions for one year at 50 cents each, or **Four** subscriptions at 35 cents each. Or we will send the Teddy Bear post-paid, without subscription to the magazine, upon receipt of 50 cents.

ABOVE: Illustration 197. Ad taken from Sunday supplements, September 12, 1915.

RIGHT: Illustration 198. Bellas Hess & Company catalog, 1915.

A Dear Little Teddy Bear

Given for Two New Yearly Subscriptions and Thirty Cents Extra, Postpaid.

Here is just what all little girls and some big ones are wishing for, a dear little Teddy Bear, a perfect little beauty just 12 inches tall when he stands up as he is in the picture we show of him. Teddy **can** grunt if you touch him in the right place, and his head and legs will all move, so he can be made to cut up lots of funny antics. When you have found subscribers enough to get this little Teddy, you can take him with you, and he will help you to get more and earn other things that you want.
Will be sold postpaid, for $1.30.

Illustration 196. November, 1907.

FINE QUALITY TEDDY BEARS

28x117. Finest grade of natural Teddy Bears, made of bearskin plush of best quality; practically indestructible. Has movable arms and legs. Comes in natural cinnamon color only.

Size 10 in....39c
Size 12 in....59c
Size 14 in....79c
Size 16 in....98c
Size 18 in..$1.29
Size 24 in..$1.89

94

Illustration 199. *The Youth's Companion* magazine, October 21, 1915.

Premium Number 2508
Teddy Bear

Given to Companion subscribers only for one new subscription and 10 cents extra; or sold for 85 cents. In either case we will DELIVER FREE anywhere in the United States. Read Premium Conditions, page 543.

This Teddy Bear is made of the finest quality cinnamon-colored plush, has jointed neck and legs, and stands 12 inches high, which is the popular size. It is a handsome little animal, too. Soft and comfortable to the touch, and will make the children a delightful bed companion. If desired, the Bear can be dressed in a variety of ways. It can also be thrown about, and is not easily injured. It is not necessary to create a demand for the Bear, for its fame has already reached every section of our land.

Illustration 200. Premium catalog, *Holland's Magazine,* 1916.

CASSINO'S LITTLE FOLKS

ABOVE LEFT: Illustration 201. *Cassino's Little Folks,* December, 1915.

ABOVE RIGHT: Illustration 202. Montgomery Ward catalog, circa 1921.

LEFT: Illustration 203. *Comfort* magazine, August, 1922.

96

Here They Are!
The Jolly Teddy Bears
10 Inch Size 54¢

These jolly little Teddy Bears,
Who always love to play,
When hugged by little boys and **girls**
Will scare all gloom away.

These chubby bears are real pals. The more you hug them the more they squeal. The little 10-inch bear, however, is not quite big enough to have a voice, but he is just as nice as the larger bears. Their bodies are covered with cinnamon-colored plush, jointed at neck, shoulders and hips. All have lifelike glass eyes.

Baby Bear. Height, 10 inches. Shipping weight, ½ pounds.
48 C 3140................................**54¢**
Mama Bear. Height, 14 inches. Shipping weight, 1 pound.
48 C 3147................................**89¢**
Papa Bear. Height, 18 inches. Shipping weight, 1½ pounds.
48 C 3143................................**$1.48**
Grandpa Bear. Height, 22 inches. Shipping weight, 2 pounds.
48 C 3150................................**$1.98**

Illustration 204. Montgomery Ward catalog, 1922.

Dressed Bears and Monkeys $3.75

—16 inches high, dressed in felt. Jointed arms and legs. Heads can be moved in any desired position by moving tail.

Illustration 205. *Bullock's Toy Time News,* 1923.

Teddy Bears

4L5763—Price, **98c**
Shipping weight, 1 lb.
Teddy Bear with Voice. Covered with **heavy** plush, closely resembling the soft **coat** of a genuine bear. Jointed head **and** legs can be placed in a variety of **positions.** Height, 14 in. Cinnamon color.

4L5764—Price, **50c**
Shipping weight, 12 oz.
Same as 4L5763. Height, 10 in.

4L5760—Price, **25c**
Shipping weight, 8 oz.
Same as 4L5763. Height, 8 in.

Illustration 206. Montgomery Ward catalog, 1914.

Plush Teddy Bears
Sleeping Eyes

Makes a hit wherever displayed. Note our very low prices.

MOVING EYES

SLEEPING BEAR

Cinnamon long pile fine quality plush, well stuffed, full size bodies, cork stuffed turning head, composition moving eyes, jointed limbs, felt soles, stitched mouth and nose, ribbon bow and band, strong voices. 1 in box.

F5107—15 in. . . . . Each, $2.00

F5108—17 in. . . . . Each, $2.25

F5109—19 in. . . . . Each, $2.50

Plush Teddy Bears

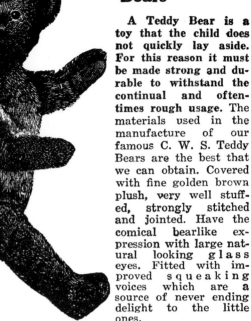

A Teddy Bear is a toy that the child does not quickly lay aside. For this reason it must be made strong and durable to withstand the continual and oftentimes rough usage. The materials used in the manufacture of our famous C. W. S. Teddy Bears are the best that we can obtain. Covered with fine golden brown plush, very well stuffed, strongly stitched and jointed. Have the comical bearlike expression with large natural looking glass eyes. Fitted with improved squeaking voices which are a source of never ending delight to the little ones.

37R921	Height, 10 in.	Shpg. wt., 12 lbs.	Price	$0.65
37R922	Height, 12 in.	Shpg. wt., 1 lb.	Price	.89
37R924	Height, 16 in.	Shpg. wt., 1½ lbs.	Price	1.10
37R926	Height, 20 in.	Shpg. wt., 2 lbs.	Price	1.45
37R928	Height, 24 in.	Shpg. wt., 2½ lbs.	Price	2.10

ABOVE LEFT: Illustration 207. Butler Brothers catalog, Fall, 1923.

ABOVE RIGHT: Illustration 208. Charles William Stores, New York, 1919.

BELOW: Illustration 209. Montgomery Ward catalog, 1923.

Fuzzy Bear With Voice

When you roll this playful Bear over on his back he growls—"Grr-grr." He is mounted on four wheels, so you may pull him along the floor by the chain. Imitation leather muzzle. Papier mache body, covered with soft silky imitation bearskin in dark color. The very small child will find endless amusement with a toy like this. Length, 10 inches. Imported.

48 E 3276 . . . . $1.49

Postage, 8¢ extra

Here We Come—The Teddy Bears with Voices

$1⁴⁸

$1⁸⁹

55c

85c

$2⁴⁸

10-inch Bear
With Voice
We have endeavored to give the little tots the best bear we could procure at a low price. Made of good quality cinnamon color plush. Glass eyes. Also has voice. Head, arms and legs are jointed. Ship. Wt. ¾ lb.
48E3176—Price...**55c**

12-inch Bear
With Voice
This popular sized bear has a voice. Made of good quality cinnamon color plush, with glass eyes. Head, arms and legs are jointed. Height, 20 inches. Shipping weight, ¾ pounds.
48E3204—Price...**85c**

16-inch Bear
With Voice
For a good sized bear with voice, this one will bring happiness to the children. Made of good quality plush, cinnamon color. Head, arms and legs are jointed. Shipping weight, 1¼ pounds.
48E3199—Price...**$1.48**

20-inch Bear
With Voice
This pleasant looking bear has a voice. It is made of good quality cinnamon color plush. Fully jointed. We offer this serviceable toy at a very low price. Shipping weight, 2½ pounds.
48E3201—Price...**$1.89**

24-inch Bear With Voice
"My. What a wonderful large bear." Has jointed head, arms and legs. Made of good quality cinnamon color plush. Large glass eyes. Also has voice. Shipping weight, 3¾ pounds.
48E3176—Price...**$2.48**

Illustration 210. Montgomery Ward
catalog, circa 1921.

Cinnamon Plush Teddy Bears

As popular as ever. These soft cuddly playthings have stood the test of time and are in large demand wherever toys are sold.

Well stuffed, good quality, brown plush, turning head, glass eyes, jointed limbs, felt soles, stitched mouth and nose, all with voices. $\frac{1}{12}$ doz. wrapped.

F5070—12 in	Doz.	**$8.00**	F5073—18 in	Doz.	**$12.75**
F5071—14 "	"	**9.50**	F5074—20 "	"	**16.50**
F5072—16 "	"	**11.25**	F5075—22 "	"	**19.25**

Illustration 211. Butler Brothers catalog, Fall, 1923.

"Mr Whitewash"—11 in. high, white plush head, chest, arms and feet, sateen trousers, gingham check & sateen vest, glass eyes, stitched nose and mouth.

F5152—1/12 doz. in box.

Doz. **$8.75**

Illustration 212. An example of Uncle Wiggily Bedtime Animals, universally known to many children. Wide publicity was given to Uncle Wiggily stories through newspapers and radio broadcasts. The various characters were dressed in varied-colored outfits. In addition to "Mr. Whitewash," there was 13 in. (33cm) "Uncle Wiggily," 10 in. (25.4cm) "Nurse Jane Fuzzy Wuzzy," 7½ in. (19.1cm) "Jackie Bow Wow" and 9 in. (22.9cm) "Billie Bushy-Tail." Butler Brothers catalog, Fall, 1923.

Shaggy Teddy

Reward No. 9992

Lovey Teddy

Given for Two Subscriptions.

Dear old Teddy, playmate to millions of boys and girls all over the nation! He's a dandy, big, lovable, hugable, cuddly fellow and best of all he's made to stand all kinds of rough usage. Ted is 10 inches tall.

Illustration 213. *Comfort* magazine, August, 1924.

Growling Bear

$3.25

A soft, woolly fellow who growls when you pick him up — but is a very peaceful citizen otherwise. *Other Animals up to $25.00.*

Illustration 214. Washington State newspaper, Christmas, 1924.

Teddy Bears

Every little girl or boy loves a soft, woolly teddy bear. We offer them in two different sizes.

9½ inch, each **85c**

15½ inch, each **$1.35**

Illustration 215. Advertisement from "Santa Claus Headquarters" booklet for Globe Manufacturers Teddy Bears. Milton G. Cooper Dry Goods Co., circa 1925.

Illustration 216. *Ladies' Home Journal* magazine, December, 1923.

The Children Will Love This Big 16-inch
Teddy Bear
*Given for **Four** Subscriptions*

WE know that all the girls and boys in the homes of our readers must have a Teddy Bear to play with, so we shall make it very easy for every mother to secure this one without cost. Teddy will withstand the rough handling of children, because he is well made of fine-quality plush with felt-lined paws, solidly stuffed and strongly sewed. His head is movable, and his legs may be placed in all positions so that you can make him look in any direction, stand upright, sit down, stand on his head, or go on "all fours." And Teddy has a strong, lusty voice, too. Press him gently in the body, and he makes a loud, squeaking noise that is not unlike the cry of a real live baby bear.

We send Teddy carefully packed, by prepaid parcel-post, and guarantee that he will reach you safely. When ordering please mention **Gift No. 6948.**

Illustration 217. *Needlecraft* magazine, January, 1924.

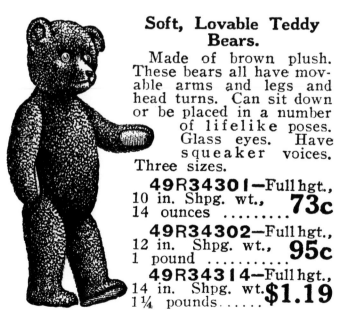

Soft, Lovable Teddy Bears.

Made of brown plush. These bears all have movable arms and legs and head turns. Can sit down or be placed in a number of lifelike poses. Glass eyes. Have squeaker voices. Three sizes.

49R34301—Full hgt., 10 in. Shpg. wt., 14 ounces **73c**

49R34302—Full hgt., 12 in. Shpg. wt., 1 pound **95c**

49R34314—Full hgt., 14 in. Shpg. wt. **$1.19** 1¼ pounds......

Illustration 218. Sears, Roebuck and Co. catalog, 1924.

Squawking Teddy Bears
25c

Made of brown plush, size 8½ inches.

Illustration 219. Newspaper advertising, circa 1925.

Illustration 220. Montgomery Ward catalog, 1921.

102

From Toyland's Zoo

Here They Are!
The Jolly Teddy Bears

These jolly little Teddy Bears,
Who always love to play,
When hugged by little boys and girls,
They'll scare all gloom away.

These chubby Bears are real pals. The more you hug them the more they squeal. The little 10-inch bear, however, is not quite big enough to have a voice, but he is just as nice as the larger bears. Their bodies are covered with cinnamon brown plush, jointed at the neck, shoulders and hips. All have lifelike glass eyes.

48 E 3140—Baby Bear. Height, 10 inches **$ .82**
Postage, 6¢ extra
48 E 3147—Mama Bear. Height, 14 inches **1.29**
Postage, 6¢ extra
48 E 3143—Papa Bear. Height, 17 inches. **1.89**
Postage, 8¢ extra
48 E 3150—
Grandpa Bear. Height, 21 inches......... **2.49**
Postage, 8¢ extra

10-Inch Size 82¢

Illustration 221. Montgomery Ward catalog, 1923.

GET YOUR PICK

TAN TEDDY
BEARS

Very well made.
Very special. Now
69 c

Best for the Little Tots
TEDDY PULL TOYS

Their antics delight the kiddies. Guaranteed
fast colors. Teddy Locomotive, Teddy
Soldier and Gun, Teddy Blue Sailor, Teddy
Acrobat   Regular $1.00
Values cut to, each . . . . 69 c

Illustration 222. Newspaper advertising, circa 1925.

Growling Bear

GROWL

Growling Grizzly with rumbly voice that
seems to come from the bottom of his feet,
and gleaming glass eyes. Coat is golden
brown plush; extra strong papier mache
body. Collar and muzzle; nose ring and
chain. Length, 9½ inches. A wheel on
each foot.
48 E 3277 . . . . 98¢
Postage, 10¢ extra

Illustration 223. Montgomery Ward catalog #105, 1926.

Imported Teddy Bears

We are sure that no better
values in Teddy Bears are offered
anywhere else in America. Specially
made for us in Europe. Covered
with a golden brown plush that has
the very finest close pile and rich
luster.

Honest Proportions

These bears have not been
stretched out in order to get
greater length. The limbs
are correctly formed and the
bodies are comfortably plump
like a real baby bear with the
hump at the back of the
shoulder. Cunningly formed
heads with perky inquisitive
noses and fine clear selected
glass eyes.

Each with Voice

He growls nearly every
time he moves, in a gruff
voice. But that's just for fun
because he really has a happy
disposition. Fine lustrous
close pile golden brown plush.
Long arms with inside joints
at shoulders; fat chubby legs,
set well up on the side.
Head turns; glass eyes.
Heights do not include ears.
48 E 3162—Height, 15½
inches. Each. $1.59
48 E 3161—Height, 12½
inches. Each. . . . . 89¢
48 E 3160 — Height, 10
inches. Each. . . . . 59¢
Postage: 12¢, 10¢ and 8¢
extra

WITH GROWLER VOICE

The Three Bears

The very Three Bears that Goldilocks ran
away from—Big Papa Bear in his overalls and
spectacles, middle size Mamma Bear in her
kitchen apron (she cooked the soup, you know),
and wee Baby Bear all pinned up in his diaper.
Each is made of golden brown plush with jointed arms and legs so they can run like everything after Goldilocks. Shining glass eyes and
inquisitive noses. Height of papa bear, about
7 inches; mamma, 5⅛ inches; baby, 4 in. 98¢
48 E 3272—Three bears. . . . . 98¢
Postage, three bears, 8¢ extra

Illustration 224. Montgomery Ward catalog #105, 1926.

104

The Children will Love This Big 16-inch
Teddy-Bear

*Given for **Four** Subscriptions*

WE know that all the girls and boys in the homes of our readers must have a Teddy-bear to play with, so we shall make it very easy for every mother to secure this one without cost. Teddy will withstand the rough handling of children, because he is well made of fine-quality plush with felt-lined paws, solidly stuffed and strongly sewed. His head is movable, and his legs may be placed in all positions so that you can make him look in any direction, stand upright, sit down, stand on his head, or go on "all fours." And Teddy has a strong, lusty voice, too. Press him gently in the body, and he makes a loud, squeaking noise that is not unlike the cry of a real live baby bear.

We send Teddy carefully packed, by prepaid parcel-post, and guarantee that he will reach you safely. When ordering, please mention **Gift No. 2460.**

Illustration 225. *Needlecraft* magazine, 1924.

Shuco Patent Toys

A GERMAN craftsman perfected the marvelous movement for the Shuco animals' heads, controlled by manipulating the tail as a lever. Just move the tail from left to right, up and down, or in a circular motion and the animal will then move his head in any direction. Ask them questions—they'll cock their heads in the cutest sort of a knowing way, and nod "yes" or shake their heads "no"!

Shuco Teddy Bears

Knowing black eyes, fat tummies, jointed arms and legs. Made of fine golden brown plush.

48 E 3212— Height, 11 in. **$1.98**
48 E 3213— Height, 13 in. **2.89**
Postage: 10¢ and 12¢ extra

Some Views of Shuco Teddy

A Shuco Cub

Wise looking little Cub with spectacles. Jointed limbs and head that turns in any direction. Unbreakable metal body covered with soft, lustrous golden brown plush. Height, 5 inches.

48 E 3211 **73¢**
Postage, 8¢ extra

Illustration 226. Montgomery Ward catalog #105, 1926.

This Selection
MAKES CHRISTMAS SHOPPING EASY

Fine Quality Bears
In Three Sizes

Teddy Bears! The favorite toy of all. How the little ones love these cunning bears with their cute faces and fat little bodies. Baby can turn their jointed head, arms and legs in any direction. They have squeaker voices and bright glass eyes. Covered with golden brown plush.

36 B 201—10-inch bear..... Post. 4¢ extra. **55¢**

36 B 202—12-inch Bear...... Post. 6¢ ex. **79¢**

36 B 203—14-inch Bear...... Post. 8¢ ex. **98¢**

55¢ up

Sleeping Bear

1.89

36 B 205—This 16-inch Teddy Bear is especially popular for the little one to take to bed. Teddy can go to sleep, too. Has movable glass eyes; jointed head, arms and legs that can be turned in any direction. Squeaker voice; smart ribbon bow. Covered with golden brown Mohair plush.
Postage 10¢ extra. **$1.89**

Illustration 227. Ad placed by the National Cloak & Suit Company, National Caraley Company, New York and Kansas City, Missouri, 1926.

TEDDY BEARS

Teddy Bears, made of long, brown or black silk plush bear cloth. Similar to the fur of the real bear, imitation claws; this is also one of the best made real lifelike articles, and we only carry the cleanest and best made of these goods in the following sizes:

10 in. high.	Doz...........	**$5.75**
12 in. high.	Doz...........	**$7.00**
14 in. high.	Doz...........	**$8.25**
16 in. high.	Doz...........	**$10.00**
18 in. high.	Doz...........	**$12.25**
20 in. high.	Doz...........	**$14.50**
22 in. high.	Doz...........	**$16.75**
24 in. high.	Doz...........	**$19.75**

Illustration 228. Called "Novelty Goods," a Teddy Bear advertised in Singer Brothers catalog #37, New York, 1926.

$10.00 Retail Value Only $6.67

Child Can Ride This Beautiful Plush Bear on Wheels

The delight of all kiddies. Built on steel frame and consequently strong enough to hold 150 pounds. Safe, practical and beautiful. Can be used either to ride or to pull. Made by a fine maker of quality toys. Is made of good quality plush and is exceptionally well shaped. Natural looking glass eyes. Leather collar. Pulling cord is attached to front axle. Length, over all, 21 inches; height, over all, 15½ inches; depth, widest point, 8 inches. Shipping weight, 8 pounds. 79 F 34030 . . . . $6.67

Illustration 229. Sears, Roebuck and Co. catalog, 1926.

Bear on Wheels

Y36 B 206—The youngster's delight—Strolling Bear strong enough to ride on. Built on a heavy steel frame and will hold up to 150 lbs. Made of good quality Plush, is well shaped and has squeaker voice. Glass eyes. Pulling cord on front axle. About 22x16 inches. Shipping weight, 8 lbs. See p. 457 for shpg. charges. **$5.89**

Illustration 230. Ad placed by the National Cloak & Suit Company, National Caraley Company, New York and Kansas City, Missouri, 1926.

Illustration 231. Steiff catalog, 1926.

Our Best Quality Mohair Bears

These are beautiful, realistically shaped teddies with charming expression in their cute faces. Made by one of the finest makers of stuffed animals, out of a fine grade, fluffy, long pile, mohair brown plush. They have natural looking glass eyes, movable head, also movable arms and legs which are longer and better shaped than the lower priced bears we show. Each bear has a squeaker voice and a pretty ribbon around its neck. Two sizes.

Usual $2.50 Retail Value for $1.98
13-In. Bear. Shipping wt., 1⅛ lbs.
49D4318. **$1.98**

Usual $3.50 Retail Value for $2.79
15-Inch Bear. Shipping wt., 1¼ lbs.
49D4319 . . . . **$2.79**

Illustration 232. Sears, Roebuck and Co. catalog, 1927.

Soft Cuddly Playfellows

Three Jolly Fellows
Our Medium Grade Teddy Bears With Voices

See these perky little faces, fat roly-poly bodies. Heads, arms and legs move. Have lifelike glass eyes. Bodies are covered with soft, long pile, brown color plush, and all have voices which squeak every time baby hugs them on the back. The bodies are better shaped than our lower priced bears and the arms are longer and more shapely.

	10-Inch Bear 49F34308 Shipping wt., 1⅛ lbs. $1.00	12-Inch Bear 49F34309 Shipping wt., 1¼ lbs. $1.48	14-Inch Bear 49F34310 Shipping wt., 1¾ lbs. $1.89

Our Leader Quantity Value $1.00

A nicely made 14-inch bear which has many points of quality as well as size, really exceptional for this price. Made by a very fine teddy bear manufacturer. Any baby would go wild over this cunning fellow. He will play with it all day and then sleep with it at night. The two will be pals. Has movable head, arms and legs, glass eyes and a squeaker voice. Made of good grade short pile plush. Comparison will prove the big value of our bear against competition. Shpg. wt., 1⅛ lbs.

49F34314............$1.00

Our Best Quality Mohair Bears

Beautifully shaped realistic looking teddies. Made of fine grade fluffy, long pile mohair plush by a high grade maker. Have natural looking glass eyes, and movable head, arms and legs. Each has squeaker voice and pretty ribbon around its neck.

$2.50 Retail Value for $1.98 13-in. bear. Shipping wt., 1¼ lbs. 49F34318 $1.98	$4.00 Retail Value for $2.98 15-in. bear. Shipping wt., 1¼ lbs. 49F34319 $2.98

Three Wonderful Values

Every Child Loves Its Teddy

The kiddies will love, cuddle and squeeze these little pals. They certainly are lovable with their cunning faces, pudgy bodies and fat arms and legs. Each has lifelike glass eyes. Baby can move and turn their heads, arms and legs, for they are made with joints. Their bodies are covered with short pile, brown plush. All bears have squeaker voices.

16-Inch Bear 49F34304 Shipping wt., 1½ lbs. $1.48	12-Inch Bear 49F34302 Shipping wt., 1 lb....87c	9½-Inch Bear 49F34301 Shipping wt., 14 oz....63c

108

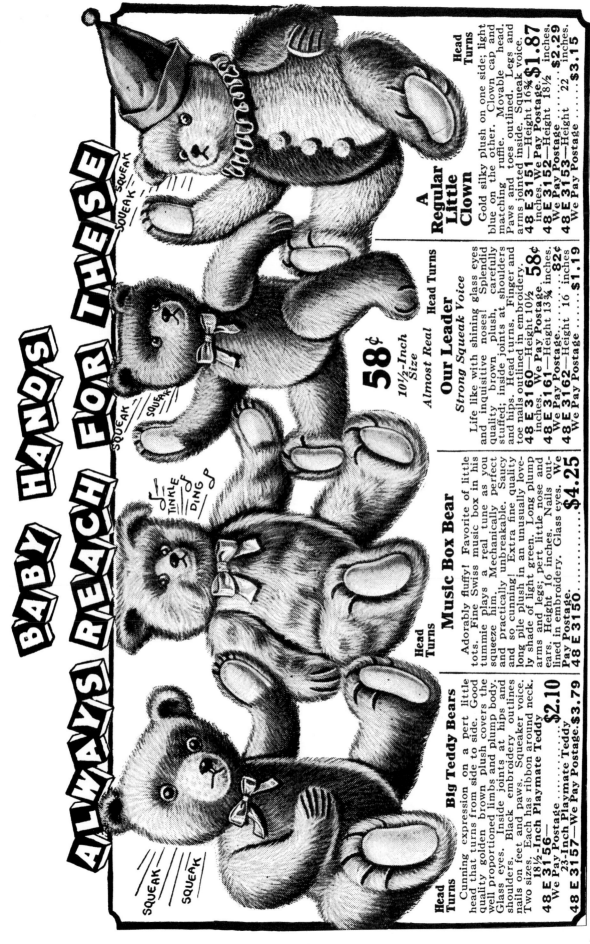

Illustration 234. Montgomery Ward catalog, 1929.

Soft Cuddly Animals

Goldie Locks' Three Bears
Every Child Loves Its Teddy!

The kiddies will love, cuddle and squeeze these little pals. They certainly are lovable with their cunning faces, pudgy bodies and fat arms and legs. Each has lifelike glass eyes. Baby can move and turn their heads, arms and legs, for they are made with joints. Their bodies are covered with short pile, brown plush. All bears have squeaker voices.

16-Inch Bear 49D4304 Shpg. wt., 1¼ lbs... $1.39	12-Inch Bear 49D4302 Shpg. wt., 1 lb....... 79c	10-Inch Bear 49D4301 Shpg. wt., 14 oz..... 59c

Our Leader Teddy Bear Value

This is a teddy the baby will go wild over. He will sleep with it and play with it all day. The two will be inseparable. Nice quality, 14-inch bear with lifelike glass eyes, movable head, arms and legs. He is made of good quality brown plush and has a squeaker voice. A dandy value for our price. Every kiddie should have one. Shpg. wt., 1⅛ lbs.
49D4314 .... 98c

Three Jolly Fellows
Our Medium Grade Teddy Bears With Voices

See these perky little faces, fat roly-poly bodies. Heads, arms and legs move. Have lifelike glass eyes. Bodies are covered with soft, long pile, brown color plush, and all have voices which squeak every time baby hugs them on the back. The bodies are better shaped than our lower priced bears and the arms are longer and more shapely.

10-Inch Bear. 49D4308 Shpg. wt., 1⅛ lbs.... 98c	12-Inch Bear 49D4309 Shpg. wt., 1¼ lbs... $1.39	14-Inch Bear 49D4310 Shpg. wt., 1¾ lbs.... $1.79

Illustration 235. Sears, Roebuck and Co. catalog, 1927.

Goldie Locks and Her Bear
Usual $1.75 Retail Value
Special for $1.00

Kiddies! Here is the famous little story character and her wee bear, so you can play the story all by yourself. Goldie Locks is 10¼ in. high and is completely dressed in pretty lace trimmed dress, full underwear, stockings, slippers and bonnet. She also has fully jointed arms and legs, and has a movable head. Her little bear is 10 inches tall, is made of good grade plush, has squeaker voice and has movable head, arms and legs. Shipping weight, 3½ pounds.
49 D 4024 .... $1.00

Illustration 236. Sears, Roebuck and Co. catalog, 1927.

39c

Little Wee Bear. Small tan plush bear with adjustable arms and legs. Height, 10¼ in. Ship. wt., 12 oz.
48E3178—Each.........39c

Illustration 237. Montgomery Ward catalog, 1927.

Ten-Inch
Teddy Bear

Given for Three
Subscriptions

Premium No. 2819

HERE is a Teddy-bear cub—just a baby bear, to be hailed with delight by the youngsters, of just the right size for the baby to cuddle, can't be spoiled with rough treatment, and is just as soft as can be. He is covered with a velvety plush and is just ten inches tall.

SPECIAL OFFER. If you will send us a club of **three** subscriptions to Hearth and Home at our regular subscription-price of **25 cents** each, we will send each subscriber this paper one year, and we will send you, prepaid, this Teddy Bear (**Premium No. 2819**).

HEARTH AND HOME, Augusta, Maine

Illustration 238. *Hearth and Home* magazine, 1928.

4 Bears
29¢

Big Value for Ward's Customers

Made of papier-mache composition covered with brown fuzzy-like material. Mama bear wears imitation leather collar and muzzle. She is 5½ inches long and 3⅛ inches high. The three cubs are 2½ inches long and 1½ inches high. Ship. weight, 10 ounces.

48 C 3163—All four bears . . . . **29¢**

Illustration 239. Montgomery Ward catalog, 1928.

55¢
10 Inch Size

Well Made Imported Teddy Bears

Imported from Europe. Well shaped limbs and body in proportion. All have voices and very cunning expressions on their faces. Very lifelike with their shining glass eyes and inquisitive snub noses. Each has been cut, stuffed and formed with great care—even the smallest size has inside joints at the shoulders and hips and is made of the same splendid golden brown plush. Jointed head turns from side to side. Measurements do not include ears.

Article No.	Height	Ship. Wt.	Each
48 C 3160	10 inches	5 ounces	$ .55
48 C 3161	12½ inches	8 ounces	.75
48 C 3162	15½ inches	1 pound	1.29

$6.69 POSTPAID

Our Big Bear on Wheels

Strong Enough for Child to Ride

Sold Elsewhere as High as $10.00

He is constructed on a steel frame mounted on strong wheels and can stand "lots" of abuse. One of our most substantial toys which is getting more popular each year.

Will Support 150 Lbs.

Made of good quality plush and is exceptionally well shaped. Has natural looking glass eyes, squeaker voice and a real leather collar. Nickel plated chain for pulling attached to front axle. Size, over all length, 21 inches; height, 14¼ inches; width at widest part, 8 inches. Every kiddie wants a bear of his own.

79 T 4030—Postpaid **$6.69**

LEFT: Illustration 240. Sears, Roebuck and Co. catalog, 1929.

ABOVE: Illustration 241. Montgomery Ward catalog, 1928.

91c

Fine
Plush
Teddy
Bear

59c

The
Whole
Bear
Family

Mamma Bear. Made of well stuffed tan plush. Glass eyes. Adjustable arms and legs. Height, 16 in. Ship. wt., 1 ½ lbs.
49E3199—Each..............91c

Big Papa Bear
A great big bear. Tan plush, shining glass eyes. Adjustable arms and legs. A dandy big bear. Height, 20 in. Ship. wt., 2 ½ lbs.
48E3201—Each..............$1.32

Little Baby Bear. A little tan plush bear with glass eyes. Adjustable arms and legs. Height, 12 in. Ship. wt., 12 oz.
49E3204—Each..............59c

Illustration 242. Montgomery Ward catalog, 1927.

EVERY CHILD LOVES HER TEDDY BEAR

All Our Bears Have
Movable Heads,
Arms and Legs

All
Bears
Postpaid

Real Values in Bears
Lifelike glass eyes, jointed head, arms and legs. Baby will have fun making it squeak, placing head, arms and legs in sleeping position and cuddling it to sleep. Short pile brown plush.

16-In. Size	12-In. Size	9½-In. Size
49T4304	49T4302	49T4301
$1.37	**85c**	**59c**

Soft Pliable
Fine Quality Mohair Bears
Exceptional Quality—Low Prices
Fluffy and lifelike, beautifully shaped. Each has natural looking glass eyes, s q u e a k e r voice, and pretty ribbon around neck.

13-Inch Size	15-Inch Size
A $2.50 value elsewhere.	Our leader, $3.50 value elsewhere.
49T4318	49T4319
$2.10	**$2.95**

$1.00

Our Postpaid
**Leader Short
Pile "Teddy"**
Here's a chubby fellow, 14 inches tall and a real playmate. Press him and hear him squeak. Many of our little friends have had hours of fun playing with him, turning his head, posing his arms and legs, and making him do all sorts of things. All movable parts firmly constructed so they will not come off. Covered with good grade short pile plush.
49T4314—Postpaid.....**$1.00**

Illustration 243. Sears, Roebuck and Co. catalog, 1929.

The Teddy Bear Sensation of 1929

These new tri-color bears went over with a Bang last year. We want every kiddie to have the thrill of owning one this year. For years bears have been made in solid colors. These bears instead of being the usual solid brown or cinnamon color, are combinations of pink, white and blue, medium pile plush. The movable heads are white plush, the bodies are one-half pink and the other half blue. The movable arms and legs are in pink and blue also, but contrast with the side of the body to which they are attached. A row of white cloth ball buttons sets off the body colors. Each has a cute little removable cloth hat jauntily perched on the side of its head and has a squeaker voice. Come in three sizes, All Postpaid.

12-Inch Bear 49T4321 $1.29	14-Inch Bear 49T4322 $1.69	16-Inch Bear 49T4323 $1.98

Our Popular Musical Bear
Usually Sold Elsewhere for $5.00

Made in color combinations like bears above, but instead of squeaking when pressed—Oh! A real surprise to hear the tinkly tones of a music box. Press a few times and hear a complete melody. Baby's eyes will just "pop" when given one of these musical surprises. Is 16 in. tall and is made of medium length pile plush.
49T4324—Postpaid.............. **$3.98**

Illustration 244. Sears, Roebuck and Co. catalog, 1929.

FAT PUDGY BABY ANIMALS

$1.98 A Dear Little Elephant

Chubby, fat little rascal with four pudgy legs and two great floppy ears. One of the finest baby toys. Little glass eyes peer out from underneath the light green fur of long soft plush. White tusks. Inquisitive trunk. Superior quality sure to please mother as well as baby. Wheels are red hardwood. 7 by 6¼ in. high. We Pay Postage. 48 E 3107. **$1.98**

Just a Lazy Baby Pup

Life for this little Puppy is just a dream in this comfy wicker basket with two pillows of bright colored felt! Plump soft body covered with golden brown and white plush. Black ears. Glass eyes; embroidered nose and mouth. Body on wire frame so he can take different poses. 8 inches long. Basket 9⅞ by 6⅞ in. wide. We Pay Postage. 48 E 3108. **$1.98**

"Was He Into the Jam Again?"

Just finished his dinner and now, with his bib still on, he is placidly nursing his pacifier. His fat little tummy is just so big he can hardly balance on his hind legs. Excellent quality long plush in a variety of solid bright colors. Nose and mouth embroidered on. Glass eyes. Bright felt shoes with pompons. Height 10¼ inches. We Pay Postage. 48 E 3106. **$1.98**

Illustration 245. Montgomery Ward catalog, 1929.

Soft Cuddly Lovable Playfellows

Goldie Locks' Three Bears.
Every Child Loves Its Teddy!

The kiddies will love, cuddle and squeeze these little pals. They certainly are lovable with their cunning faces, pudgy bodies and fat arms and legs. Each has lifelike glass eyes. Baby can move and turn their arms and legs, for they are made with joints. Their bodies are covered with short pile, brown plush. All bears have squeaker voices.

16-Inch Bear. Shpg. wt., 1½ pounds. 49T4304. $1.39	12-Inch Bear. Shipping wt., 1 pound. 49T4302. 87c	10-Inch Bear. Shpg. wt. 14 ounces. 49T4301. 67c

Our Two Leader Bear Values.

We offer here the two best values we have been able to find—one is the largest well made good grade plush bear we can find for the price. The other is a smaller bear made of better quality plush and is of much better workmanship and proportions, such as longer and better shape arms and legs and more expression throughout. These values are made possible by our tremendous purchasing power. We do not believe you can equal these values elsewhere. Each bear has a squeaker voice, lifelike glass eyes, movable head, arms and legs and is well padded with clean excelsior. Shipping weight, 1¼ pounds.

14-Inch Quality Bear. A big bear for a little price. Light brown color. 49T4314........98c	10-Inch Quality Bear. Soft, cuddly, much better shape, better grade plush. Dark brown color. 49T4308........98c

Three Jolly Fellows.
Our Medium Grade Teddy Bears With Voices.

See these perky little faces, fat roly-poly bodies. Heads arms and legs move. Have lifelike glass eyes. Bodies are covered with soft, long pile, dark brown color beaver plush, and all have voices which squeak every time baby hugs them on the back. The bodies are better shaped than our lower priced bears and the arms are longer and more shapely.

13-Inch Bear. Shpg. wt., 1¼ pounds. 49T4309. $1.48	15-Inch Bear. Shipping weight, 1¾ lbs. 49T4310. $1.87	17-Inch Bear. Shpg. wt., 2¼ pounds. 49T4312. $2.39

Illustration 246. Sears, Roebuck and Co. catalog, circa 1920s.

Cute 16-Inch Teddy Bear

**Woof! Woof! Says this bear
when you press his tummy**

Given for *Three* yearly Subscriptions
(or for Subs totaling $1.50)

Just the cutest clown Teddy-bear for the kiddies that
you ever saw. He has a blue cap and a blue ruffled
neckpiece. One side of his fuzzy clown-suit is pink
and the other is blue. He measures 16 inches from
the tip of his cap to the tip of his toes. Order by
name and by **Gift No. 3197.**

ABOVE: Illustration 247. *Hearth and Home* magazine,
November, 1929.

RIGHT: Illustration 248. December, 1931.

An Old Friend in New Dress
CUBBY BEAR

Given for *Two*
two-year
Subscriptions at 50
cents each

Hello folks, here I
am all dressed up and
n o w h e r e to go.
Everyone will recognize
me, though, as their
old friend Cubby Bear.
In his new c o l o r e d
dress Cubby Bear is
twice as gay
as he ever
b e f o r e
appeared.
His f u r is
l o n g and
f u z z y , his
arms and legs so natural
that they will let him do
all sorts of s t r a n g e
tricks. He stands 12
inches tall.

Call on your friends. Show them your copy
of Needlecraft. Tell them a two-year subscription costs only fifty cents. Ask them to sub-
scribe through you. Send us the two names,
addresses and the money collected. We will
send each subscriber this magazine two years.
We will send you, free and postpaid, this Cubby
Bear. Order by name and by **Gift
No. 3767** Address

**NEEDLECRAFT MAGAZINE
Augusta, Maine**

$5⁹⁸ — A Big Bear to Ride
Postpaid

Medium Brown Color

Strong Enough for Child to Ride

2⅝ in. dia. Rubber tired wheels
Even daddy can ride him if he does
not weigh over 150 lbs.

One of our most substantial toys
which is getting more popular each year.
He is constructed on a channel steel
frame mounted on strong wheels and
can stand "lots" of abuse. Made of good
quality cotton plush and is exceptionally
well shaped. Has natural looking glass
eyes, squeaker voice, and a real leather
collar. Nickel plated chain for pulling
attached to front axle. Size, overall,
length 21 inches; height 16 in.; width at
widest part 8 inches. Every kiddie wants
a bear. Will support 150 lbs. **$5.98**
79F4030—Postpaid....... $5.98

**Sold
Elsewhere
as
High
as
$10.00**

**Will Support
150 Lbs.**

Illustration 249. Sears, Roebuck and Co. catalog, 1931.

CHILDREN LOVE ANIMALS

Our Finest Quality Mohair Long Pile Plush Teddies

Better Quality Plush at Cheap Plush Prices

WE PAY THE POSTAGE ON ORDERS OF $2⁰⁰ OR MORE

SEE PAGE 2

15-In. Size

$2⁶⁹ *Postpaid*

Light Cinnamon Color

9½-In. Size

55c

Fine Quality Teddies

Pride of the best animal maker in this country. Soft and pliable and stuffed with kapok. Fluffy and life-like, beautifully shaped. Each has natural looking eyes, squeaker voice and pretty ribbon. Movable head, arms and legs on double washer joints which makes it almost impossible for child to pull bear apart.

13-Inch Size	**15-Inch Size**
A $2.50 Value elsewhere. Shpg. wt., 1¼ lbs.	Our Leader. $3.50 Value elsewhere. Postpaid.
49F4318	**49F4319**
$1.89	**$2.69**

Our Bears Have Well Shaped Movable Arms and Legs

An early order with the manufacturer to keep his factory open enables us to offer medium long pile cotton plush bears ordinarily sold for much more. Have double washer joints to hold limbs in place. The glass eyes, features, and ribbon bows give them their individual expressions. Each has squeaker voice.

9½-Inch Size	**12-Inch Size**	**16-Inch Size**
49F4305	49F4306	49F4308
Shipping wt., 1 lb. **55c**	Shipping wt., 1 lb. **79c**	Shipping wt., 1¼ lbs. **$1.19**

Illustration 250. Sears, Roebuck and Co. catalog, 1931.

115

MUSICAL BABY BEAR

CUDDLE BEAR

Illustration 251. Cuddle Bear.
"Give this little fellow a bear hug and hear his cute baby squeak. Deliciously soft stuffed and of pure white silky plush, with long, flexible legs for comfort in holding and jointed head and arms. 13" — 2.00, 18" — 5.00."
F.A.O. Schwarz Christmas catalog, 1932.

MUSICAL BABY BEAR

No. K-433 — A gentle bear hug and this imported Baby Bear plays music. Soft stuffed, plush covered. White or blond. 13" tall. . $5.75

Illustration 252. F. A. O. Schwarz Christmas catalog, 1932.

Illustration 253. Sears, Roebuck and Co. catalog, 1931.

Illustration 254. Steiff catalog, 1933.

Illustration 255. F. A. O. Schwarz Christmas catalog, 1935. (These are Steiff Teddies, using the same illustration as in ad in 1932 catalog, Illustration 256, this page.)

"We are proud of our teddy bear collection - - the softest finest plush procurable and all fully jointed so that they can assume many cunning positions. They have such cute expressions with ears perked high and little pudgy noses. All have growling voices. Cinnamon or white, 10" $1.50, 11½" 2.00, 13½" $3.00, 17" $4.50, 21" $7.50."

Illustration 256. This Steiff Teddy Bear came with the following specifications:

cinnamon - white	10 in. (25.4 cm)	– $1.50
	12 in. (30.5cm)	-- 2.00
	13 in. (33cm)	-- 2.50
with growling voice	14 in. (35.6 cm)	-- 3.50
	16 in. (40.6cm)	-- 4.50
	18 in. (45.7cm)	-- 6.00
	20 in. (50.8cm)	-- 7.50

F.A.O. Schwarz catalog, 1932.

Life-like Teddy Bears — Medium Long Pile Alpaca Plush

Ⓐ American Made! Don't confuse with lower priced imported cheaper quality short-pile bears. Cute faces—glass eyes; deep brown medium long pile. Movable arms, legs, head, attached with large **double washer joints, not nailed or wired as on cheaper bears.** Each has squeaker voice.

12-In. Size	15-In. Size	18-In. Size
49 K 4330	49 K 4331	49 K 4332
Shpg. wt. 10 oz.....**63c**	Shpg. wt. 15 oz.....**83c**	Shpg.wt., 1 lb. 5 oz.**$1.00**

Ⓑ **Big 14-In. Soft Cuddly Finer Quality Bear** Prettier, more shapely, softer! Soft, lustrous, dark brown alpaca **longer pile plush bear stuffed with cotton.** Squeaker voice. Glass eyes. Movable head, arms, legs on **double washer joints. $1.00** **49 K 4333**—Shipping weight, 1 pound.. **$1.00**

ABOVE: Illustration 257. Sears, Roebuck and Co. catalog, 1935.

RIGHT: Illustration 258. Butler Brothers catalog, 1936.

16 In. American Made
TEDDY BEARS
DOZ $7.20

60-5164—½ doz in box

Fine quality brown plush, **WELL STUFFED BODY**, glass eyes, stitched features, jointed hips and shoulders, felt jaws and soles, ribbon collar, press voice.

LEFT: Illustration 259. Musical Bear.

"You just squeeze his little tummy and he plays a pretty tune. Fluffily soft, too, because he's made of very special plush for the tiniest baby to safely hug. White only 13" tall. $7.50."

F.A.O. Schwarz Christmas catalog, 1935.

BELOW: Illustration 260. Three Little Bear Set.

"Well, if it isn't Father Bear, Mother Bear, and Johnny Bear looking just as though they stepped from the pages of the story book. Each one made of the softest wooly plush, plump as can be and the nicest bearskin grey color, you'd think they were real. Very carefully detailed even to natural color felt soles with fine stitching. Each one perched on its own white wooden chair ready to eat with its own little spoon from its own little porridge bowl. Folding table to match chairs and red-and-white checked table cloth also included. Father Bear 16" tall, others in proportion. Colored story book included. $25.00."

F.A.O. Schwarz Christmas catalog, 1935.

MUSICAL BEAR

Australian Bingo Bears

Illustration 261. Australian Bingo Bears.
"Just as fizzy, cunning, and snub nosed as the forefathers of this not-often-found but internationally known bear. He plays, eats, and sleeps in groups, so we kept them that way when we took the picture. Made of fine English plush. 6"—$1.75, 8"—$3.00, 12"—$5.50."
F.A.O. Schwarz Christmas catalog, 1936.

Illustration 262.
Source unknown.

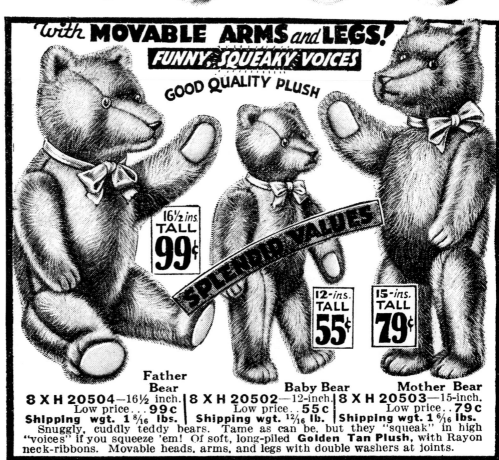

with MOVABLE ARMS and LEGS!
FUNNY, SQUEAKY VOICES
GOOD QUALITY PLUSH

16½ ins. TALL 99¢

SPLENDID VALUES

12-ins. TALL 55¢

15-ins. TALL 79¢

Father Bear
8 X H 20504—16½ inch.
Low price . . . 99c
Shipping wgt. 1 8/16 lbs.

Baby Bear
8 X H 20502—12-inch.
Low price . . 55c
Shipping wgt. 12/16 lb.

Mother Bear
8 X H 20503—15-inch.
Low price . . 79c
Shipping wgt. 1 6/16 lbs.

Snuggly, cuddly teddy bears. Tame as can be, but they "squeak" in high "voices" if you squeeze 'em! Of soft, long-piled **Golden Tan Plush**, with Rayon neck-ribbons. Movable heads, arms, and legs with double washers at joints.

Hand
Freckle-Faced
Bear

Guardsman

ABOVE LEFT: Illustration 263. Guardsman.
"His determined expression and the set of his jaw are framed by the chin strap of his tall black fur hat. His bright red flannel coat has white felt and brass buttons, his navy blue pants a red stripe down the side. Fortunately for this fellow his shoes are patent leather and always have a shine. Measures 25" from the soles of his shoes to the top of his hat. $10.00."

F. A. O. Schwarz Christmas catalog, 1936.

ABOVE RIGHT: Illustration 264A. Freckle-Faced Bear.
"All of this little fellow's charming characteristics have been faithfully portrayed- -his big round eyes, turned up nose with knobby end, shaggy fur, pointed (cloth) claws, bright red pants and most important of all each and every freckle. Exclusive with Schwarz. 9" - $2.75, 19" - $10.00. Book of *The Freckle-Faced Bear* a story and pictures of a most extraordinary bear."

F. A. O. Schwarz Christmas catalog, 1938.

BOTTOM RIGHT: Illustration 264B. Hand puppet, Freckle-Faced Bear.
"Has 10" arm spread. Body and head of short brown plush and white felt, rolling eyes, open mouth shows the red inside, button nose and lots of freckles. $1.50."

F. A. O. Schwarz Christmas catalog, 1938.

120

Illustration 265.
"We are proud of our teddy bear collection--the softest, finest plush procurable and all fully jointed so that they can assume many cunning positions. They have such cute expressions with ears perked high and little pudgy noses. All have voices. Cinnamon or white, 10"-$1.75, 12"-$2.25, 13½"-$3.00, 17"-$4.75, 21"-$7.50." Maker: Steiff.
F.A.O. Schwarz Christmas catalog, 1938.

Teddy Bears

Bear on Wheels

Illustration 266. Bear on Wheels.
"A faithful companion for the small girl or boy--one that will survive years of strenuous play. He has a voice, his strong metal frame which can support 150 pounds, has wooden wheels so that he can be easily moved about or best of all can be ridden kiddie car fashion. His round stuffed body is covered with thick brown plush and measures 15" high. The red leather collar adds colorful touch. $8.00."
F.A.O. Schwarz Christmas catalog, 1936.

FEEDME

"Feed-Me"
Bear

Illustration 267.
EATING TEDDY BEAR

M. Greenfield, President, Commonwealth Toy & Novelty Co., states that his new teddy bear called "Feedme," which actually devours real food, is meeting with widespread interest in the trade. The child pulls on a ring located at the back of the bear's neck, the mouth opens and animal crackers, dry cereal, candy, rolls, toast, etc., are really swallowed by this ingenious teddy. A zipper located in the bear's back is then opened and the crackers, etc., removed. These teddy bears are very attractively made of plush and mohair and measure approximately eighteen inches high. They are dressed in attractively colored bibs and carry a lunch box filled with animal crackers. They retail at a popular price and can be sold with or without high chairs. This enterprising firm is furnishing attractively colored counter display material free with each order. During a recent interview with Mr. Greenfield, he stated that the National Biscuit Co. were using this "Feedme" bear in their advertising material for animal crackers. He added that this advertising would be displayed in thousands of grocery stores throughout the United States and would unquestionably be an added sales help to dealers featuring this new eating teddy bear.

Playthings, August, 1937.

LAMBS WOOL TEDDY BEARS
Washable — Sanitary — Movable Limbs
With Music Box

A Swiss Music box is carefully built into "Chubby" the Golden Fleece Teddy Bear. Imbedded key has no sharp edges to cut the child. Looks so real, cute and cuddly, he makes a big appeal to parents and children alike. Made of pure natural lambskin. The wool won't pull out and can be washed. Directions for washing with every animal. Has movable legs, arms and head. Eyes are fastened in tight. Attractive ribbon around neck. Filled with genuine Kapok, such as is used in all high grade stuffed toys.

No. 630X860M—Musical Teddy Bear. Height 16". Shipping weight 5 lbs. List $6.50.
Each $4.35. Less 2% Net............................**4.26**

Without Music Box

Same materials as above but without music box. This bear has a funny squeak when he's pressed.

No. 627X810 — Teddy Bear. (Squeak Voice — No Music Box). Height 11". Shipping weight 1 lb. List $1.35. Net per dozen...........**10.00**

Each $0.90. Less 2% Net...............................**.88**

No. 628X830—Teddy Bear (Squeak Voice—No Music Box). Same as above but larger. Height 12". Shipping weight 2 lbs. List $2.50. Each $1.63. Less 2%
Net..**1.60**

No. 629X860—Teddy Bear (Squeak Voice—No Music Box). Same as above but larger. Height 16". Shipping weight 3 lbs. List $3.75. Each $2.52.
Less 2% Net...**2.47**

No. 6–48 – "Feed-Me" Bear – Having an insatiable appetite made possible by a metal lined throat and stomach. The latter empties through a zipper in his back all forms of food, welcome to the amusement of all, except liquids; by tipping his head back his jaws open. His brown plush body (with rubber bib) measures 14" tall.

$3.95

Illustration 268. F.A.O. Schwarz catalog, 1941.

Illustration 269. National Porges Corporation catalog, Winter, 1939.

Hand Panda Bear

RIGHT: Illustration 270. Hand Panda Bear.

"It does not require an expert to animate most amusingly this 8" bear. He fits over hand glove-fashion and then his white and black plush head and arms can be moved grotesquely. $1.00."

F.A.O. Schwarz Christmas catalog, 1938.

BELOW: Illustration 271. Cubbie Bears.

"Not unlike the popular Australian Bingo Bear in conformation. Has the same round body and head with snub nose. He is tan, however. His soft body is covered with a thick, soft, short plush. Jointed head, arms, legs. Toy and companion. 14"-$5.75, 9½"-$2.50."

F.A.O. Schwarz Christmas catalog, 1938.

Cubbie Bears

MEET HONEY BEAR AND HIS "DUDE" BROTHER

CUDDLY!

At left are two cute cuddly bears with soft stuffed bodies. Each has movable head, arms and legs, and can stand alone. Honey Bear, at far left, is 10 in. high. His "dude" brother is dressed in velvet overalls, comes in two sizes.

Honey Bear
N25246......$2.20
Dressed Bear
N25247 9 in.-$1.40
N25248 13 in. 2.00

Illustration 272. John Plain catalog, 1940.

PINKIE TEDDY
Pink and White Fur

A cuddly bear with washable coat of fluffy pure cotton, Pink and White. He is 15 in. high, will sit up by himself. He has pretty eyes that move and flirt with you! Wears a blue silken ribbon around his neck; floppy ears, arms and legs. His body is soft and cuddly; squeeze him and he delights you with his concealed voice.

N25237 PRICE.......$1.65

Illustration 273. John Plain catalog, 1940.

PANDA—TWO SIZES

Soft stuffed body, with coat of Black and White silky mohair plush. Has hidden voice, floppy arms and legs. An adorable plaything, your choice of two sizes, 12 in. or 19 in. high. Each Panda has flirting eyes that roll and flirt with you!

N25240 Small Panda.................$1.40
N25241 Large Panda................. 3.00

MADE OF PURE LAMB'S FLEECE
Teddy Bear and Lamb

The above two animals are made of pure lamb's fleece, perfectly odorless, washable; they are ideal playthings for any youngster. The teddy bear, shown above at the left, has a luxurious coat of genuine Lama-Fur, a pleasure to caress. When he sits, like he is in the picture, he is just 7½ in. high. The lamb is 6 in. high and 8 in. long. She's a lovable darling, and you can treat her just like you would a real live pet, for you can wash her with soap and water.

N25242 Teddy Bear.................$1.80
N25243 Lamb 1.65

Illustration 274. John Plain catalog, 1940.

No. 5 – 67—Musical Bear

No. 5–67 – Musical Bear – Small children have real affection for their animal friends and more so if their bodies are soft stuffed and the plush is downy. These are features of this bear to a marked degree. His soft thick piled plush is pink or blue with tan velvet paw pads, brown nose, red tongue. His body contains a Swiss music box and he is 14" tall. STATE COLOR. EXCLUSIVE WITH US. $5.95

Illustration 275. F. A. O. Schwarz catalog, 1941.

Illustration 276. Musical Shag.
"14" tall, he has very wooly and yellow feet, hands and face, with brown wooly ears, large blue button eyes, black nose and red tongue, sweater and cap. His body contains a Swiss music box. $5.75."
F.A.O. Schwarz Christmas catalog, 1938.

Musical Shag

MOHAIR PLUSH BEARS
Teddy Bears Salute You!

Here come two proud teddy bears, just as cute as they can be. They salute you! No wonder they are proud, for they have coats of the finest long pile silky mohair plush, Cinnamon Brown in color, with a lustrous sheen that shows how healthy these darling teddy bears are! The two bears are 13½ in. and 18 in. tall. Each bear has a concealed voice—hug him and he answers with a cheerful call. Each bear is lifelike as can be, with movable head, arms and legs; dressed with bright silken ribbon around neck. Two star performers from the greatest show on earth!

N25235   Bear 13½ in. Tall.....................$2.95
N25236   Bear 18   in. Tall..................... 5.00

Illustration 277. John Plain catalog, 1940.

Illustration 278. Ad placed by Dolls of Hollywood, Inc., Hollywood, California. Designed by Eli Brucker, circa 1945.

RIGHT: Illustration 279. Autograph Bear.
"Instead of being hunted, this fellow does the hunting. He hunts for autographs and his pure white closely woven fabric exterior provides the surface on which your friends, and his friends, can write in ink without blurring, making a permanent record of interest and value. He is soft stuffed with floppy arms and legs and measures 36" tall. $8.75."
F. A. O. Schwarz Christmas catalog, 1941.

Musical Mama and Baby Bear

LEFT: Illustration 280. Musical Mama and Baby Bear.
"While Mama can't sing to her baby she can be made to play her music box concealed in her soft, round and roomy body. She measures 20" tall, is covered with soft white plush with jointed arms. She wears red striped pajamas and a red bath robe. In her arms she holds her 8" white plush baby that has red ears and blue eyes. $9.95."
F. A. O. Schwarz Christmas catalog, 1941.

126

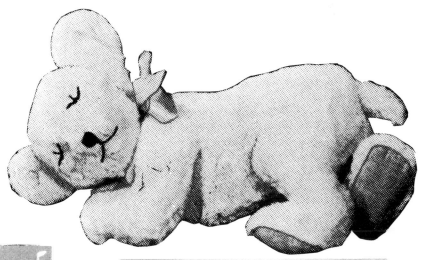

Illustration 281. Snoozing Animals.
"Every age adores these famous 'softies'. Whether for boudoir decoration or for babies to cuddle, we never seem to have enough of these downy favorites. Softest, silky plush with back 'zipper' closing. About 15" long. Bear, light blue or pink. $3.00."
F. A. O. Schwarz Christmas catalog, 1941.

MUSICAL SLEEPING BEAR

To see him is to love him! He's down-soft and sleeps like a babe. The little Swiss music box inside him plays 'Rockabye Baby' when wound. Luxurious Pink or Blue rayon plush, soft cotton filled. 14 1/2 inches tall. Specify Pink or Blue.

81674 B595   With music box $8.50
81675 B315   Without music box 4.50

SQUEAKING VOICE "TEDDY"

Cuddly Brown Teddy Bear . . . "growls" just like the bears at the zoo. Head turns completely around. Jointed arms and legs. All Brown plush with embroidered nose and mouth. Black plastic eyes give him a capricious look. Certain to be well loved!

81680 B245   12" Jointed Bear $3.49
81681 B472   18" Jointed Bear 6.75

COWBOY BEAR

Howdy pardner--got room for me in your bunkhouse? I'll make a real buddy to any little boy or girl! 26 inches tall. Cinnamon colored rayon plush over soft, cotton stuffing. Cream colored hands, ears, feet. Dressed in Yellow Western style chaps, plaid kerchief, holster, gun.

81679 B385   Cowboy Bear, 26" tall . .$5.50

Illustrations 282, 283 & 284. All from John Plain catalog, 1950.

127

627 Mutzli stehend C, W,   3³/₄''   9¹/₂ cm
611 *Mutzli debout*   W,   3¹/₂''   9   cm
      standing

640 Mutzli Flexy, C, R, Bl (Umschlagseite 1)
      biegsame Glieder   7¹/₂''   19 cm
      membres flexibles
640-2 C   flexible arms and legs   11''   28 cm

600-55 cm   50   43   40

MUTZLI

Mutzli-Gliederbären, die besten Spielkameraden unserer
Kinder, bewegl. Arme, Beine, Kopf;

*Mutzli, Ours articulé, les camarades de jeux préférés de
nos enfants; têtes, jambes et bras
mobiles*

Mutzli, jointed Bears, movable head, arms and legs.
W, G, Br, C

600-15 -22 -25 -28 -30 -35 -40 -43 -50 -55 cm
6 8¹/₂ 10 11 11³/₄ 13³/₄ 15³/₄ 17 19⁵/₈ 21¹/₂ inches

mit Druckstimme	mit Brummstimme
voix à pression	*voix grognante*
with Squeaker	with Growler

35   30   28   25
22   15   627   611

22 B   22 M

610-2   610   620

				cm
22 M, B, col. C	Mutzli 22 cm	bekleidet Mädchen, Bub *habillé fille, garçon* dressed girl, boy	8¹/₂''	22
687 M, B, col. C	Mutzli stehend 14 cm	bekleidet Mädchen, Bub *debout, habillé fille, garçon* standing, dressed girl, boy	5¹/₂''	14
687 H	Mutzli stehend 14 cm col. C	bekleidet Koch *habillé Chef de Cuisine* dressed Cook	5¹/₂''	14
610	Mutzli-Floppy, C, R, Bl,	Schlenkerbär weichgestopft mit Schellen *bourré ouate, avec grelots*	7¹/₂''	19
610-2		soft stuffed	10''	25¹/₂
620	Mutzli-Bébé C, R, Bl,	weichgestopft, mollig *bourré ouate, mou* soft stuffed	9¹/₄''	23¹/₂

687 H   687 M   687 B

Illustration 285. The Teddy Bears of MCZ Schweizer Pluschtierchen, Switzerland's finest plush stuffed animals, circa 1950.

993/40   981/12   992/18   993/25   993/30   992/20   992/15   981/10   992/36

993/0/45   992/55   993/70   993/60   993/50

Illustration 286. Taken from ELI—Puppen und Spieltiere, Germany, circa 1950.

966/60   966/2/70   966/45   967/2/60

966/80

967/45   967/2/50   966/2/45   966/2/40   966/2/50   966/55   102

Illustration 287. From ELI—Puppen und Spieltierre, Germany, circa 1950.

Illustration 288. Steiff catalog, 1953.

Illustration 289. Newspaper advertising for *Dean's Rag Book* Teddy, England, 1953.

Illustration 290. The first issue of "Smokey Bear" with wire-on vinyl head, hands and feet, 1953.

Nationally Famous SMOKEY BEAR

Now the famous symbol of forest-fire prevention is a cuddly toy—acts as a reminder to be careful. Smokey is a plaything for children—a mascot for adults. 18" tall; stuffed rayon plush with Vinyl face. Wears "Smokey" trousers, hat, badge, belt buckle, carries famous shovel. It's a wonderful toy—it's "Ideal." $4.98. Others at $6.98 and $14.98.

Illustration 291. The second version of "Smokey Bear" with vinyl head. The ad is Ideal's publicity for "Smokey Bear," 1954.

B 40-210 TEDDY ON WHEELS Wt. 19 lbs. Exp. only **$25.00**
Long to be remembered are the enjoyable rides on the
broad soft back of this lovable playmate. Fitted with concealed strong steel frame with rubber tired disc wheels.
With leather collar, voice and pull cord. 25" long, 19" high.
40-230 ROCKER FOR ABOVE BEAR 45" long. Ship. wt. 8
lbs. Express only...**$7.50**
C 15-202 STANDING YOUNG BEAR Wt. 3 lbs.......**$7.50**
Brown mohair plush with collar, bell and voice. 13" long.
D JUBILEE BEAR "JACKIE"—Long honey color mohair plush,
moving arms, legs and head. With ribbon bow. A squeeze
of his fat tummy produces a voice.
15-111 JUBILEE BEAR "JACKIE" 6½" tall. Wt. 1 lb....**$2.75**
15-197 JUBILEE BEAR "JACKIE" 9" tall. Wt. 2 lbs....**$4.50**
15-194 JUBILEE BEAR "JACKIE" 13" tall. Wt. 3 lbs....:**$7.75**

Illustration 292. F. A. O. Schwarz catalog, 1954.

Illustration 293. The third version of "Smokey Bear"
with plush face, circa 1960s.

LE BON GROS NOU-NOURS TRADITIONNEL,
A L'EPAISSE TOISON BLANCHE.
(MERY GUTMAN.)

Illustration 294. Traditional white Teddy
Bear. *Le Jouet Francais* toy magazine, 1956.

E ZOTTY BEARS — Long shaggy, sand colored, mohair plush. Jointed and
with ribbon and voice.
15-98 ZOTTY BEAR 7" tall. Ship. wt. 1 lb.............................**$3.00**
14-66 ZOTTY BEAR 11" tall. Ship. wt. 3 lbs.............................**$6.75**
F 16-71 TEDDY BABY BEAR..............................**$5.95**
11" tall. Dark brown mohair plush. Collar with bell and voice. Ship. wt. 2 lbs.
G ORIGINAL TEDDY BEAR — Of soft mohair plush cinnamon color with
jointed head, arms and legs. Has voice and pert ribbon bow around neck.
15-83-8 ORIGINAL TEDDY 11½" tall. Ship. wt. 2 lbs.................**$4.00**
15-52-8 ORIGINAL TEDDY 13½" tall. Ship. wt. 2 lbs.................**$5.95**

Illustration 295. F. A. O. Schwarz catalog, 1954.

MARJO-REIMS

Illustration 295. Teddy Bear advertised as an Easter gift. *Le Jouet Francais* toy magazine, France, 1956.

Teddy Bears...

LARGE TEDDY BEAR comes in honey-colored or brown plush. There's a Swiss music box inside him. 18" tall............8.95

BEAR WITH DRUM. His big red drum really makes music because it conceals a fine Swiss music box. Honey color or brown. 8" high.................7.95

a Panda...

BOY TEDDY BEAR is cream color. He is dressed in orange and green, has a daisy in his buttonhole. He's musical, too. 18" tall.................10.95

PANDA WITH BALL is black and plays appropriate tune. Ball contains winding mechanism. 11" high....................7.95

Illustration 296. Musical Toys — Schirmer's Musical Christmas list, circa 1955.

Cette firme présente d'origi-
naux animaux bourrés, parmi
lesquels il faut citer un ours
en peluche blanche. A remar-
quer la conception nouvelle des
pattes de devant.

Illustration 297. French
white plush cub. *Le Jouet
Francais* toy magazine,
France, 1956.

62-14   626

Miniature Teddy Bear. Made of plush and fully jointed.
No. 62-14 5", 8 oz $2.50 ea

Red Pajama Teddy Bear. These are the most adorable of all. Oh, gosh!
but he is cute with his white plushy head and paws, and his red suede
cloth pajames.
No. 626 13" 2 lbs $6.50 ea

Illustration 298. Mark Farmer Company catalog, 1957.

Illustration 299.   Mechanicals from the National
Bellas Hess catalog, 1957.

Moves His
Body, Beats
His Drum

89¢ Up

Drumming Bear

**Musical bear beats 3-in. circus
drum, moves his body and head
in time to music. Soft rayon
plush. Steel coil-wound motor.
Attached key. Comes in two
sizes. Imported.**
16 AN 3156–6 in. Wt. 6 oz. . . .89¢
16AN3155–9½ in. Wt. 8 oz.$1.89

1966

Illustration 300. Steiff catalog, 1966.

Steiff toys... the gentlest playmates

Every moment, in every nation of the world, a Steiff toy is part of the life of some little boy or girl. One may be found in the arms of a sleeping child or several may decorate a nursery. A Steiff lion or Teddy Bear may be companion to a little boy on his flights into fancy. A little girl may be seen placing a loving kiss on the soft cheek of her Steiff lamb or kitten.

A Steiff toy will share a child's busy day and listen patiently to its joys and sorrows. It will withstand ferocious hugging and furious play, yet when bedtime comes, it is ready to sleep quietly beside its daytime playmate providing the assurance of a friend close by. Steiff toys are made in much the same way they were more than 85 years ago when the deep love a kindly seamstress had for children prompted her to produce the world's first stuffed toy. The same highstandards of craftmanship and quality first set down by Margarete Steiff in the year 1880 are still maintained today. Though thousands of toys leave daily from the little German town of Giengen on the Brenz where the Steiff factory is located, each has been individually created in the gentle hands of a skilled toymaker. The individual handcrafting of Steiff animals produces slight variations in facial expression, giving each a personality of its own. Thus some may appear to be pondering a deep thought while others may seem on the verge of a mischievous gambol or smiling a gentle puppy-dog smile. All, though, bear the characteristic, very spezial charm that unmistakably identifies a Steiff toy. Steiff is now the world's largest producer of stuffed animals. A variety of more than 600 toys, representing practically every member of the animal kingdom, is contained in the Steiff zoo and their appeal is universal. Collectors in every corner of the globe are filling their shelves with miniature Steiff trophies. Teenagers are using them as top of bed decorations or "gab session" companions and owners of earlier Steiff toys are handing them down as heirlooms. Steiff toys are placed at the top of gift lists as appropriate for just about any occasion.

Unless otherwise indicated, all Steiff toys are made of the finest obtainable grade of lustrous mohair plush. Where size permits, all are equipped with voices. Each Steiff toy carries the world famous trademark . . .

Steiff

Button in Ear Brand

All of fine Mohair Plush if no other description

Illustration 301. Steiff catalog, 1966.

134

1 Original TEDDY
Woven synthetic fur
10.5" V fs   0205/26
13.5" V fs   0205/35

2 20" V fs   0205/50

3 ZOTTY Bear
Mohair plush
8.5" A   0300/22
11" A   0300/28
13.5" A   0300/35
17" A   0300/43

4 ZOTTY
Mohair plush
8.5" A fs   0305/22
12.5" A fs   0305/32
18" A fs   0305/45

Original TEDDY
Mohair plush
honey color
5 4.5" A   0201/11
6 10.5" A   0201/26
7 13.5" A   0201/36

8 Original TEDDY
Mohair plush
caramel color
4.5" A   0202/11
10.5" A   0202/26
13.5" A   0202/36
16.5" A   0202/41
20" A   0202/51

9 TODDEL Bear
Dralon plush
12.5" A fs   0290/32

75 years ago, Steiff invented the Teddy Bear. When your grandmother was a little girl, she had a Teddy Bear.

Illustration 302. Steiff catalog, 1978.

135

Naiadene Thompson Blackburn and her Teddy Bear. 1914.

V. Teddy Bears
Bears in Order of Dates

ABOVE: Illustration 303. 18 in. (45.7cm) Teddy Bear. Gold mohair, excelsior stuffed. Fully jointed, worn felt pads, embroidered paws. Shoe button eyes. Squeeze mechanism in body plays music. Circa early 1900s. *Beverly Port Collection.*

ABOVE: Illustration 304. 10 in. (25.4cm) Steiff bear, button in ear. Deep gold short pile plush, squeaker. Fully jointed 5 in. (12.7cm) front legs, 4½ in. (11.5cm) back legs. Tan peach felt pads. Embroidered black claws and nose. Brown glass eye, dark pupils. Old ribbon woven in metallic silver reads: "Merry Christmas." Circa 1904. *Judy Johnson Collection.*

RIGHT: Illustration 305. 10 in. (25.4cm) Steiff bear, button in ear. White mohair, fully jointed and embroidered claws. Shoe-button eyes. Circa 1905. *John Stafford Collection.*

Illustration 306. 21 in. (53.3cm) Steiff bear, original button in left ear. Button eyes. Originally white; obvious when looking at creases at swivel joints of neck, arms and legs. Now soft grey. Brown embroidered nose and mouth. Extra long curved arms and big feet. Circa 1907. *Beverly Port Collection.*

Illustration 307A. 14 in. (35.6cm) bear. Very fine soft gold mohair. Fully jointed, 7½ in. (18.4cm) front legs, 6½ in. (16.5cm) back. Four black claws, beige felt pads. Shoe-button eyes. Circa 1906.

Illustration 307B.

Illustration 308. 24 in. (61cm) short brownish-gold mohair bear. All straw stuffing. Fully jointed. Beige felt pads and no claws. Original black floss embroidered nose. Replaced glass eyes. Ears sewn on. Note particularly rounded head. Circa before 1910. *Margaret Mandel Collection.*

Illustration 309. 21 in. (53.3cm) cinnamon long mohair bear. Stuffing of kapok and straw mixture. Fully jointed. Felt pads and no claws. Replaced eyes (early celluloid buttons). Long nose, embroidery missing. Ears sewn on. At one time this bear had a squeaker. Very long feet and hands. Circa before 1910. *Margaret Mandel Collection.*

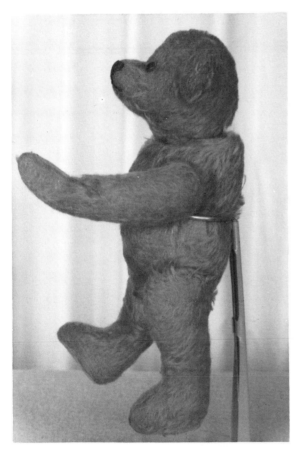

Illustration 310. 11 in. (27.9cm) dark gold mohair bear. Straw head, kapok body and straw limbs. Fully jointed. Felt pads and no claws. Flat footed with long and thick feet. Original glass eyes and black embroidered nose. Ears sewn on. Squeaker present. Circa before 1910. *Margaret Mandel Collection.*

Illustration 311. 16 in. (40.6cm) off-white long mohair bear. Straw stuffed head, body and limbs. Fully jointed. Ears sewn on (one missing). Original beige felt pads. Embroidered black floss claws and matching nose. Original shoe-button eyes. Squeaker. Long arms and big feet. Circa 1910 or before. *Margaret Mandel Collection.*

Illustration 312A. 16 in. (40.6cm) Clown Bear. Short wool mohair, fully jointed. Thin tan felt pads, three black embroidered claws. Right back front legs are pink, left are blue. Right side torso is blue, left is pink. Growler. Head is white with brown glass eyes and dark pupils. Pointed hand-embroidered nose. Neck ruff missing. Sears Roebuck and Company, 1920s.

Illustration 312B. Showing head contour and long, thin front legs.

Illustration 313. 14 in. (35.6cm) off-white mohair bear. All straw stuffing. Fully jointed. Beige felt pads and very dark brown embroidered claws with matching embroidered nose. Original glass eyes. Ears sewn on. Long feet and squeaker. Circa before 1920. *Margaret Mandel Collection.*

140

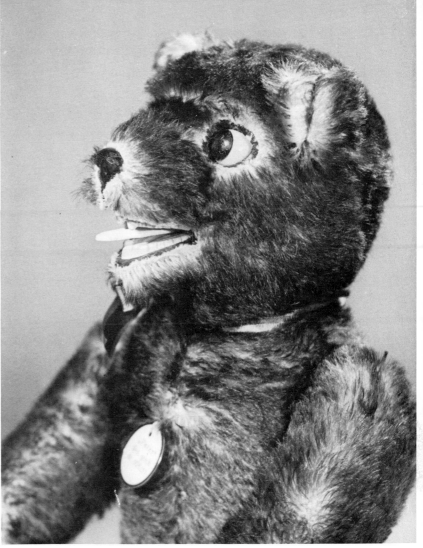

Illustration 314A & B. 14 in. (35.6cm) "Peter"/Gebrüder Süssenguth Box marked Neuheit, (novelty) Neustadt, Thuringia, Germany. Head is formed of hard material covered with dark brown plush; lighter underneath. Full set of upper and lower teeth (bisque-like). Pinkish inner mouth. Movable bisque tonque. Front paws curve up at end. Brown felt paws. Solid black round pupils in flirting eyes. Tag on chest: "Peter"//Ges. gesch//Nr. 895257. Circa 1925. *Helen Sieverling Collection.*

Illustration 314C. Neuheit (Novelty) Ges. gesch (legally protected). *Helen Sieverling Collection.*

Illustration 315. 20 in. (50.8cm) dark gold long mohair bear. All straw stuffing. Fully jointed with felt pads. No embroidered claws. Original glass eyes, embroidered nose and blue silk bow. Ears cut into head. Purchased in London by owner before 1930. *Margaret Mandel Collection.*

Illustration 316. 16 in. (40.6cm) light gold very long mohair bear. Fully jointed. Straw head, arms and legs and kapok body. Beige felt pads and no claws. Nose re-embroidered in brown. Glass eyes and ears sewn on. Squeaker. Circa 1930 or before. *Margaret Mandel Collection.*

Illustration 317. 14 in. (35.6cm) off-white very long mohair bear. Head stuffed with straw and body and limbs with cotton. Gold velveteen pads (foot pads in shape of triangle). No claws. Fully jointed. Black floss embroidered nose and ears sewn on. Original glass eyes. Squeaker and replaced bow. Circa 1930s. *Margaret Mandel Collection.*

ABOVE: Illustration 318. 12½ in. (31.7cm) yellow long mohair bear. Straw stuffed head and kapok body and limbs. Fully jointed. Rust brown flocked canvas pads. No claws. Original glass eyes and embroidered black floss nose. Ears sewn on. Sewn on tag:
"Hygienic Toys
Made in England by
The Chad Valley Co. Ldt."
Circa. 1930. *Margaret Mandel Collection.*

RIGHT: Illustration 319. 19 in. (48.3cm) long gold mohair bear. Straw sutffed head with cotton stuffed body and limbs. Fully jointed. Felt pads and no claws. Original glass eyes and metal nose. Circa 1930s. *Margaret Mandel Collection.*

Illustration 320. 13 in. (33cm) black and white cotton plush bear. Straw stuffed head and cotton body and limbs. Unjointed. Same cotton plush pads. Metal nose and replaced button eyes. Black tail. Circa 1930s. *Margaret Mandel Collection.*

Illustration 321. 13 in. (33cm) gold very long mohair bear. Straw stuffed head and kapok body and limbs. Felt pads and no claws. Fully jointed. Original orange tin eyes, black embroidered yarn nose. Snout is matching bristle-type mohair (set in). Ears sewn on. Squeaker. Early 1930s. *Margaret Mandel Collection.*

LEFT: Illustration 322. 13 in. (33 cm) bear. Brown composition head with black ears. Print material with red roses and blue background. White cotton pads. Satin chest. No joints. Black painted eyes. Open-closed red mouth with molded pink tongue. Appears to be a product of war time shortages. Circa 1940s.

Illustration 323. 12 in. (30.5cm) standing bear. Dark brown wool plush. Stuffed with all cotton, straw only in haunches. Jointed head and arms only. Legs are rigid. Note the haunches. Gold velveteen arm pads and nose. Black felt foot pads (flat footed). Original glass eyes and metal nose. Ears sewn on. Growler still operable. Original waterstained pink taffeta type bow. Childhood bear of owner. Circa 1936-38. *Margaret Mandel Collection.*

Illustration 324. 21 in. (53.3cm) cinnamon brown cotton plush bear. All cotton stuffing. Only legs jointed. Beige felt pads and no claws. Ears sewn on. Original glass eyes and embroidered black floss nose. Very thick legs. Late 1940s. *Margaret Mandel Collection.*

Illustration 325. 9 in. (22.9cm) "Teddy Baby" standing cub by Steiff. Cream color mohair, fully jointed. Tan felt pads. Brown glass eyes with dark pupils. Label: "Made in U. S. Zone, Germany." 1950s. *Judy Johnson Collection.*

ABOVE: Illustration 326. 12 in. (30.5cm). Bear on left is brown; the one on right is white. Stuffed with excelsior. Long, shaggy fur. Fully jointed. Noses are short mohair. Felt paws and felt inside the open mouth. "Made in Western Germany" on bottom of teeter-tooter platform. Also "Beimo-Heinz Mordelt-Mech., beweal Dehovalions Figaree-Telepon Berlichingen 321." Electrified. Circa 1950s. *Susan Gaskill Collection.*

RIGHT: Illustration 327. 11½ in. (29.1cm) Steiff bear. Soft gold mohair. Fully jointed with felt tan pads and four black claws. Brown glass eyes and black embroidered nose. Label in front leg seam: "Made in Western Germany." 1950s.

Illustration 328. 7 in. (17.8cm) "Zotty" Teddy Bears, Series #0300/18. Caramel golden orange mohair plush. Orange tinted chest hair. Brown glass eyes with black pupils. Dark brown embroidered nose. Open mouth lined with peach felt. Red gun-sprayed tongue. Peach felt pads. Jointed at neck, shoulders and hip. Arms curved downward. Growler. Original Steiff labels in ears. Made in Germany. 1969. *Patricia Rowland Collection.*

Illustration 329. 14 in. (35.6cm) "MISHA" bear (available in several sizes) by Dakin. Rich brown and beige plush. No joints. Black felt pads and felt claws. Original tag shows art work of VIKTOR CHIZHIKOV, Russian artist, chosen to create MISHA official mascot of 1980 Moscow Olympic Games. Label: "R. Dakin & Co. Product of Korea. 1979."

Illustration 330. 12½ in. (30.5cm) bear made by "Anker." Frosted brown long pile plush with short mohair on ears. Peach felt mouth and red tongue. Jointed head only. Peach felt pads, painted claws on hind feet. Brown glass eyes with dark pupils. Black hand-embroidered nose. On one side the tag is blue and gold with symbol of a lion with anchor super imposed. Reverse side reads: "ANKER//(beneath black rectangle)//PLUSCHTIERE AUS MUNCHEN." Circa 1960.

RIGHT: Illustration 331. 8½ in. (21.6cm) bear. Orange plush, pink ribbon bow. Jointed legs and pink felt pads. Glass eyes with black pupils. Velvet nose, embroidered mouth. Red, white, black and gold label, front: "Made in China." Label back: "B. Shackman & Co. skin, cotton and wool." 1970s.

146

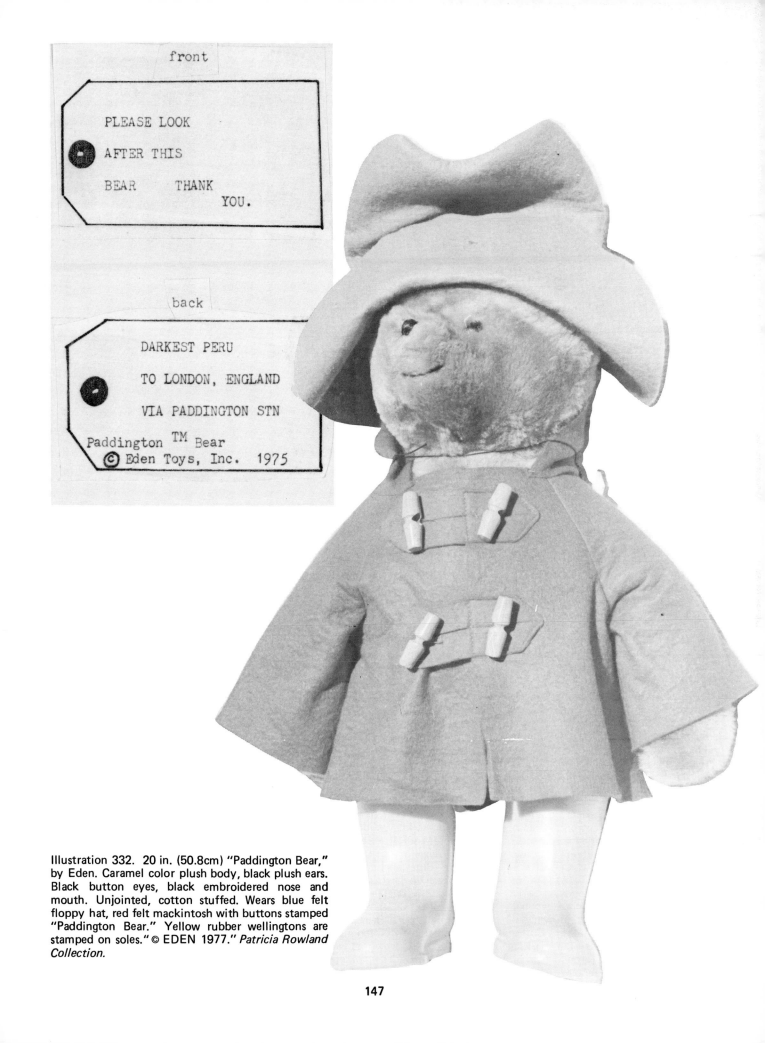

front

PLEASE LOOK

AFTER THIS

BEAR   THANK

            YOU.

back

DARKEST PERU

TO LONDON, ENGLAND

VIA PADDINGTON STN

Paddington ™ Bear
© Eden Toys, Inc. 1975

Illustration 332. 20 in. (50.8cm) "Paddington Bear," by Eden. Caramel color plush body, black plush ears. Black button eyes, black embroidered nose and mouth. Unjointed, cotton stuffed. Wears blue felt floppy hat, red felt mackintosh with buttons stamped "Paddington Bear." Yellow rubber wellingtons are stamped on soles." © EDEN 1977." *Patricia Rowland Collection.*

147

Steiff Teddy Bears

Illustration 333. **(A)** 11 in. (27.9cm) "Petsy" Teddy Bear, Series #0241/30. Light golden Dralon. Brown glass eyes with black pupils. Dark brown embroidered nose and mouth. Synthetic velvet foot pads same color as body. Jointed at neck, shoulders and hips. Fat tummy. Cotton stuffed. Original mint green ribbon. Labels read: chest -"STEIFF·ORIGINAL·MARKE [around top half of label]//Petsy// [flat printed bear head beneath]." Ear - "Made in//Austria// covering - 80% Dralon// 20% cotton." Orange, rose and purple label tied around neck with washing instructions in four languages: "OUTER COVERING WASHABLE." 1975. **(B)** 4 in. (10.2cm) "Original Teddy," Series #0202/11. Caramel colored mohair plush. Black metal eyes. Brown embroidered nose and mouth. Cotton stuffed. Labels read: chest - "STEIFF· ORIGINAL·MARKE [around top half of label]//Original//Teddy// [emboss-

ed printed bear head beneath]." Ear - "Made in//Germany//covering - 59% wool//41% cotton." **(C)** 14 in. (35.6cm) "Original Teddy Bear," Series #0202/36. Caramel colored mohair plush. Synthetic velvet pads same color as body. Brown glass eyes with black pupils. Dark brown embroidered nose and mouth. Jointed at neck, shoulders and hips. Small hump. Original red ribbon. Cotton stuffed. Labels read: chest - "Original//Teddybar// [printed bear head beneath and Steiff in script beside the head]// KNOPF IM OHR." Ear - "Made in// Austria//covering - 80% Dralon//20% cotton." Blue label tied around neck with washing instructions in three languages: "OUTER COVERING WASHABLE." 1975. **(D)** 5 in. (12.7cm) "Young Bear," Series #12/ 1312,0. Caramel colored mohair plush. Tan felt pads. Brown glass eyes with black pupils. Dark brown embroidered nose and mouth. Shoulders, tail and

claw pattern - painted. Jointed at the head. Small hump. Excelsior stuffed. Green leather collar with bell. Label: white cloth label with black printing "MADE IN US-ZONE GERMANY." Manufactured with no button in ear. Circa 1950s. **(E)** 2-5/8 in. (6.7cm) bear. Dark golden yellow mohair plush. Black metal eyes. Black embroidered nose and mouth. Jointed at neck, shoulders and hips. Appears and feels to be a metal covered body. Label: white paper tag with black printing "MADE IN WESTERN GERMANY." Manufactured with no button in ear. **(F)** 12 in. (30.5cm) bear. Caramel colored mohair plush. Peach colored felt pads. Black embroidered nose, mouth and claws. Jointed at neck, shoulders and hips. Small hump. Growls when squeezed. Wood shaving stuffed. Thread still intact where label was sewn on chest. Manufactured with no button in ear. *Patricia Rowland Collection.*

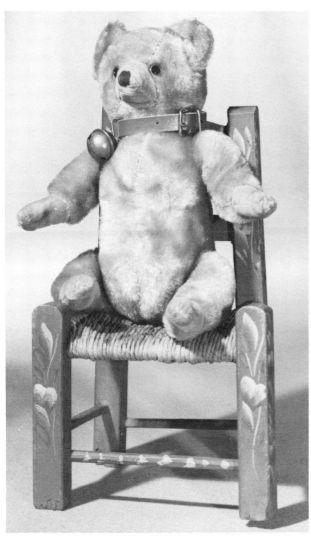

RIGHT: Illustration 335. 12 in. (30.5cm) Steiff "Teddy Baby" bear. Gold mohair with paler gold muzzle, chest and feet. Fully jointed. Paws turn under. Open-sewn type mouth. Excelsior stuffed. Brown glass eyes. Original tag says "STEIFF·ORIGINAL·MARKE [around top half of tag] //Teddy-//Baby//[bear head beneath]." *Beverly Port Collection*

Illustration 334. 7 in. (17.8cm) sitting bear. Orange rayon plush. Wired legs, no joints. Four feet and muzzle are yellow velvet. Embroidered black nose and orange mouth. Red leather collar with bell.

Illustration 336. 13 in. (33cm) Kathe Kruse bear. Soft brown plush over foam rubber form. No joints. Pearlized button eyes, two sewn holes form pupil. Gold tag, red printing: "Original// Kathe Kruse//, MODELL//HANNE KRUSE// made in Germany."

Illustration 337 A & B. 13 in. (33cm) bear by Bruin Manufacturing Company. Light brown mohair. Hump, long curving front legs with long feet. Fully jointed. Embroidered claws on peach pads (faded to tan). Brown glass eyes. Blue and gold woven label, "B.M.C." *Helen Sieverling Collection.*

Illustration 338. 23 in. (58.4cm) bear. Deep gold long pile wool mohair. Head stuffed with excelsior; the rest kapok stuffed. Fully jointed, cream velvet pads. Black embroidered nose and mouth. Brown glass eyes with dark pupils.

Illustration 339. 23 in. (58.4cm) bear. White long pile wool mohair. Short pile muzzle. Head stuffed with excelsior. The rest of the bear stuffed with kapok. Squeaker. Fully jointed. White velvet pads. Brown glass eyes and hand-embroidered nose.

Illustration 340. 13½ in. (34.2cm) bear by Knickerbocker Toy Co. Inc. White plush, fully jointed with red felt paws. Three silver bells indicate clown bear. Brown plastic eyes with threaded iris. Velvet muzzle and black felt nose. Embroidered mouth. Satin label: "Knickerbocker Toy Co. Inc. Animals of Distinction."

Illustration 341 A & B. 22 in. (55.9cm) two-face "Bear - Orangutan" by "Merrythought Hygienic Toys." Light golden mohair wearing red jacket with white braid. Velvet stitched forepaws and gold velvet feet. Black glass eyes, long pointy hand-embroidered nose. Two labels. Top label reads "REGD. DESIGN//No. 83D449." Second label, "REGD. DESIGN// No. 801863//MERRYTHOUGHT//HYGIENIC TOYS// MADE IN ENGLAND." *Helen Sieverling Collection.*

Illustration 342. 7 in. (17.8cm) Steiff "Zotty" bears. Brown silver tipped long mohair. Gold on chest. Fully jointed. Peach felt pads and peach mouth with deeper tint. Brown glass eyes with dark pupils. Paper tags: "STEIFF·ORIGINAL· MARKE [around top half of label] // Zotty//[bear head printed beneath] ." *Left: Helen Sieverling Collection.*

Illustration 343. 9 in. (22.9cm). Early white wool mohair bear. No joints. Wired arms. Red velvet ears, unusual red front mitten paws with back pads. Very pointed nose. Brown glass eyes with dark pupils. Squeaker.

152

ABOVE LEFT: Illustration 344. 11½ in. (29.1cm) short plush, faded soft blue bear. Legs jointed on WIRE. Bright red cotton ear linings and pads. Deep set gray glass eye. Nose of stitched felt and embroidered black mouth.

ABOVE RIGHT: Illustration 345. 9 in. (22.9cm) bear. Reddish brown rayon plush. Fully jointed with pink embroidered claws. Deep yellow velvet pads with black markings. Brown glass eyes, velvet muzzle, and black embroidered nose. Green leather collar with bell, cloth label in back: "Made in Japan."

RIGHT: Illustration 346. 8½ in. (21.5cm) baby's bear "Mutzli," from Switzerland. Rattle in paws. Wool mohair, white head and pale blue body. White feet with peach felt pads on bottoms. Short plush on muzzle, hand-embroidered brown nose. Brown glass eyes with dark pupils.

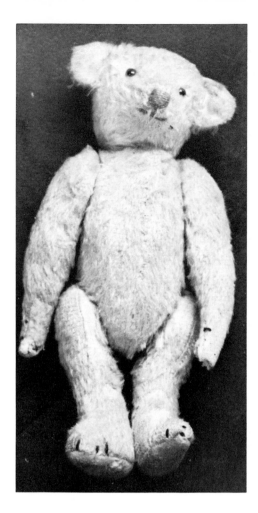

Illustration 347A & B. 9½ in. (24.1cm) Teddy Bear. White mohair with white felt pads. Eyes have been replaced. Gold brown embroidered nose and mouth. Five black embroidered claws. Jointed at neck, shoulders and hips. Hump and growler. Stuffed with excelsior. *Patricia Rowland Collection.*

Illustration 348A & B. 21 in. (53.3cm) Teddy Bear. Gold mohair plush with heavily painted tan gauze pads. Brown glass eyes with black pupils. Black embroidered nose, mouth and claws. Jointed at neck, shoulders and hips. Small hump and growler. The back of the head is unusually flat. Stuffed with excelsior. There is a yellow knotted thread in his ear where possibly a label was sewn on. *Patricia Rowland Collection.*

Illustration 349A & B. 18 in. (45.7cm) Teddy Bear. Caramel golden brown mohair plush with tan felt pads. Black shoe-button eyes and black embroidered nose, mouth and claws. Jointed at neck, shoulders and hips. Hump and long curved hands and large feet. Long snout and growler. Stuffed with excelsior. *Patricia Rowland Collection.*

Illustration 350. 15 in. (38.1cm) bear. Very early yellow cotton string-type plush. Head stuffed with straw, body and limbs with cotton. Off-white felt pads and no claws. Fully jointed. Black floss embroidered nose. Original glass eyes. Squeaker. Ears sewn on. Acquired from original owner who was born in 1906. *Margaret Mandel Collection.*

Illustration 351. 22 in. (55.9cm) Teddy Bear. Deep chestnut brown mohair plush. Light chestnut brown plush snout (mohair?). Tan peach pads. Brown glass eyes with black pupils and black felt circle behind each eye. Black embroidered mouth. Black nose (feels like deteriorated rubber) with red painted nostrils. Jointed at neck, shoulders and hips. Body and head stuffed with excelsior; arms and legs stuffed with cotton. Growler. *Patricia Rowland Collection.*

155

Illustration 352. 17 in. (43.2cm) rose color long mohair bear. All kapok stuffing. Fully jointed with hardwood discs. Beige felt pads and no claws. Black embroidered nose. Original but larger than shoe-button type eyes. Ears sewn on. Nice big feet and long arms. *Margaret Mandel Collection.*

ABOVE: Illustration 353. 11½ in. (29.1cm) musical Teddy Bear. White mohair with tan felt pads. Deep golden orange glass eyes with black pupils. The back of the eyes are painted over with white sealer. Black embroidered nose. Claws are made with black marker. Jointed at neck, shoulders and hips. Plays "Brahm's Lullaby." Stuffed with cotton. *Patricia Rowland Collection.*

LEFT: Illustration 354. 9 in. (22.9cm) bear. Light tan mohair. Fully jointed. Creamy tan felt paw pads; black claws are hand-embroidered. Hand-embroidered nose and mouth. Brown glass eyes. Elongated feet. Squeaker. *Helen Wilburn Collection.*

Illustration 355. 18 in. (45.7cm) dark gold cloth with nap wool bear. All straw stuffing. Fully jointed, hard cardboard discs. Brown canvas pads and embroidered claws. Shoe-button eyes. Ear sewn on and stuffed. Original embroidered black nose. *Margaret Mandel Collection.*

BELOW: Illustration 356A & B. 12 in. (30.5cm) Teddy Bear. Chestnut brown mohair plush with tan felt pads. Black shoe-button eyes. Black embroidered nose, mouth and claws. Jointed at neck, shoulders and hip. Hump, long curved hands, large feet and long snout. Stuffed with excelsior. *Patricia Rowland Collection.*

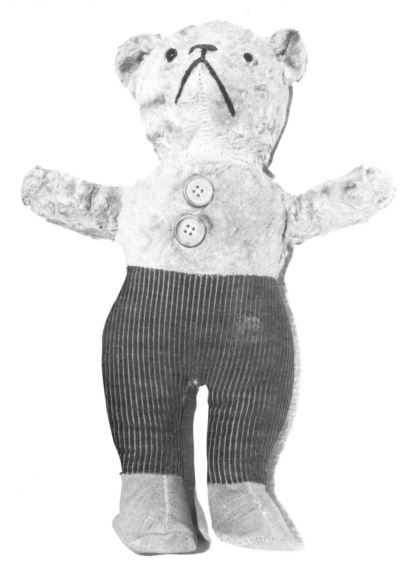

Illustration 357A & B. 12½ in. (31.7cm) Teddy Bear. Cinnamon mohair plush upper torso with two buttons, head and arms are sewn to the body. (Buttons are replacements -- same size as marks left on body; old buttons.) Navy blue wide-ribbed corduroy lower torso and legs. Orange flannel feet (shoes) with heavy cardboard soles inside to give them shape. Glass eyes with black pupils. The back of the eyes are painted brick red and from the front side show as iris'. Black embroidered nose and mouth. Circular bent wire inside arms where they connect with body, perhaps to give strength. Excelsior stuffed head and cotton stuffed body. *Patricia Rowland Collection.*

LEFT: Illustration 358. 15 in. (38.1cm) bear. Fuzzy dark brown. Straw stuffed. Fully jointed with dark brown glass eyes. Sits in an old Buddy L truck. *Kay Bransky Collection.*

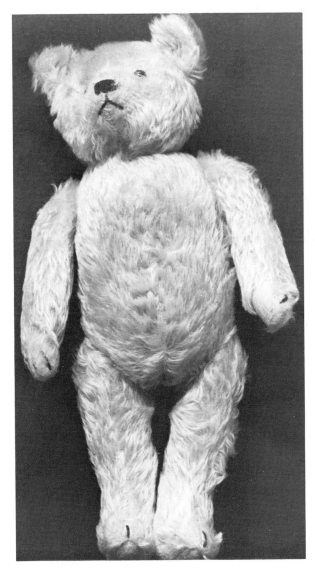

ABOVE: Illustration 359A & B. 16 in. (40.6cm) Teddy Bear. Pink mohair plush with cream-colored felt pads. Glass eyes with black pupils. The back of the eyes are painted brown and from the front side show as iris'. Black embroidered nose, mouth and claws. Jointed at neck, shoulders and hips. Small hump. Growler. Stuffed with excelsior. *Patricia Rowland Collection.*

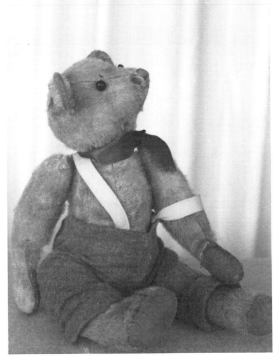

Illustration 360. 12 in. (30.5cm) brown gold mohair bear. Head stuffed with straw, body mixture of kapok and straw with straw limbs. Fully jointed. Brown cotton pads. Original orange wool claws and remnant on nose. Original shoe-button eyes and cardboard discs. Ears sewn on. *Margaret Mandel Collection.*

159

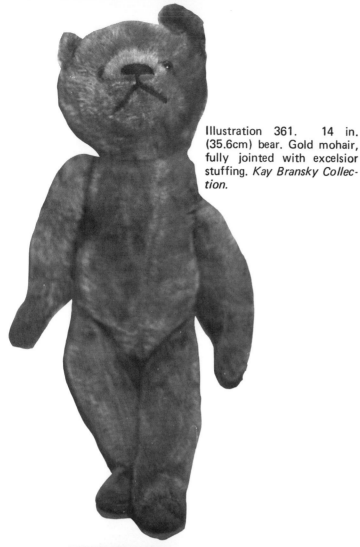

Illustration 361. 14 in. (35.6cm) bear. Gold mohair, fully jointed with excelsior stuffing. *Kay Bransky Collection.*

Illustration 362. 11 in. (27.9cm) Teddy Bear. Gold long mohair plush with tan felt pads. White hand-blown glass eyes with golden yellow iris' and black pupils. Made with wire rings like shoe-buttons. Black embroidered nose and mouth. No claws. Jointed at neck, shoulders and hips. Very pronounced hump. Small, funny little feet. Growler. Over-stitched with army green thread. Stuffed with excelsior. *Patricia Rowland Collection.*

Illustration 363. 18 in. (45.7cm) bear. Dark brown with lighter brown chest, paws and ears. Fully jointed with dark brown glass eyes. Straw stuffed. Sitting on straw stuffed Steiff riding pony. *Kay Bransky Collection.*

Illustration 364A & B. 22½ in. (57.1cm) Teddy Bear. Black long mohair plush. Flesh colored soft plastic vinyl pads with brown spray-painted toes. Circular white felt iris' with black celluloid button eyes. Rubber snout with painted features. Brown nose and whiskers. Deep orange mouth and nostrils. Red tongue and one white tooth. Jointed at neck, shoulders and hips. Hump and growler. Stuffed with cotton. *Patricia Rowland Collection.*

Illustration 365. 17½ in. (44.4cm) Teddy Bear. Dark brown mohair plush. Peach velvet pads and brown glass eyes with black pupils. Black embroidered nose and mouth. Jointed at neck, shoulders and hips. Fat tummy. Stuffed with cotton. Growler. *Patricia Rowland Collection.*

Illustration 366. 12½ in. (31.7cm) Teddy Bear. Gold short mohair plush. Brown glass eyes with black pupils. Black embroidered nose and mouth. Tan foot pads. Jointed at shoulders and hips. Fat tummy. Head stuffed with excelsior and body stuffed with cotton. *Patricia Rowland Collection.*

ABOVE: Illustration 367. Left: 14 in. (35.6cm) rare black bear. Black long pile mohair. Fully jointed. Claws embroidered on felt pads. Gold glass eyes with black centers. Flat feet for standing. *Helen Sieverling Collection*. Right: 14½ in. (36.9cm) bear. White mohair. Fully jointed. Three black claws. Black embroidered nose. Dark brown eyes with black pupils. *Helen Sieverling Collection*.

ABOVE RIGHT. Same black Bear as shown on the left of the above photo.

RIGHT: Illustration 368. Left: 10¼ in. (26cm) baby's bear. Pink cotton eiderdown cloth. All legs jointed. No pads on front paws, white felt pads on rear. Brown glass eyes with dark pupils. Pink embroidered nose. Cotton stuffing. Right: 9¼ in. (23.5cm) baby's bear. Tan cotton plush. Fully jointed with peach cotton velour pads. Cotton stuffed.

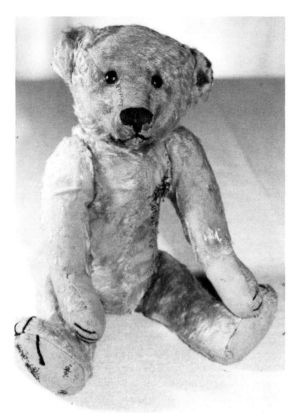

Illustration 369. 20 in. (50.8cm) Teddy. Gold mohair with excelsior stuffing. Fully jointed with large paws and feet. Shoe-button eyes. *Beverly Port Collection.*

Illustration 370. 24 in. (61cm) Teddy Bear. Gold plush with excelsior stuffing. Large hump and fully jointed. *Beverly Port Collection.*

Illustration 371. 19½ in. (49.5cm) German musical squeeze bear. Gold mohair, fully jointed, excelsior stuffed. Three black claws and embroidered nose. Gold glass eyes with black pupils. Tan felt pads. (By grasping torso in both hands and squeezing, music box is activated.) *Helen Sieverling Collection.*

Illustration 372. 14½ in. (36.8cm) bear by Chad Valley. Bright gold long pile mohair. Fully jointed, cotton stuffed. Red brown felt pads. Brown glass eyes with dark pupils. Label on chest: "Hygienic Toys of England by Chad Valley, LTC." On foot: "THE CHAD VALLEY CO. LTD//By appointment//Toy makers to the Queen."

Illustration 373. 17 in. (43.2cm) bear doll. Golden mohair plush. Completely jointed. Embroidered paws and shoe-button eyes. Old blue knit cap covers baby head. Baby face, open-closed molded mouth and blue glass sleeping eyes. Patented June 9, 1914, by Louis S. Schiffer, New York. *Beverly Port Collection.*

Illustration 374. 20 in. (50.8cm) bear. Gold plush, excelsior stuffed and fully jointed. Extra long, curved arms. Embroidered claws and working growler. Eyes: electric eye bulbs, wire from eyes goes through tube in neck to battery and control in body. Porcelain "tummy-button" to light eyes. *Beverly Port Collection.*

Illustration 375. 9½ in. (24.1cm) Steiff bear, button in ear. Red, white and blue figured dress with white puffed sleeves, gathered by red cord. Body is pink stockinette material. Brown glass eyes with dark pupils. Brown plush head with cream muzzle. Plush on backs of front paws and top of back paws. Open mouth, felt lined. *Helen Sieverling Collection.*

Illustration 376A & B. 17 in. (43.2cm), two-face. Golden mohair plush, fully jointed. Very prominent black claws. Excelsior under bear nose. Entire bisque head under hood and multi-stroke brows. Blue open mouth, two teeth and lashes above and below. Patented June 9, 1914, by Louis S. Schiffer, N.Y. *Helen Sieverling Collection.*

Illustration 377. 13½ in. (34.2cm) "Floppy" bear. Cream colored mohair. Peach felt open-mouth and tan felt pads on rear legs. Embroidered nose and brown felt circles for eyes with pink embroidery stitches for eyelids. No joints. Very early model. *Helen Sieverling Collection.*

Illustration 378. 8 in. (20.3cm), gold Steiff bear, button in ear. Fully jointed with peach pads and four claws. Foot measures 1¾ in. (4.4cm). Glass eyes and dark pupils. *Private Collection.*

Illustration 379. 14 in. (35.6cm) Steiff Teddies, button in ears. White mohair plush, excelsior stuffed. Fully jointed. Shoe button eyes and peach felt paws. Paper left attached to button in ear is white, the earliest used. *Beverly Port Collection.*

Illustration 380A & B. 9½ in. (24.2cm) Steiff bear. Soft gold short pile mohair plush. Front legs 5 in. (12.7cm) long, back legs 4½ in. (11.5cm) long. Fully jointed. Hump, but not large. Paw pads once peach color. Squeaker and shoe-button eyes. *Helen Sieverling Collection.*

Illustration 381A & B. 8½ in. (21.6cm). "Father Christmas Bear." White plush face with black bead eye. Black embroidered nose. Hood and body garment of maroon blanket cloth. White felt pads on arms and white felt feet. Used on Christmas tree. *Helen Sieverling Collection.*

Illustration 382. 11 in. (27.9cm) bear by Kersa. Light beige mohair. Fully jointed. Peach felt pads on paws. Hand-embroidered nose. Clear glass eyes with black pupils. Oblong metal tags fastened in feet inscribed "KERSA//Made in// Germany." *Helen Sieverling Collection.*

Illustration 383. 28 in. (71.1cm) gold short pile mohair bear. Firmly stuffed with excelsior. Fully jointed tan felt pads and medium hump. Brown glass eyes with dark pupils. Nose is black material sewn into pattern. Embroidered mouth. *Helen Sieverling Collection.*

Illustration 384. Left: 14 in. (35.6cm) standing cub. May have had leash. Steiff button in ear. White mohair, fully jointed. Foot pads were once peach felt. Black hand-embroidered claws. Brown glass eyes with dark pupils. Collar clamped on with two Steiff buttons, half the size of button in ear. Bits of material under button are dark orange. Right: 14 in. (35.6cm) standing cub. Steiff button in ear. Cream long pile mohair and fully jointed. Faded peach color felt open mouth. Short pile plush on nose and feet. Brown embroidered claws. *Judy Johnson Collection.*

Illustration 385. 20 in. (50.8cm) "Zotty" bear by Steiff. Fully jointed, brown frosted long pile mohair. Large hump on back and growler. As of 1978, these bears are no longer jointed. *Beverly Port Collection.*

Illustration 386. Left: 10 in. (25.4cm) bear. Light gold sparsely woven mohair. Excelsior stuffed. Fully jointed. Tan felt worn pads. Three black claws. Brown glass eye on glass pin (one missing). Squeaker. Right: 11 in. (27.9cm) bear. Gold sparsely woven mohair. Jointed on wire through legs. Pale pink felt pads on paws. Very short feet and three black claws. Gold eyes with dark pupils. Blown glass eyes; the stems to insert are glass. Squeaker. *Judy Johnson Collection.*

Illustration 388. 12 in. (30.5cm) Teddy. Gold plush and fully jointed. Dark brown pads and button eyes. Made by Dean's Childsplay Co., England. *Beverly Port Collection.*

Illustration 387. 11 in. (27.9cm) bear. Gold mohair, fully jointed. Four black claws, pink-tan felt pads. Large oblong working squeaker. Brown glass eyes.

Illustration 389. 20 in. (50.8cm) bear. Cotton stuffed with squeaker in stomach. Gold long and shaggy mohair. Fully jointed, brown yarn stitched nose. Felt pads on paws, worn. *Susan Gaskill Collection.*

Illustration 390. 5 in. (12.7cm) bear. Body is pressed wood form covered with brown plush, fully jointed. Not cuddly. No pads on front paws; material covers pads on back feet. Eyes are clear glass with small black pupils. Nose looks like the head of a straight pin. *Susan Gaskill Collection.*

Illustration 391. 19½ in. (49.6cm) bear. Dark brown mohair. Fully jointed. Peach felt pads on paws. Rather straight front legs. Embroidered claws and nose. Gold glass eyes with large black pupils. *Helen Sieverling Collection.*

Illustration 392. 22 in. (55.9cm) "Trudi," two-tone brown with buff nose, paws and feet. Pale pink blush on cheeks under eyes. Italy. *Beverly Port Collection.*

Illustration 393. Left: 24 in. (61cm) Teddy. Tan mohair with glass eyes. Right: 14 in. (35.6cm) "Merrythought," gold. *Kimberlee and John Port Collection.*

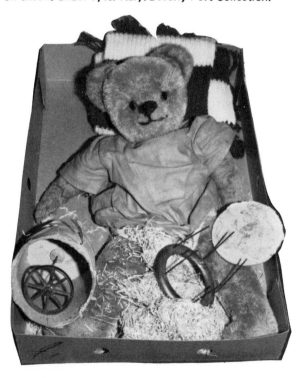

Illustration 394A. 17 in. (43.2cm) golden mohair plush, fully jointed with brown glass eyes. Metal wheel on left goes around inside metal ring on right, hitting the upright metal tines producing a melidious tune. Early German bear. *Beverly Port Collection.*

Illustration 394B. 17 in. (43.2cm) Christmas bear. Golden mohair plush, fully jointed with brown glass eyes. Red and green with knitted muffler and hat. Green sweater. Early German bear. *Beverly Port Collection.*

Illustration 395. 16 in. (40.6cm) bear manufactured by Merrythought. Fully jointed, brown plush, embroidered claws. Velvet nose. Bells in ears. "Made in England" on foot. *Beverly Port Collection.*

Illustration 396. 11 in. (27.9cm) bear. Cotton plush head, once white. Front paws match the head material. Velvet nose and embroidered mouth. Maroon velvet shirt and feet, deep blue velvet trousers. Shoe button eyes. *Bill Boyd Collection*

Illustration 397. 24 in. (61cm) bear. Zipper in back for pajamas. Golden long pile mohair. Fully jointed with tan felt pads on paws. Brown eyes with dark pupils. *Sara Barrett Collection.*

Illustration 398. Left: 6 in. (15.2cm) bear by Berg. Red metal heart on chest marked: "Berg-Herr mit Herr." Fully jointed. White mohair with peach felt pads on all feet. Brown glass eyes. Hand-embroidered nose. The label on the back seam of the right arm is undecipherable. Right: 6 in. (15.2cm) bear by Berg. Red metal heart reads "berg" on the back. Cream gold mohair and red rayon ribbon. Fully jointed with no pads. Brown glass eyes. Hand-embroidered nose.

Illustration 399. 18 in. (45.7cm) bear. Gold wool mohair, fully jointed. Tan felt pads, large brown glass eyes and dark pupils. Metal nose piece, embroidered mouth. Broad face and shorter nose. Orange sweater.

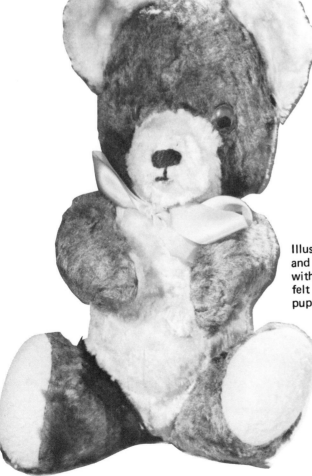

Illustration 400. 12½ in. (31.7cm) bear. Gold and blue rayon plush. Vivid blue head and legs with gold chest. Fully jointed. Deep yellow felt pads on paws. Goggle eyes, a floating black pupil inside a clear container. Cotton stuffed.

Illustration 402. 12 in. (30.5cm) bear. Brown long pile mohair. Reddish brown short pile muzzle. Hand-embroidered nose and mouth. Fully jointed with brown glass eyes and dark pupils. *Bill Boyd Collection.*

Illustration 401. 16 in. (40.6cm) Steiff rust color bear, button in ear. Different shape of head, ears set low. Felt pads. 9½ in. (24.2cm) front legs, 7½ in. (19.1cm) back legs. *Private Collection.*

Illustration 403. 13½ in. (34.2cm) bear. White wool mohair, fully jointed. Beige felt pads on feet. Gold glass eyes, dark centers. Hand-embroidered black nose. *Judy Johnson Collection.*

LEFT: Illustration 404. 25 in. (63.5cm) Steiff cinnamon bear. Long plush mohair, fully jointed. Black claws and shoe-button eyes. *Private Collection.*

ABOVE: Illustration 405. 14 in. (35.6cm) Steiff bear, button in ear, white tag #5325, white long pile mohair, hump. Fully jointed, three brown claws and brown nose. Felt pads. (He is standing in rear on right in "Family Reunion", Illustration 406.) *Private Collection.*

LEFT: Illustration 406. "Family Reunion". Group of all white bears with brown noses. Largest: 14 in. (35.6cm). Smallest: 8½ in. (21.6cm). *Private Collection.*

176

Illustration 407. 25 in. (63.5cm) Steiff bear. Faded apricot long pile plush mohair. Foot is 5½ in. (13.9cm) long. Fully jointed with felt paws and shoe-button eyes. *Private Collection.*

Illustration 408. 21 in. (53.3cm) Teddy. Faded gold long pile mohair. Fully jointed. Beige felt paws. Four black claws-feet. 11½ in. (29.2cm) front legs, 9 in. (22.9cm) back legs. Shoe-button eyes. Roosevelt button (not from Steiff). *Private Collection.*

Illustration 409A & B. 21 in. (53.3cm) matched pair of Steiff bears, button in ear. Fully jointed, black claws, seam down middle of nose. Felt pads, feet almost 4½ in. (11.5cm). Shoe-button eyes. Girl, on right, has long and curly pile of deep gold mohair. Boy, on left, has long and curly pile of pale gold mohair. His Roosevelt button has been added. *Private Collection.*

LEFT: Illustration 410. Official Walt Disney version of Winnie-The-Pooh. Gold-tan plush. Came with a Pooh "Golden Book" and record in mid 1960s. Legs sewn in sitting position. 10 in. (25.4cm) tall sitting-size. Gold and red sweater, red bat with gold tassel. *Beverly Port Collection.*

Illustration 411. Winnie-the-Pooh, inspired by the books by A. A. Milne. A rare version. *Playthings,* August, 1930.

Miniature Bears

Illustration 412. (A) 4 in. (10.2cm) bear. Light brown mohair. Button eyes. Fully jointed. Tag: "Original Teddy." (B) 3½ in. (8.9cm) Steiff bear. White mohair. Button eyes. *Helen Wilburn Collection.* (C) 2¾ in. (7cm) Steiff bear. Pale gold mohair. Fully jointed.

Illustration 413. Left: 3¾ in. (9.5cm) Steiff bear. White mohair. Fully jointed. Button eyes. Well-shaped long feet. Japanese bamboo chair, 1903. *Helen Wilburn Collection.* Right: 2¾ in. (7cm) bear. Light gold mohair. Fully jointed over hard form. Black button eyes. Tag in leg seam inscribed "Made in Western Germany." Japanese bamboo chair, 1903. *Helen Wilburn Collection.*

LEFT: Illustration 415. Left: 6 in. (15.2cm) Steiff. Gold mohair, jointed. Middle: 6 in. (15.2cm) Steiff. Candy Box body, jointed. Right: 6½ in. (16.5cm). Gold mohair, early, jointed. *Beverly Port Collection.*

Illustration 414. 5 in. (12.7cm) Theodore B. Bear. Fully jointed. Button eyes. Hand-embroidered nose and mouth. Theodore B. Bear, noted journalist, writing his articles with phone "at the ready." Just came back from a visit to Peter Bull in England where he attended the "Great Teddy Bear Rally." *Beverly Port Collection.*

ABOVE: Illustration 416. 2¼ in. (5.7cm) high x 4 in. (10.2cm) long miniature "Bruin-Teddy." Hard form covered by golden bristly mohair (more sparsely woven). Remnants of a collar. Non-jointed. Brown glass eyes with dark pupils and a tail. Circa 1906.

Illustration 417. 5½ in. (14cm) Teddy Bear. White mohair plush. Snout and foot pads are short white mohair. Brown glass eyes with black pupils. Black embroidered nose and mouth. Jointed at shoulders and hips. Fat tummy. Stuffed with excelsior. When purchased in 1976, he came with the basket carved from a fruit pit and tied with a ribbon to a small safety pin in his paw. *Patricia Rowland Collection.*

RIGHT: Illustration 419. 5 in. (12.7cm) childhood bear. Only one leg. Golden mohair. Button eyes. *Gerrie Voorhees Collection.*

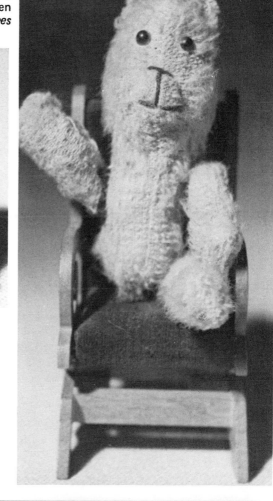

Illustration 418. 2½ in. (6.4cm) baby bear with bottle. Yellow gold with red pads. Metal nose and eyes. *Gerrie Voorhees Collection.*

BELOW: Illustration 420. Three Bears and Goldilocks. Steiff. Papa 8½ in. (21.5cm), golden mohair with peach felt pads. Fully jointed. Brown eyes with dark pupils. Four black claws and hump. Mama 6 in. (15.2cm), no pads. Brown glass eyes with dark pupils. Baby 3½ in. (8.8cm), bead eyes and embroidered nose. Embossed tag: "STEIFF·ORIGINAL·MARKE [around top half of tag] // Original Teddy//[bear head beneath]." *Helen Sieverling Collection.*

181

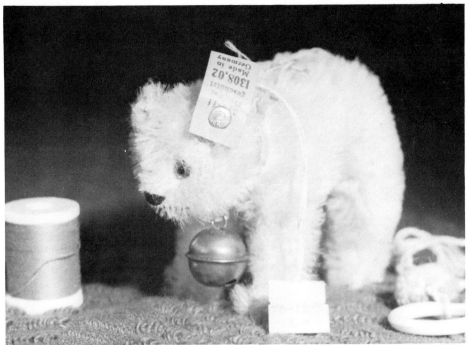

Illustration 421. 3 in. (7.6cm) high x 4 in. (10.2cm) long standing bear by Steiff. Cream color with gold bell. Brown glass eyes. Deep orange tag under button. Ring and pompom on cord for baby toy. Original price: $1.00. *Private Collection.*

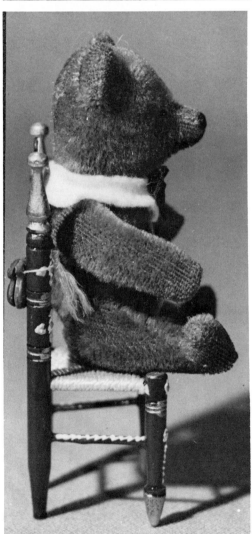

Illustration 423. 4¾ in. (12.1cm) twin gold bears. "GERMANY" stamped on rayon ribbons. Short, wide bodies. Bright gold mohair. Wired-on arms and legs. Head stationary. Very short feet. Glass eyes and ears cut into head. Japanese rattan furniture, 1903. *Helen Wilburn Collection.*

Illustration 422. 5¼ in. (13.3cm) bear. Chestnut brown mohair. Fully jointed. Beady eyes and pointed nose. No pads on paws. *Helen Sieverling Collection.*

182

Illustration 424. 5½ in. (14cm) bear. Light tan mohair, excelsior stuffed. Fully jointed. No pads on paws. Brown glass eyes. Hand-embroidered nose. *Helen Wilburn Collection.*

Illustration 425. 4 in. (10.2cm) bear. Currently available. Label on right has Chinese characters in red and on reverse reads "Pure Wool" in green script. Pink neck bow. Label of outer gold rim, red inside, black center. Made in China. Brown glass eyes. Non-jointed.

Illustration 426. 6 in. (15.2cm) childhood bear of author's daughter. Steiff. No button in ear. Label: "Original Teddy." Gold mohair. No pads or claws. Fully jointed. Original red bow. Brown glass eyes. Circa 1955. *Willa Koenigsaecker Collection.*

Illustration 427A & B. 4 in. (10.2cm) bear. Some of these bears were sent on mail tags from Yellowstone National Park. Dark green gold sparsely woven mohair. Fully jointed, no paw pads or claws. Brown glass eyes on glass rod. Hand-embroidered nose and mouth. Ears inserted into head.

Illustration 428. 3½ in. (8.9cm) Steiff gold bears. Mohair over hard form. Fully jointed with hand-embroidered noses and mouths. Button eyes. Original cotton bows, two red and one green.

Illustration 429. 5 in. (12.7cm) Steiff bear baby rattle. White with brown nose. Fully jointed. Steiff button in ear inscribed "Steiff." Bell inside body in metal container. Button eyes. *Private Collection.*

Illustration 430. 6 in. (15.2cm) bear. Original red ribbon. Light brown mohair. No pads or claws. Jointed on wires. Head stationary. Ears cut into head. German (Occupied Zone).

Illustration 431. 2¾ in. (7.1cm) Steiff bear and German dollhouse boy doll. Light brown mohair over a hard form. Fully jointed. Black button eyes. Hand-embroidered nose. Tag reads "A toy for you from Christopher Mott." A favor given at a baby shower. The real child Christopher is now six feet tall!

Mechanical Bears

Illustration 432. Far Left to Far Right: Plush-covered black Teddy riding metal rocking horse. Teddy's face is metal, brightly colored like the horse. The sitting Teddy is fabric-covered with glass eyes. When his arms are wound "round and round," he turns somersaults. He and his friend, the roller skating Teddy, are probably from the 1930s. The others date from the 1940s - 50s. The roller skater is also fabric-covered and has glass eyes. Mechanism is in his oversized skates instead of inside his body like the others. The short all metal fellow, next to the skater, is bright and colorful. Marked "Chein U.S.A." He is the only one from this group that is American. The others are from Japan and Germany. Teddy on the far right is plush-covered, but has rubber hands. One hand holds a boot, the other a hammer — a busy shoemaker, this bear! They are all under 8 in. (20.3cm) tall. *Beverly Port Collection.*

Illustration 433. Approximately 4 in. (10.2cm) tin mechanical bears from Germany. Made by the Kohler Co. Keywind in chest. They dance around in a circle. Red ribbon at neck printed on metal. Felt ears inset in holes in head. Gold brown color with dark brown ears. *Beverly Port Collection.*

LEFT: Illustration 434. Approximately 14 in. (35.6cm) mechanical Teddy. Nods "yes" when his tail is pushed up and down, and shakes his head "no" when his tail is pushed from side to side. Brown plush. Brown glass eyes. Fully jointed. Squeaker in stomach. Rare old fellow. Not many have tails. Paws turn under. *Beverly Port Collection.*

Illustration 436. 3 in. (7.6cm) high x 5 in. (12.7cm) long mechanical bear. Chestnut brown mohair plush covering with a small piece cut to simulate a tail. Oval shaped yellow cotton pads glued on. Tan short mohair snout. Brown glass eyes with black pupils. Black metal nose. Body made from tin beer cans. When wound with a key, he walks and turns his head from side to side. *Patricia Rowland Collection.*

Illustration 435. 14½ in. (39.9cm) blue mechanical bear. Long mohair plush. Metal box in torso padded with excelsior. Wind-up key in back. Metal legs are covered by long pile plush. Hand-embroidered brown nose, black claws. Tan felt pads on front legs. Back feet have painted claws. Walks along, growls and walks again. *Helen Sieverling Collection.*

Illustration 437. 10 in. (25.4cm) high bear. Excelsior stuffed. Once white mohair. Shoe button eyes. Heavy metal wheels. *Helen Sieverling Collection.*

187

Illustration 438. 6½ in. (16.5cm) tall x 9 in. (22.9cm) long pull toy by Steiff, Germany. Original residual pull string, red, green and yellow, twisted and braided. Cast iron wheels. Bear dark brown WORSTED WOOL/NAP. No jointing and all straw stuffed. Beige felt pads. Black floss embroidered claws and nose. Shoe-button eyes. Pewter Steiff clip with "ff" underscored. "STEIFF" imprinted on brown leather collar. Circa before 1905. *Margaret Mandel Collection.*

Illustration 439. Bruin-Teddy pull toy in red muzzle. 9½ in. (24.1cm) long x 3¼ in. (8.2cm) wide platform. Bear 6 in. (15.2cm) at shoulder. Bright gold mohair over a hard form. Lightweight metal wheels. Gold eyes with black pupils. *Helen Sieverling Collection.*

Illustration 440. Left: 14 in. (35.6cm) rare mechanical bear. Swiss music box plays "Teddy Bears Picnic" and head turns from side to side to the music. Completely jointed. Circa 1972. *Beverly Port Collection.* Right: 17 in. (43.2cm) rare old mechanical bear. To open and close mouth, press bear's stomach. Excelsior stuffed and completely jointed. Glass eyes. Early 1900s. *Beverly Port Collection.*

Illustration 441. 14 in. (35.6cm) high x 21 in. (53.3cm) long riding toy. Very dark brown long mohair with gold cast. All straw stuffed. Unjointed head with hump. Early cast iron wheels. Beige felt pads and black (floss) embroidered nose. Original glass eyes. Blue silk bow, possibly original. Circa 1910 or before. *Margaret Mandel Collection.*

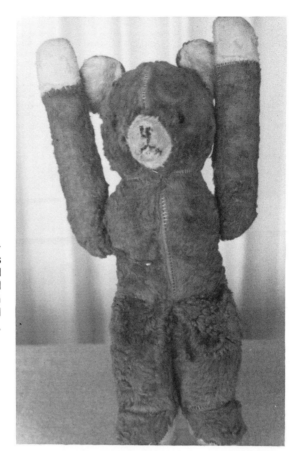

Illustration 442. 15 in. (38.1cm) cinnamon cotton plush mechanical bear. Arms wind up. Arms only jointed. Head stuffed with straw, cotton body and legs and metal arms. Yellow cotton plush sewn on ears, pads and snout. Embroidered nose and mouth. Original glass eyes. Circa 1930s. *Margaret Mandel Collection.*

Illustration 443A & B. 11 in. (29.9cm) mechanical "Shuco Bear." Deep gold long pile mohair. Fully jointed, tiny short feet with tan felt pads. Hand-embroidered nose. Squeaker. Orange glass eyes with dark pupils. Tail (see view B) causes bear to say "yes" and "no." *Helen Sieverling Collection.*

Illustration 444. 20 in. (50.8cm) brown Teddy Bear can sing and speak in German. Fully jointed. Cream color plush on paws and feet. Small record inside body can be turned over. One side talks and the other sings. This bear is circa 1975 and was still available in 1979. *Beverly Port Collection.*

Illustration 445. 10 in. (25.4cm) "DEAR HEART" Teddy Bear has a heart that really beats. It has a battery-run "thumping" heart. Made by Kamar Toy Co. The tag claims that "the sound will lull Baby off to sleep." *Beverly Port Collection.*

Illustration 446. 18 in. (45.7cm) tall x 29 in. (73.7cm) long very early Bruin-Teddy on cast iron wheels. Excelsior stuffed. Mohair almost grayish in color. Shoe-button eyes. Growler cord. 30 in. (76.2cm) clown composition boy by Electra T.N.C., New York. *Kay Bransky Collection.*

Illustration 448. 20 in. (50.8cm) bear, Heunec Co., Germany. Wooly cream color plush. Fully jointed with brown paws and dark button eyes. Ordered from Quelle German catalog, Spring, 1976. Tag: "HEUNEC//Sprech//Bar." *Beverly Port Collection.*

Illustration 447. 9¾ in. (24.8cm) music box bear plays "The Blue Danuhe." Light brown wool mohair. Fully jointed. Three black embroidered claws. Peach felt pads. Embroidered mouth and nose. Brown glass eyes with dark pupils. Red and white button in ear inscribed "Swiss Made//"MUTZLI M.C.Z."//

Illustration 449. 9¾ in. (24.8cm) mechanical "Bing." Stiff body. Brown mohair head, paws and feet. Button eyes. Blue felt jacket with two gold buttons. White vest and red trousers. Germany. Red metal button with black printing fastened into right arm. *Private Collection.*

An early Teddy with his modern counterpart. Bust of T.R. is an Avon bottle. *John Zimmerman Collection. Photograph by John Zimmerman.*

VI. Bearmobilia - Related Items

Nothing could make a collector more aware of the tremendous imprint the Teddy Bear made upon the world than a study of the related items that allude to him. There seem to be few facets of life he did not enter.

There were garments to wear, buttoned on with Teddy Bear buttons. One could carry a Teddy Bear purse, intended for adults as well as children. There were also Teddy Bear cases and bags with the furry shaped head on display.

A fortunate child of 1907 had a sterling Teddy rattle, as well as sterling spoons or fully formed Teddies on the handles of a knife and a fork. He could don his Teddy decorated bathrobe, and cover himself with a similar blanket for his crib, with a Teddy shaped hot water bottle at his feet.

Grown-ups had pillow tops, autograph books, china and metal ornaments, Teddy handkerchief boxes and stationery decorated with Teddies. It went on and on. It seems nostalgia revived the Teddy craze in the 1970s, as new items continue to come on the market. Some of these have been included.

Illustration 450A & B.
Rare "Humpty-Dumpty" Teddy Bear sits on a bench beside his head. Body opens down center seam and contains a miniature compact with oval mirror and powder section with tiny original powder puff. Oblong metal bracket has removable section containing a small tube of lip gloss. Everything handy for the little girl who owned it. Close the body, put the metal bracket at neck section up into Teddy Bear's head and there he sits, "All together" again! And his secret compartment completely hidden. Head swivels on bracket and arms and legs are jointed. Old, worn, dark-gold mohair plush. Early 1900s. A tiny friend only 3¾ in. (9.6cm) tall — just right for a child's small hand. Little black button-like eyes.

Doll News

Beverly Port Collection

Illustration 451A & B. Left: 5 in. (12.7cm) perfume bear. Gold mohair plush with embroidered nose. Fully jointed, no pads. Black button eyes, removable head. Right: 3½ in. (8.9cm) compact bear. Lavender plush mohair. Fully jointed. Body opens to reveal compact inside with powder puff and mirror. *Helen Sieverling Collection.*

Illustration 453. 3½ in. (8.9cm) novelty Teddy. Made from a lump of black coal. Cub with front paws on stomach.

Illustration 452. 5½ in. (14cm) celluloid bear. Deep pink body, yellow suspenders and black belt. Lighter pink pouty baby has movable head strung to opposite arm of the mother. Mother has white eyes, black pupils. Baby's eyes are black dots. Marked:

MADE IN
OCCUPIED
JAPAN

JAPAN

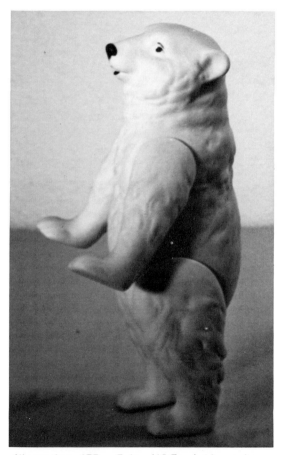

Illustration 454. 5 in. (12.7cm) white papier-mache. Fully jointed with glass eyes. *Mrs. William Ballard Collection.*

Illustration 455. 5 in. (12.7cm) bisque bear. Elastic jointed at shoulders and hips, painted features. Capable of sitting with back legs straight out and, of course, standing on all fours as well as in this upright position. *Beverly Port Collection.*

Illustration 456. Left: 2½ in. (6.4cm) panda bear. Black and white hand-crocheted. Red pupils and mouth. Black iris' and nose and white claws. Made in Communist China, 1977. Middle: Wooden bear with 1½ in. (3.8cm) torso. Unstained natural plywood, hand-painted black features on both sides of face -- ears, nose and mouth. White eyes with black pupils. Head and limbs are jointed with round-headed metal rivets. The head, which pivets, fits into a notched slit in body and is held in place by the rivet which passes through it and connects the front legs. Right: 4 in. (10.2cm) light, golden-yellow mohair plush bear. Black French knot eyes. Nose and mouth missing; only what appears to be a hard glue spot remains. Arms are one connected piece which are pulled through a hole in the body enabling them to move up and down. Original faded red ribbon. Wire armature body stuffed with cotton. Oval blue tag with white edge and white printing inscribed: "MADE IN POLAND." All from *Patricia Rowland Collection*

Illustration 457. 5 in. (12.7cm) celluloid rattle. White Bruin-Teddy. Red cap, black binoculars and silver sword. Red cape lined in yellow. *Billie Tyrrell Collection*

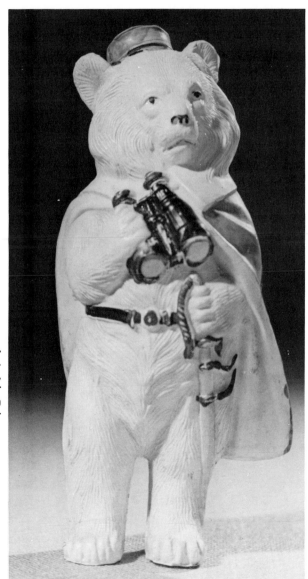

Illustration 458. Three bisque miniatures. 1¾ in. (4.3cm) old stone bisque bear with red bow. 3 in. (7.6cm) doll figure with brown teddy. Marked: "MADE IN JAPAN." 2 in. (5.1cm) small girl with large Teddy. Marked: "Germany."

Illustration 459. Left: 2½ in. (6.4cm) "Rupert." Red sweater with yellow plaid scarf and trousers. Flocked material. Middle: 2¾ in. (7cm) "Paddington." Black hat, tan fur (flocked) body and blue coat. Right: "Smokey" marked on hat. Bisque with brown and yellow hat, blue water pail and blue-gray trousers.

Illustration 460. Left to Right: 3¼ in. (8.2cm) brown and black bear. Wood and leather ears. Gold label: "MOC — Japan." 2¼ in. (5.7cm) light wood bear. Painted eyes, nose and nails. 2 in. (5.1cm) wooden hand-carved bear. Extraordinary detail; excellent proportion. 3¾ in. (9.5cm) standing; 2¾ in. (7cm) sitting bear. Natural wood. Head moves up and down. Movable legs.

196

Illustration 461. Pair of old Teddy Bear muffs. The one on the left has glass eyes and squeakers in both hands. Reddish brown plush. 1920s to 1930s. The one on the right has black shoe-button eyes and a squeaker in the chest. Golden mohair plush with original Steiff button in ear. Early 1900s. *Beverly Port Collection.*

Illustration 462. 9 in. (22.9cm) hand puppet. Japan. Dark brown mohair. Ears set in head. Outlined peach mouth and white muzzle. Inside of paws, peach velvet. Three black claws. Dark brown eyes. *Bill Boyd Collection.*

Illustration 463. Child's cinnamon mohair coat, circa 1907, with gold finish Teddy Bear buttons. *Helen Sieverling Collection.*

Illustration 464. 12 in. (30.5cm) child's muff. Short nose. Gold-brown very soft mohair. Coarsely embroidered nose. Three claws on feet. Lined in flannelette. *Private Collection.*

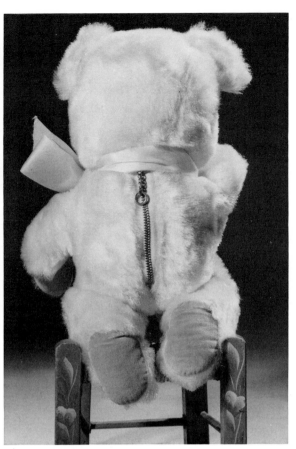

Illustration 465A & B. 13 in. (33cm) "Teddy Purse." Pink rayon plush with blue velvet ears and pads. No joints. Red circle felt underneath brown glass eyes. Hand embroidered black nose and mouth. Red felt tongue. Zipper in back.

Illustration 466A & B. 14 in. (35.6cm) "Teddy-Doll Muff" Two-face. Celluloid face with blue eyes. Mohair, faded blue body, white arms and legs. Embroidered claws. Cotton cord with tassels to go around child's neck. *Helen Sieverling Collection.*

198

BEAR RUG

IT'S A RUG
IT'S A HIDE-A-BAG
IT'S A WALL
OR BED DECORATION

Illustration 467.

Give this exciting trophy to your favorite youngsters . . . an adorable pet to use and to amuse. Children love to decorate their rooms this way. They can hang it up or lay it flat . . . toss it on the floor or bed. Meanwhile zippered compartment on underside performs useful function of holding pajamas, bed linens, laundry or secret treasures. Top is of silky soft, curly plush, underside is felt. Head swivels and tail has ring for hanging. Color is a bearlike brown. 24" overall.

A RARE BUY AT
$2.98
postpaid

Home Book, December 1956.

Illustration 468. Plush Teddy Bear Slumber Bag. Attractive sleeping bag, head becomes pillow. R & R Toy Mfg. Co., Inc., Pen Argyl, Pennsylvania. *Playthings,* July, 1970.

Illustration 469. Large adult umbrella with brown wooden handle. Marked: " © 1978 Stella Olsen." Imprinted "teddy·teddy·teddy" in brown on beige silk. Made in U.S.A.

Illustration 470. Modern child's sweater to which Teddy Bear buttons of 1907 have been sewn. *Helen Sieverling Collection.*

Illustration 471. 23 in. (58.4cm) x 23 in. (58.4cm) Smokey scarf. Pale green cotton with designs in pink, blue, white, black, dark green and shades of brown. Border of small bears show methods of preventing forest fires: pouring water on campfires, shoveling dirt on campfires, crushing out cigarettes and breaking matches in half. Printing on scarf, "BY LICENSE U. S. DEPT. OF AGRICULTURE//APPROVED BY STATE FORESTRY DEPT'S." Seal: *Patricia Rowland Collection*

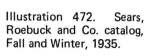

Illustration 472. Sears, Roebuck and Co. catalog, Fall and Winter, 1935.

Illustration 473.
3-Pc. Hot Water Bottle Sets — 9 in. rubber bottle, wash cloth and cake of soap. Each set in asstd. pink and blue boxes with gift card. Cellophane wrapped.
90-8516 — ½ doz in carton, 5 lbs . . . . . Doz 4.20
Butler Brothers catalog, 1936.

Illustration 474. Baby hankie with embroidered motif in pink and blue on white lawn. 25¢ ea. Child's teddy bear fishing scene in gay colors makes this hankie fun to use. 20¢ ea.

Washington State newspaper, 1945.
(Exact paper unknown)

Illustration 475. Oblong hanky signed "Tony Sarg." Beige bear with brown apron. Blue hanky edge and other accents. Circa 1945. *Beverly Port Collection. Photograph by Beverly Port.*

TEDDY BEARS INVADE STATIONERS' STORES.

"The Teddy Bear, who has made himself so conspicuous in the toy departments, has now stepped into the stationery stores and is appearing in many forms. The monogramed paper proved a great success for the manufacturers and likewise did the novelty thin tissue with colored linings, but we are informed that the new fad impresses "Teddy's admirers on a much larger scale and he will probably be sent to the four corners of the earth. Some of the very pretty cards had Teddy embossed upon them, and in the corner of each was a verse begging the guest to "feel at home." The Teddy Bear is cherished by many a young debutante. One prominent New Yorker went so far as to have her calling cards cut in the shape of Teddy Bears. Needless to say, it caused no little sensation among her friends. One glance into a fashionable woman's writing desk would reveal the secrets of her character. Her inkstand was a glass Teddy; her pen wiper a very elaborately dressed Bruin and her stationery of the Teddy Bear style. We are apt to wonder how a young man would feel were he to be handed a Teddy Bear envelope in the presence of his fellow acquaintances."

Playthings, 1907.

"Hardly a day passes but that a new Teddy Bear article is brought before the public, and the latest use is as a decoration for paper napkins. The bear is brown and is placed in one corner, making a most attractive article for children's parties."

Playthings, 1907.

THE ORIGINAL TEDDY BEAR TABLET.

The hit of the season, you won't be able to keep them.

F 1800—Teddy Bear Tablet. This is the original Teddy Bear Tablet. There are numerous imitations, but the cover designs on this tablet are reproductions of all the illustrations in the original F 1800. Teddy Bear book, as published by Edward Stern & Co.; 10 entirely different and exceedingly interesting illustrations. The paper is a good quality, ruled, pencil stock. Size 6½x9½; 100 sheets. A decided novelty and a great seller.
Per doz. . . . . **.39** | Per gross **4.40**

Illustration 476. G. Sommers catalog, 1907.

THE LATEST TEDDY BEAR NOVELTY.
The name and design will do the work.

F 1369 – Teddy Bear Stationery. The ever popular subject in a new idea, this box is beautifully lithographed and does full justice to the "Teddy Bear" idea; the paper is the finest quality of cloth finish stock with wallet velopes.
Per doz **1.85**

Illustration 477. G. Sommers catalog, 1907.

Illustration 479. Pyrographic novelties displaying the Teddy Bear theme. G. Sommers catalog, Fall, 1907.

D 8175—New Teddy Bear auto; the very latest; silk plush; fancy shape; each in box.
Per doz. **6.95**

Illustration 478. Autograph album. G. Sommers catalog, 1907.

D 9326—Teddy Bear panels; measuring 6x18 in.; comical group of 6 Teddy Bears; will be a winner.
Each . . . . **.15**

Illustration 480. G. Sommers catalog, Fall, 1907.

Illustration 481. 11 in. (27.9cm) x 12 in. (30.5cm) doll's pink and white eiderdown blanket. Circa 1920s. *Phyllis Roberts Collection.*

Illustration 482. 3-5/8 in. (9.1cm) china wall plaque, Hummel style. Child teaching Teddy to walk. Legend: "That's my good boy." Paper sticker: "Japan." Gold edges, green dress and white Teddy.

Teddy Bear Robes

For Little Bare Skins

Also Crib Covers

We make beautiful soft "comfy" Bath Robes for girls, boys and grown-ups. Every one ought to know the luxurious, downy comfort of a good Bath Robe.

The little Teddy Bears do not show very plain on the picture here, but on the Robes themselves they are very attractive and will delight any child.

In material and workmanship these Robes are excellent. The colors are absolutely fast, and will wash. The Robes are finished with girdles and neck cords to match, and made in Navy Blue, Tan, Red, Brown, Baby Blue and Baby Pink, with Teddy Bears in contrasting colors.

CRIB COVERS, ribbon bound, colors to match Robes, $2.25

ROBES, sizes 1 to 6 years, $3.00
    "   " 8 " 12   "   3.50
    "   " 14 " 16   "   4.00
Men's and Women's
ROBES, sizes 34 to 44 bust, 5.50

Send to your local dealer for these garments. If he cannot supply you, they will be sent direct upon receipt of price.

THOMPSON & KENT

Wholesale Manufacturers

59 Fourth Avenue   **New York City**

"THE NEW LOVE"

This is the most delightful picture of the year.

Copy't, 1907, by Gutmann & Gutmann, N.Y.

The Teddy bear and the sleeping child are exquisitely drawn. The size is 18 x 14 inches. All ready to frame — this most artistic photogravure will make a charming gift.

Sent by prepaid express on receipt of $1.00
Or in high class hand coloring for $1.50.

NEW YORK ART CO., 56 W. 34th St., New York City

Illustration 484. 18 in. (45.7cm) x 14 in. (35.6cm). Print for framing. Also issued as a postcard. *Ladies' Home Journal,* 1907.

Illustration 483. *Ladies' Home Journal,* November, 1907. *Courtesy Beverly Port.*

Big Teddy Bear Free for You

They are all the Rage

Teddy Bear is a fine specimen of his kind, made of **Shaggy Cinnamon Bear Plush**, and 12 inches tall. His **head**, his **arms** and his **legs** are **jointed** on to the body so that they can all be turned in any direction, And you should see him shake his head and hear him **grunt** when you hit him in the stomach! **Teddy** is all the rage in the cities. The children carry him to school and even the grown-up ladies carry him with them when they go out for a walk or ride, or to the theatre. The more costly Teddys sell as high as **$25.00** each. We have picked out this one for you on account of his good **size**, his **jointed head, arms** and **legs**, his **cute grunt** and his **fine cinnamon color**. We will send him to you **free by mail**, together with one of these fine latest hand-tinted novelty **"WHOLE=BEAR=FAMILY"** **Pillow=tops**, if you will get **six** of your friends each to give you **25 cents** to pay for their subscription to our popular WOMAN'S HOME JOURNAL for **two whole years**. This is surely the easiest way you will find of owning one of these fine Teddys yourself or of getting one to give to some friend. We make our plan very clear and simple because we want every one to understand it thoroughly and to be pleased when they get the Bear, the Pillow-top and the magazine. Remember, if they do not all reach you just as we describe them we want you to let us know. **We guarantee satisfaction.**

WOMAN'S HOME JOURNAL, Dept. 9,
291 Congress St., Boston, Mass.

12 INCHES TALL

THE WHOLE BEAR FAMILY

Pillow-Top is 21 inches square.

THE MAGAZINE: THE WOMAN'S HOME JOURNAL is one of the best of the popular priced magazines. It gives you every month 32 pages or less of interesting stories, household departments, fancy work, etc. The regular price is 15 cents a year, two years for 25 cents. For that small sum you get an amount of good stories and reading matter that would cost you five or ten times as much if bought in book form.

TEDDY IS FREE. Remember we send you this fine Teddy Bear and a beautiful tinted "WHOLE-BEAR-FAMILY" pillow-top **Free of charge. The bear and pillow=top are for yourself.** Just take this advertisement along with you to show to your friends, and tell them about it and you can easily get the **six** subscribers and we will send the Teddy Bear and Pillow-top just as soon as we receive the money for the six subscriptions. **$1.50 in all.** We hope you will go right out and get them at once so that we can send you the Teddy Bear. We know you will like him as he is very good company and we guarantee that you and your friends will like the magazine and the beautifully tinted pillow-top. We will be glad to send you sample copies of the magazine if you need them to show your friends, but we think you can easily get them to subscribe without waiting so long. We send the Teddy Bear and pillow-top to you **at once and guarantee them** to be as here described. Write your letter to

WOMAN'S HOME JOURNAL, Dept. 9
291 Congress Street, = = = = Boston, Mass.

Illustration 486. *Woman's Home Journal*, Boston, Massachusetts, 1907.

Esmond Crib Blanket

Soft as Rabbit-Skin—to wrap your baby in

THIS double cotton blanket is just the thing for the wee tot who must be kept snug and warm. It is about 36x50 inches—large enough to allow for a most generous tucking-in.

Comes in blue or pink, with cute animal-figures in white woven in it. Order by name and number.

Gift No. 2225 given free and postpaid for Four yearly subscriptions at 50c each

Illustration 488. Circa 1920s.

LEFT: Illustration 487. Black bear models dressing gown of old flannelette in shades of soft rose and gray. Boy and girl Teddies are on their way to bed, candle in hand. One glances nervously at his shadow. *Helen Sieverling Collection.*

Illustration 489. Carriage Set: Happy Bear Cub. Newspaper pattern offer, 1948.

Illustration 490. Fancy goods novelties. Cushion slips (pillow cover); colored art ticking with stitched Teddy Bear subject. No embroidery. 22 in. (55.9cm) x 22 in. (55.9cm). Price - $.49. Teddy Bear is shown bowling. Siegel Cooper Co. special Christmas catalog, 1907.

Inside the bottom of base:

Illustration 491. Snow globe (appears to be snowing after globe has been shaken). Glass globe with black plastic base. Gold and black decal inscribed "Yosemite National Park." Brown painted bisque bear with one arm held across his stomach and waving with the other. Black hand-painted eyes and nose, red hand-painted mouth. Globe unscrews. Bear is molded on a base and held in place with two small pieces of wood which are wedged between base and rim.
Patricia Rowland Collection.

Dorothy Neighbors Daily Pattern

R2478

PATTERN No. R2478

Here is a colorful and practical present for a bride-to-be. The cunning little bears are embroidered in simple stitches and work up so quickly you'll want to make another set for your own use.

Pattern Envelope No. R2478 contains hot-iron transfer for 6 designs, color chart, embroidery stitch illustrations and full directions.

To obtain this pattern, send 15 cents, giving pattern number, your name, address and zone number to PATTERN DEPARTMENT, Seattle Times, Seattle 11.

Illustration 492. *The Seattle Times,* circa 1945.

Illustration 493. 2¾ in. (6.9cm) salt and pepper shakers. Brown ceramic set, with white faces, green bows and black eyes and noses. Yellow pads and ears. Marked: "JAPAN." Circa 1935.

Illustration 494. Left: Decorated yellow plaster bear bank. Green muzzle and pink nose, ears and pads. Black stitch marks. Marked: "KOREA." *Jonathan Koenigsaecker Collection.* Middle: Silver finish bear bank. Blue and silver label: "Tarnish Resistant - Japan." *William Koenigsaecker Collection.* Right: Light brown flocked bear bank. Deep brown pads, black nose and brown glass eyes. *William Koenigsaecker Collection.*

Illustration 495. 5 in. (12.7cm) yellow bear candle with red red ribbon. Mexican. *Beverly Port Collection.*

Illustration 496. 6¼ in. (15.8cm) candle in rich brown. Black eyes, nose and mouth.

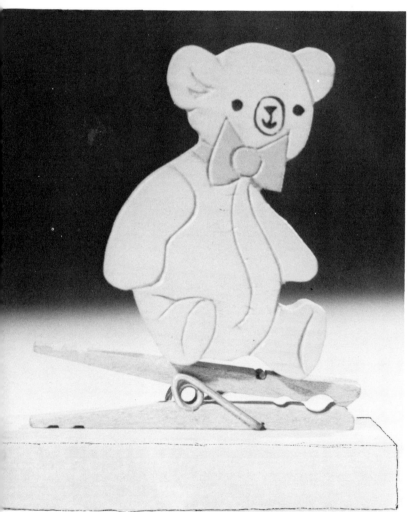

Illustration 497. 4¼ in. (10.8cm) wooden handmade letter holder. Marked: "Lois Hubbard//North Kingston, R.I."

Illustration 498. 3¼ in. (8.2cm) bear soaps. Marked: "Copyrighted H & H 1907." Each holds a set of paper cards. Creamy-white color. *Beverly Port Collection.*

208

Illustration 499. Tobaggan Teddies soap.

"3 cuddly teddy bears of castile soap. Soap laden sled will look adorable peeking out of a stocking . . . on a dresser. 8 N 9905 — Shpg. wt. 1 lb . . . Toboggan with 3 bears gift boxed 59c"

59c

Sears, Roebuck and Co. catalog, 1947.

Illustration 500. 2½ in. (6.3cm) Pincushion Teddy, reddish-brown plush with glass eyes. Has a tape measure inside. Original ribbon and tag on neck. 1920s. *Beverly Port Collection.*

LEFT: Illustration 501A. Left: Bear button with "CUB" on chest, red and gold letters. Brown bear in white suit with paw in shoe. Reverse: "A Sunday Shine All The Time CUB Shoe Polish Only A Dime." Middle: Steiff Toy Animal button. These buttons are found in animals' ears. Right: "SHE'S A BEAR" button. *Helen Sieverling Collection.*

RIGHT: Illustration 501B. Three old brass buttons on right. All approximately 1 in. (2.5cm) in diameter. Middle one has the most "Teddy-like" bear. The large tin coin-like medal on the far left has a Teddy in the middle and says, "Won't you be my Teddy Bear." It is approximately 2 in. (5.1cm) in diameter. *Beverly Port Collection.*

LEFT: Illustration 501C. Button has small painted brown bear and is marked "Genuine Satsuma." The tag is an old souvenir label, also from Yellowstone Park. *Beverly Port Collection*

Illustration 503. Sears, Roebuck and Co. catalog, 1936.

Illustration 502. 5¼ in. (13.3cm) glass paperweight. Model of koala bear. Marked: Lenwile glass//ARdalt//Japan. Multi-colors in body of bear.

Illustration 504. Left to Right: 1¾ in. (4.4cm) fine china panda, excellent model. Baby on front feet under adult panda. 1½ in. (3.7cm) reclining bear, blue tipped ears and feet with pale pink body. Marked: "Made in Occupied Japan." Glazed ceramic. 1¾ in. (4.4cm) bear with baseball mitt behind head. Blue-green with blue feet and ear tips. Glazed ceramic. 2¾ in. (7cm) bear with gold fly. Pointed nose, brown ear markings and paws. Blue bow. Glazed ceramic.

Illustration 506. 3½ in. (8.8cm) Twin figurines. Blue coat, lavender bow, white rabbit. Pink coat, blue bow, white Teddy. Each marked: "KW 3120." Red and gold sticker: "Lefton// Reg. U. S. Pat. OFF.//Exclusives'//Japan." Circa 1950s. *Willa Koenigsaecker Collection*

Illustration 505. 9 in. (22.9cm) toothbrush holder. Maker: Gantoy - England//REGD. DES. 678517. Soft blue early plastic, black ears and nose. Brown glass eyes with dark pupils. Red buttons on trousers.

Illustration 507. 2¾ in. (6.9cm) high x 3¾ in. (9.4cm) long bisque boy modeling military hat. Grasping blue Teddy. Deeper blue ears, pads and black eyes. Lefton trademark.

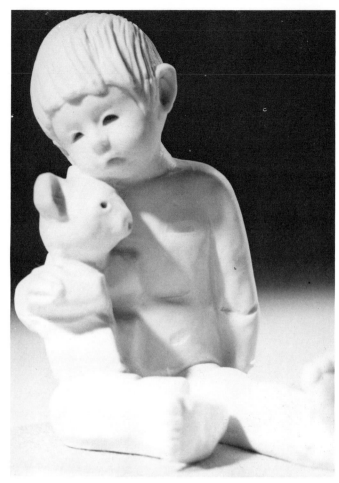

Illustration 508. 5¼ in. (13.3cm) white bisque figurine. Signed: "Ann Centes// © 1972//Grossman Designs, Inc."

Illustration 509. 5 in. (12.7cm) porcelain figurine, "Sleepy head" on paper label. From the Charlotte Byj (BYJ) painting. Blue ink: "V with symbol of a bee   by//W. Goebel//West Germany." Incised: "Byj 77." Golden brown hair, blue pajamas, gray Teddy, pink pads and bow, white face and black eyes.

Illustration 510. 4 in. (10.2cm) glazed ceramic pitchers. Bears are gold tinted and have black eyes. Circa 1930s. *Diana Downing Collection.*

Illustration 511. 3½ in. (8.8cm) Milk mug, white glazed ceramic. Clown handle is hand-trimmed in red and yellow. Mug is hand-trimmed in red with back printed, "I LIKE MILK." The design is stamped on, color scheme green, black, brown, yellow and blue. Mark stamped in red on mug bottom: "JAPAN." *Patricia Rowland Collection.*

Illustration 512. Left: Ceramic honey container with place for ladle in back. Marked: "H 16149." Yellows and browns. Right: Ceramic saccharin and honey container. Saccharin goes in container in lid and comes out hole in bear's head. Sugar in bottom. Cream and brown. *Bill Boyd Collection.*

213

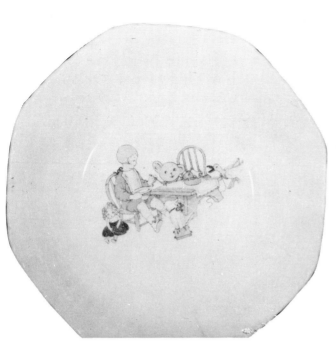

Illustration 514. 8½ in. (21.5cm) diameter. Ceramic child's dish with recessed center and gold edge. Child feeds large brown-gold Teddy from bowl.

Illustration 513. 6 in. (15.2cm) diameter. Cream color ceramic bowl. Christopher Robin-type child feeding big Teddy while doll, lamb, and duck observe. A premium dish marked ''WHEATIES.'' Circa 1920s.

Illustration 515. 5 in. (12.7cm) diameter porcelain child's dishes. Gold designs on rim. Left: Girl with Teddy on leash frightens small girl with doll. Middle: Girl bathes large Teddy while second Teddy in towel on floor attempts to creep away. Neglected doll is submerged in wash basin. Right: Girl prepares to feed Teddy; bowl on table.

214

Illustration 516. 7 in. (17.8cm) diameter china feeding dish. Gold ABC's around outside rim. Winking bear on roller skates. Marked: "Made in Japan." *Bill Boyd Collection*

Illustration 517. 7¾ in. (19.6cm) diameter porcelain plate with gold rim. Teddy at sports including soccer, golf and roller skating. Marked: "BS" over symbol of a crown with "Austria" beneath.

Illustration 518A. 6 in. (15.2cm) ceramic bowl. Oversize golden brown Teddy with blue bow fills blue wicker carriage. Small boy policeman watches girl. English artwork.

Illustration 518B. 6 in. (15.2cm) ceramic bowl. Time for bed. Teddy has fallen asleep while Golliwog snuggles up. Golden brown Teddy. Yellow, orange, blue and green colors.

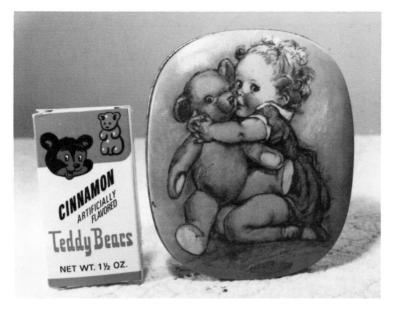

Illustration 519. Even candy has come in a Teddy Bear shape. The candy bears (left) are red, chewy and cinnamon flavored. Made by the Howard B. Stark Co. of Pewaukee, Wisconsin. The metal box 5¼ in. (13.3cm) (right) once contained toffee from England. 1930s. *Beverly Port Collection.*

Illustration 520. Bowl of early sterling silver spoon with caption "Teddy Bears" above embossed Roosevelt Bears holding cowboy hats. One holds "big stick" and the other has gunbelt. Both wear glasses. *Beverly Port Collection.*

Illustration 521. Left: As advertised in *Delineator,* 1907. Rogers, Lunt, and Bowlen, sterling. Right: Curved handle baby spoon. "Teddy Bear" embossed on shaft. Bowl: "Teddy Bear Toboggan." Maker: Watson Company. *Bill Boyd Collection.*

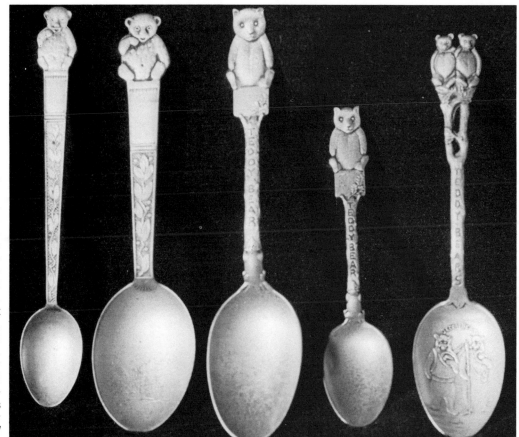

Illustration 522. Left to Right: (a) Feeder spoon. Marked: Nils Johan, Sweden. (b) Teaspoon. Marked: Nils Johan, Sweden. (c) Teaspoon patented 1907, The Mauser Mfg. Co. (d) Feeder spoon patented 1907, The Mauser Mfg. Co. Detailed design front and back. (e) Teaspoon. Twin Teddies. Embossed "Teddy Bears" on shaft. Detailed on back; toy Teddies have arms around each other. Bowl embossed "Teddy Bears" details "Teddy B" and "Teddy G" Bruin-Teddies. *Bill Boyd Collection.*

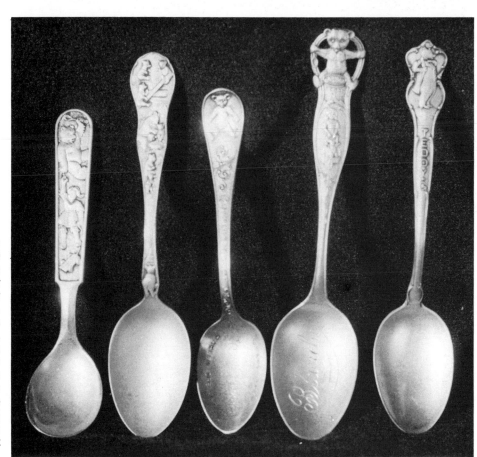

Illustration 523. Left to Right: (a) Feeder spoon marked: "830 S" (European). Bear raising spoon over head. (b) Teddies on teeter totter. Maker: Niagra Falls Silver Co. (c) Teddy on handle top. Embossed on shaft "Compliments of" and in bowl "5 Ave. Theatre, Harlem Opera House, Keith & Proctor." (d) Embossed "Teddy at dinner." Teddy has food dish between legs. Child pushes Teddy in buggy. Sterling. Maker: Paye and Baker Mfg. Co. (e) Full length dressed bear (Bruin-Teddy) marked "Teddy G.", a Roosevelt bear. *Bill Boyd Collection.*

217

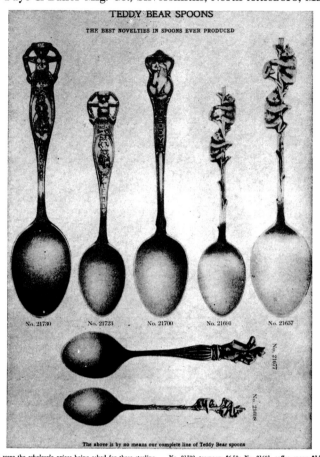

Illustration 524. By kind permission of Mr. Albert Christian Revi, *Spinning Wheel,* January-February, 1963.

Illustration 525. Child's toy silverware with Bruin-Teddy on the handles. Marked: "Germany." *Helen Sieverling Collection.*

Illustration 526. *Delineator,* 1907.

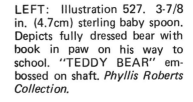

LEFT: Illustration 527. 3-7/8 in. (4.7cm) sterling baby spoon. Depicts fully dressed bear with book in paw on his way to school. "TEDDY BEAR" embossed on shaft. *Phyllis Roberts Collection.*

Illustration 529. 5½ in. (14cm) spoon. Marked: Winthrop Silver Plate. Bear at table eating with dish, cup and spoon falling down stem. *Phyllis Roberts Collection*

Illustration 528. 3½ in. (8.8cm) "Teddy And The Bear" china toothpick holder. Marked: "Made in Germany//3573//souvenir, Norfolk, Virginia." White with shades of green. *Bill Boyd Collection.*

Illustration 530A. 2 in. (5.1cm) tall tooth-pick holder. K. and Co. (Kronheimer Olden-bush N.Y. Co.) Souvenir, County Court House, Spokane, Washington. *Bill Boyd Collection.*

Illustration 530B. 2 in. (5.1cm) tall toothpick holder. Meriden Silverplate Co. Quadruple plate. *Bill Boyd Collection.*

Illustration 531A. 2¾ in. (6.9cm) silver jigger Marked: "KI." "Made in Japan" on paper label. *Bill Boyd Collection.*

Illustration 531B. 1½ in. (3.7cm) hammered silver napkin holder. Full Teddy on front. *Bill Boyd Collection.*

Illustration 532A, B & C. (a) Teething rattle, sterling with mother-of-pearl handle. Webster Company, North Attleboro, Massachusetts. (b) Teething rattle, sterling. Handle of horn. English hallmark, Birmingham, 1910. Bear facing front on both sides. (c) Silverplate bear on bone ring. *Bill Boyd Collection.*

Illustration 533. 1904 campaign item. Bread plate. Bruin-Teddies surround the profile of President Roosevelt. Marked: "A Square Deal." Teddies play at golf, tennis, and are shown with gun and musical instruments. *Robert Zimmerman Collection. Photograph by Robert Zimmerman.*

Illustration 534. Left: First Christmas handmade ornament by Jean Anderson. December 25, 1976. Red felt, top of head pink felt. Pink scarf, black nose and hand-embroidered eyes. *Jonathan Koenigsaecker Collection.* Middle: Gold ball, "Hallmark Cards, Inc. 1978." *Jonathan Koenigsaecker Collection.* Right: William's first Christmas ornament by Jean Anderson. December 25, 1978. Yellow-tan felt, hand-knit red scarf, black nose and eyes and red mouth. *William Koenigsaecker Collection*

Illustration 535. Left to Right: (a) 3½ in. (8.9cm) old Christmas ornament. Teddy with red vest and black tie. White frosted surface. (b) 3½ in. (8.9cm) same as "a". Gold bear with red vest and green tie. (c) 5 in. (12.7cm) blown glass brown bear and baby. Larger bear has flocked stomach. (d) 3½ in. (8.9cm) flocked brown over hard surface. Red bows at neck. Red ears and googly eyes.

Illustration 536. Left: 3¾ in. (9.4cm) white handmade bear with black eyes, pink in ears and pink pajamas. Ornament signed: "Phyllis Hull." Middle: 3¾ in. (9.4cm) bread dough, cream colored bear ornament with big red bow and brown eyes. Handmade. Right: 4 in. (10.2cm) tan cookie cutter bear ornament.

Illustration 537. Left to Right: (a) 3 in. (7.6cm) Joan Walsh Anglund Christmas ornament bear. ©1972. Red Santa cap and white scarf. (b) 4¾ in. (12.1cm) brown Teddy Christmas ornament with green suit. (c) 3½ in. (8.8cm) hollow paper ornament, hand-painted. Teddy playing xylophone. (d) 3 in. (7.6cm) stuffed cloth Teddy ornament, brown and yellow. B. Shackman & Co.

Illustration 538. Pin at top: 1½ in. (3.7cm) Teddy with black inset eyes, shiny finish on ear tips and pads. "8091P" on back. Quality item. Soft gold finish. Twins sets are cheaper copies of above Teddy in gold color and white. Smaller pins, gold finish. Tagged: "Bear by Hallmark."

Illustration 539A. Brass-finish child's pin. *Helen Sieverling Collection*

Illustration 539B. Left: Silver Teddy Bear Pin. Middle: Perfume bear by Max Factor. Gold finish with inset eyes (eyes inset with synthetic topaz stones). Right: Gold plated Teddy Bear pin with inset eyes (eyes inset with synthetic ruby stones). All three under 1½ in. (3.7cm). *Beverly Port Collection.*

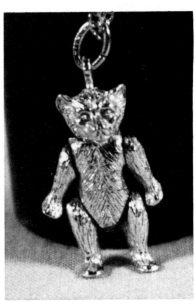

Illustration 539C. Sterling silver 1 in. (2.5cm) Teddy with swivel neck. This neck charm can sit, stand on all fours or stand upright. *Beverly Port Collection*

Illustration 540A & B. Winsome Teddy Bear necklace charm of 14KT gold with garnet eyes wears his very best sailor coat and cap on his way to sail his favorite boat. His legs are movable as well as his free arm. Looking similar to the early *Boston Globe* 1907-08 Teddy Bear paper doll series, he was created by well known artisian and sculptor, Beth Garcia of Carmel-By-The-Sea, California. *Elayne C. Shuman Collection*

Illustration 541. 2½ in. (6.3cm) sterling Teddy Bear necklace with jacket and ribbon.

Illustration 542. Left: ½ in. (1.2cm) snap-ons by Nemo, gold color. Middle: 1 in. (2.5cm) bear on chain, gold color. Right: 1½ in. (3.7cm) key ring, inset red stone eyes.

4510 — Teddy Bear hat pins. The most popular novelty of the season for ladies' bonnets. Gold finish. Per doz 69

Illustration 543. Bruin-Teddy with Roosevelt glasses and hat. G. Sommers catalog, 1907.

Illustration 544. 5/8 in. (1.55cm) bear. *Spare Moments* magazine, April, 1907.

"Little Bill" (the late Willis Bouchey, actor) and his Teddy Bear, 1910.

VII. Teddy Bear Music

The collecting of sheet music relating to Teddy Bears is a fascinating possibility of the hobby, but a painstakingly slow one for the average collector. With much effort, five editions that have not been published previously have been located and a few others have been loaned.

The Teddy Bears Picnic by John W. Bratton was first published in 1907 by M. Witmark in New York and later in London. This was an instrumental piece alluding to the bear hunting picnic by Theodore Roosevelt. It was not until 1930 that Jimmy Kennedy, author of *The Isle of Capri,* was asked to write lyrics for this old tune. In 1932 it was used on a children's program by Henry Hall in England. The B. B. C. was deluged with requests for sheet music and recordings. A recording had to be rushed into completion and was in its third million in the 1960s. All of the outstanding American and English singers recorded this piece of music, enough to make a collection within a collection! Jimmy Kennedy was able to buy himself a villa in Switzerland, a far cry from the one-room flat where he did his inspired composing. Oh, the power of a Teddy Bear!

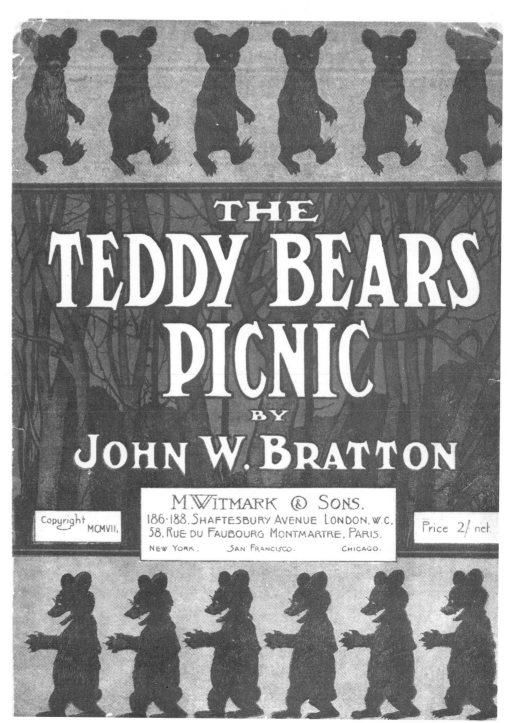

Illustration 545.   10 in. (25.4cm) x 14 in. (35.6cm), *The Teddy Bears Picnic* by John W. Bratton. Published by M. Witmark & Sons, London. Copyright MCMVII. Shades of brown and orange.

227

Illustration 546. 10¼ in. (26.05cm) x 13-5/8 in. (34.58cm) *Teddy Bear Pieces* by J. S. Fearis. Published by McKinley Music Co., Chicago and New York. This piece was entitled *Teddy Bear Waltz* and sold for $.50. Other titles were *March of the Teddy Bear* and *Dance of the Teddy Bear.* Copyright date: 1903. *Helen Sieverling Collection.*

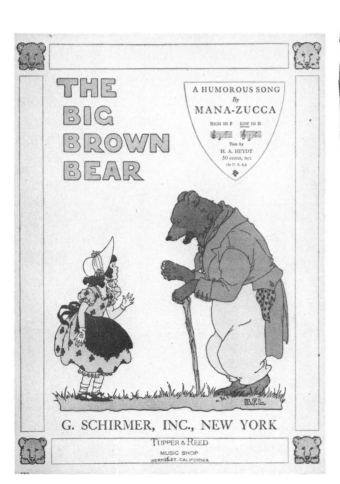

ABOVE: Illustration 547. 13½ in. (34.6cm) x 10½ in. (25.4cm), *Will You Be My Teddy Bear* by Vincent Bryan and Max Hoffmann. Published by Jerome H. Remick & Co., New York and Detroit. Copyright 1907. Deep pink edges with pink, yellow and green on figure. Brown Teddy has a blue bow.

RIGHT: Illustration 548. 10 in. (25.4cm) x 12 in. (30.5cm), *The Big Brown Bear* by Mana-Zucca. Brown bear with blue coat and light blue trousers. Girl has red curls and a dark blue apron. Copyright date: 1919. *Helen Sieverling Collection.*

Illustration 549. 10½ in. (26.7cm) x 11½ in. (29.2cm) *Stung* by Theron C. Bennett and artist, Charles Twelvetrees. Published by Victor Kremer Co., Chicago and New York. English copyright. Copyright 1908. Title in red on deep green background. Brown Teddy in same pose as on a post card.

Illustration 550. 10½ in. (25.6cm) x 13½ in. (34.2cm),
Be My Little Teddy Bear by Vincent Bryan and Max
Hoffmann. Published by Jerome H. Remick & Co., New
York and Detroit. Copyright MCMVII. White, gray-blue
and brown. *Patricia Rowland Collection.*

Illustration 551. 10½ in. (26.6cm) x 13¾ in. (34.8cm),
Teddy Bear's Lullaby by Agnes Hull Prendergast. Published
by Chandler-Held Music Co., Brooklyn, New York. Copyright 1907. White with shades of tan and brown.

Ted the Hunter March and Two-Step

Dedicated to the Readers of Pictorial Review

By M. Greenwald

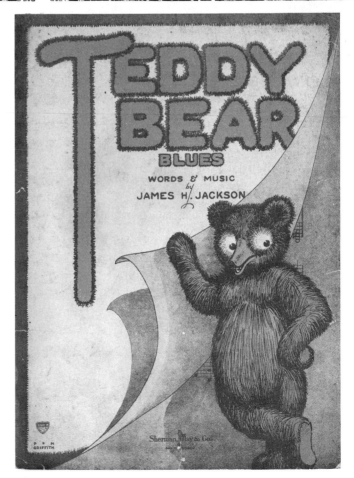

ABOVE: Illustration 552. *Ted the Hunter March and Two-Step* by M. Greenwald. Copyright 1909, Leo Feist, New York. Sections included in the piece are: Ted, the Hunter, starts for Africa; Ted's Arrival; Monkey Dance-They start for the Jungle; The Hunt Begins; The Queen of the Hottentots visits Ted; Getting ready for the Return; and Triumphal return of Ted, the Hunter. Published in *Pictorial Review*, 1909.

RIGHT: Illustration 553. 9 in. (22.9cm) x 12 in. (30.5cm), *Teddy Bear Blues* by James H. Jackson. Published by Sherman Clay & Co., San Francisco. Copyright MCMXXII. Title in navy and yellow.

231

Divided back post card showing Theodore Roosevelt as a "Teddy Bear" showing his teeth, and "Billy Possum" starting down the path to White House in the background. The legend reads, "Good Bye Teddy."

VIII. Bear Post Cards

This writer is by no means an authority on post cards, but an enthusiastic collector of them and especially of those relating to Teddy Bears. The cards do tell a large part of the Teddy Bear story. Not all of the bear sets are Teddies. In fact, a great many of them are Bruin-Teddies following the great popularity of the Roosevelt Bears in Seymour Eaton's books.

It was against postal regulations to write anything but the address on the face of the card before March 1, 1907, so people often wrote on the picture side. After this date, the divided-back post card came into being. Therefore, an undivided-back post card is usually earlier than 1907.

The Roosevelt Bear cards were published by Edward Stern and Co. of Philadelphia, who also did the first four Seymour Eaton books. The cards were taken from the colored book illustrations. Sally Carver, post card collector and authority, has stated that there are three sets of Roosevelt Bear cards. The first set is numbered 1 - 16 with titles. The second set is numbered 17 - 32 with titles. The third set of 16 cards is also numbered 17 - 32 minus titles, but with quotes from the book which correspond to the pictures. It would be a challenge indeed to assemble all three sets.

> "Among the new cards just off the press is a set of thirty designs of new 'Teddy Bear' cards that are meeting with instant success. They are copyrighted, and consequently cannot be imitated. They are also printed with a correspondence space on the address side, in accordance with the new postal ruling to take effect March 1st, permitting writing other than the address on the face of the card. The series is printed in bright colors on a very fine paper stock, and glazed. The bears are shown in characteristic attitudes, and are accompanied with quaint and pertinent sayings. They sell for $1.25 per hundred."
>
> *Playthings, 1906.*

Raphael Tuck and Sons of London published a set of 12 cards curiously entitled "Little Bears." They were enormous "Bruin-Teddies" dressed in clothing and portrayed in humorous situations. The much sought after "Cracker Jack Bears" were Bruin-Teddies as well. (*see history chapter.*) There were 16 cards in the set, slightly smaller than the average card and done in flat print. Copyrighted in 1907 by B. E. Moreland, the entire set could be obtained free by sending ten sides of Cracker Jack packages to Rueckhelm Brothers and Eckstein, Chicago, Illinois. Today these cards are very expensive and difficult to locate.

Another set is known as The Tower Bears, Tower Manufacturing and Novelty Company, New York. These Teddy Bear cards were said by *Playthings* magazine in 1908 to be the creations of Mr. Stephen T. Buckhan, for 11 years the buyer and manager of the post card department at Tower. (It is doubtful that he was the artist involved; possibly the planner.) These bears are dressed in stripes and polka dots; number 97-5 even smokes a pipe. They are very rounded and have more appearance of Teddy than Bruin.

A set of Bruin-Teddies by the comic artist, Crane, has been reported. They were issued by the Zim Company with a Days-of-the-Week set as well as a Months-of-the-Year set and are signed by the artist. They have a long, pointed muzzle and large feet.

The Hillson Bear set has a cloth embossed look similar to another identified set which are actual oilcloth cards. The latter are rather comical line drawings in Days-of-the-Week occupations. The former Hillson Bears are Series 600 "Bears in Green," 1907. Green and white are the only two colors.

One set of cards that are definitely Teddy Bear are the work of the prominent artist, Charles Twelvetrees. (Doll collectors know him as the creator of the He-bee, She-bee doll.) We do not have information as to the number in the complete set. Number 206 is "A Little Bear Behind" show-

Illustration 555. Little Bear Behind (waving goodby to a train in the background) post card. White bear on dark green background. Copyright 1906, C. Twelvetrees 206; National Art Co. *Patricia Rowland Collection*

Illustration 554. Raphael Tuck "Little Bears" one from a set of 12 cards. Bright, intense colors on this cards. The grey and brown bears are zooming along in their vintage auto and "Breaking the Record." 1915. *Beverly Port Collection*

ing a small bear from the rear waving to someone leaving on a train in the distance. Number 207 shows a scowling bear with paw to the rear; this same pose was used for the sheet music, "Stung." A bumblebee flies just above Teddy's head. Number 208 is entitled "The Bear on the Dark Stairway." Number 210 is entitled "A Bear Impression," showing a pure white Teddy who sat on a freshly painted red bench leaving stripes on his back and bottom. These are one of the earlier sets, copyright 1906. Some of them have the divided back and others do not. They must have been popular over quite a period of time as one is postmarked 1912.

W. S. Heal issued a set of Days-of-the-Week bears in 1907. Though not identified, this entire set was included in Peter Bull's *The Teddy Bear Book* by Random House.

Three sets of post cards, at least, began as illustrations in children's story books, the well-known Roosevelt Bears, *Mother Goose's Teddy Bears* and *The Busy Bears*. The original advertising for *The Busy Bears* (*see book section*) lists only six color pictures, but actually there are two additional on the front and back cover. J. I. Austen published the book but the Ullman Company published the post cards. Bobbs-Merrill published the Mother Goose book but the post cards were done by The Thayer Publishing Company of Denver.

The J. Ottmann Lithographing Company placed a full-page advertisement in *Playthings* for their ten post cards. These have not been identified before as there was no company name printed on them anywhere. They are obviously the work of the same artist who created the famous Teddy Bear, done by the same company.

Illustration 556. *Playthings*, 1907.

ABOVE: Illustration 557. "First Love." Salon de Paris, mark "AN Paris" #6033. Circa 1906. *Anita Wright Collection.*

RIGHT: Illustration 558. Early divided-back post card, requiring one cent postage. Circa 1906.

TEDDY BEAR

Shown by The Souvenir Novelty Co.

Illustration 559.

"Mr. 'Teddy Bear' is responsible for a great deal these days, and 'Teddy' is now made up in plush, canton flannel, canvas and is even carved in wood, but the latest is leather. 'Barrels' of people are now buying him in leather attached to a "tag" on which directions may be written so that he may be sent through the mails as a post card, "Teddy" being attached firmly to the tag by a small riveted eyelet. The accompanying cut illustrates the gentleman to a nicety."

Playthings, 1907.

"These bears are made of real fur, and come in cinnamon, black and white. They are shown in a variety of positions, and are cleverly executed. The cards will retail for 15 cents each, or $10.00 per hundred, and are already having a phenomenal sale. Dealers are reordering, and the only difficulty which stands in the way at present will be in supplying the demand."

Playthings, 1906.

LEFT: Illustration 560A. Teddy is father to English Golliwog doll. Circa 1907.

RIGHT: Illustration 560B. Golliwog doll is father to Teddy. Circa 1907.

Illustration 561. "This is the strenuous Life." Golden and white bear. Green and red bows on golden bear. Blue and white and plaid bows on white bear. Red-brown background. Tower M. & N. Co., N.Y. Copyright 1907.

Teddy be nimble,
Teddy be quick,
And Teddy jump
over the candle-
stick.

To make your candles last for aye
You wives and 'maids give ear-o!
To put 'em out's the only way,
Says honest Ted Boldero.

Illustration 563. Verse on post card:
"To make your candles last for aye
You wives and maids give ear-o!
To put 'em out's the only way,
Says honest Ted Boldero."
Poem is printed in red on yellow tinted background. Brown bear wears white sweater with mint green collar, cuffs and waist band. Copyright 1907 by Frederick L. Cavally, Jr., The Thayer Publishing Co., Denver, Colorado. Reproduced from *Mother Goose's Teddy Bears,* published by Bobbs-Merrill Co. *Patricia Rowland Collection.*

Illustration 562. Verse on post card: "Teddy be nimble, Teddy be quick, and Teddy jump over the candlestick." Brown bear with red sweater. Reproduced from *Mother Goose's Teddy Bears,* published by Bobbs Merrill Co. The Thayer Publishing Company, Denver, Colorado. Copyright 1907 by Frederick L. Cavally, Jr.

Illustration 564. Caption reads, "Mary had a little bear, and it was white as snow." Number 1 of a set. Ullman Manufacturing Company, 1907.

Illustration 565. Published by National Manufacturing Co., Boston, Massachusetts. Copyright 1907 by H. N. Northrop.

236

F 420

F 422

F 420—Teddy Bear Album. Will prove a tremendous seller, bound in dark green cloth with bears embossed in gold and a lithographed bear center figure, size 9x11 inches, capacity 200, 2 to page, a very attractive number. Per doz 8.00

Illustration 566. This album shows a "Days-of-the-Week" card on cover. G. Sommers catalog, 1907.

Not yet but Soon

Said Father Stork wisely one day
Our Stock in trade is getting passe
for Kids no one cares,
They all want Teddy Bears
so I'll order some right away.

COPYRIGHTED, 1907, BY W™ S. HEAL, N.Y.

Illustration 567. Copyright 1907 by William S. Heal, New York. Bright red bow on brown Teddy. *Courtesy Jane Thomas.*

Illustration 568. "Delighted" post card. Brown bear and boy wearing a red sweater, brown pants, tan spats and hat, and black shoes and gun. Copyright 1907, Gutmann & Gutmann. Published by Reinthal & Newmann, N.Y. Chas. H. Hauff, London, England. Printed in America. *Patricia Rowland Collection.*

Illustration 569. ME AND TEDDY post card. Chestnut brown bear. Blue sky and green water. Child has blond hair with a red bow. Copyright 1907 by U. Co., N.Y. Artists intitials are M.D.S.

238

Inside the card:

I'm Teddy Bear,
I'll love you hard
If you will take me
Off this card.

Illustration 571. Souvenir card showing typical sweater and toque of 1907. *Loraine Burdick Collection.*

Mary with her little bear behind.

Illustration 572. Mary with her little bear behind post card. Tinted photograph look. White bear with a red ribbon. Child has auburn hair and white pantaloons. Marked: Bamforth & Co., Publishers, Holmfirth (England) and New York, No. 1254. Copyright 1910, Bamforth & Co. *Patricia Rowland Collection.*

No. 15. The Roosevelt Bears in New York City
"They spent some days in seeing the town,
Doing Fifth Avenue up and down."

Illustration 573. Roosevelt Bears in New York, #15, 1907. *Beverly Port Collection.*

S630Z—Extra large asst., all beautifully colored, big variety catchy designs, reproductions of pictures by well known artists, etc. Many styles will be snapped up by collectors for framing, wall decoration, etc. 100 in box, asstd. Per 100, 15c

Illustration 574. The price of 100 beautiful post cards for 15¢ is scarcely comprehensible today. Butler Brothers catalog, 1908.

239

Illustration 575. Marked: "Boots Cash Chemists, Real Photograph Series, England." Postmarked 1909.

Illustration 576. Marked: "Davidson Bros., London and New York. Printed in England." Postmarked 1910. Note large Steiff Golliwog in chair on right.

Illustration 577. John Winsch, 1911.

RIGHT: Illustration 578. Marked: "This card is a real photograph on bromide paper. The Rotograph Co., New York City, Printed in England." #B2226. Circa 1910.

TWO LITTLE BARES

MERRY CHRISTMAS

May 🎅 fill your 🧦 to the
🎈 and load your 🎄
with 🧸 and 📚 and
🍬candy 🍭 and
a teddy 🧸 may 🐝

Illustration 579. 1921.

My Christmas Greeting
That all my best wishes
for you come true.

Illustration 580. Gibson Art Co., 1918.

LEFT: Illustration 581. By Margara, #676/4, Marked: "Made in Spain." Child holding large Teddy and jointed S.F.B.J. bisque head doll. Circa 1920.

BELOW: Illustration 582. Marked: "Made in Spain." By Margara. Circa 1920.

Illustration 583. This undated card shows two bears with bright yellow-gold fur. The bear on the left has blue and black striped pants; bear on the right has red and black striped pants and a tux collar. They both have inset movable "googlie" eyes with black pupils. The card is extra thick to accommodate a "squeaker" in the middle. G.N.C.O.//N.Y. Printed in Japan. *Beverly Port Collection.*

Illustration 585. Child wearing blue pajamas with bow holding dark sock with brown Teddy. Series 315C.

Illustration 584A. Many happy returns post card. Brown bear wearing a blue tuxedo, black bow tie and shoes, and yellow slacks. J. Ottmann Lithographing Co. *Patricia Rowland Collection.*

Illustration 584B. Golden brown bear on green bank. Red bait dangled before bright red lobster. J. Ottmann Lithographing Co. *Beverly Port Collection.*

Illustration 586. Child wearing pink pajamas. Blue stocking. Brown Teddy. Series 315E.

Illustration 587A & B. Artist, Mary Evans Price. Series 734B & F.

Illustration 588. Child's cloche hat has Teddy Bear head, similar to muffs. Series 736A. Stecher Litho Co.

Illustration 589A. White post card with blue border. Bear is navy blue silk applique, embossed.

Illustration 589B. White post card with red border. Bear is red embroidered patch with black eyes and nose. Take special note of Theodore Roosevelt's silhouette in upper left-hand corner and early style bears. *Patricia Rowland Collection.*

Illustration 591. Where am I at post card. Embossed brown bear in black top hat with a red bow and cane. J. Ottmann Lithographing Co. *Patricia Rowland Collection.*

Illustration 590. A Roosevelt Bear card — one of a series of the grey bear and brown bear in various adventures all over the world. This colorful card is #14 and entitled "The Roosevelt Bears on the Iceberg."

"Teddy B put a match to a pile of wood and made a fire and cooked the food." They are accompanied by a large polar bear, and all waiting for their pile of fish to cook. *Beverly Port Collection.*

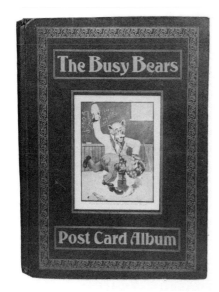

Illustration 592. 8 in. (20.3cm) x 10 in. (25.4cm) album, black with gold lettering. Post card affixed to cover reads: "Busy Bears - - Getting it in the Usual Place." *Betty Brink Collection.*

Illustration 593. Marked: "Artchrom, Deposee Copyright Printed in Saxony, Series 3028."

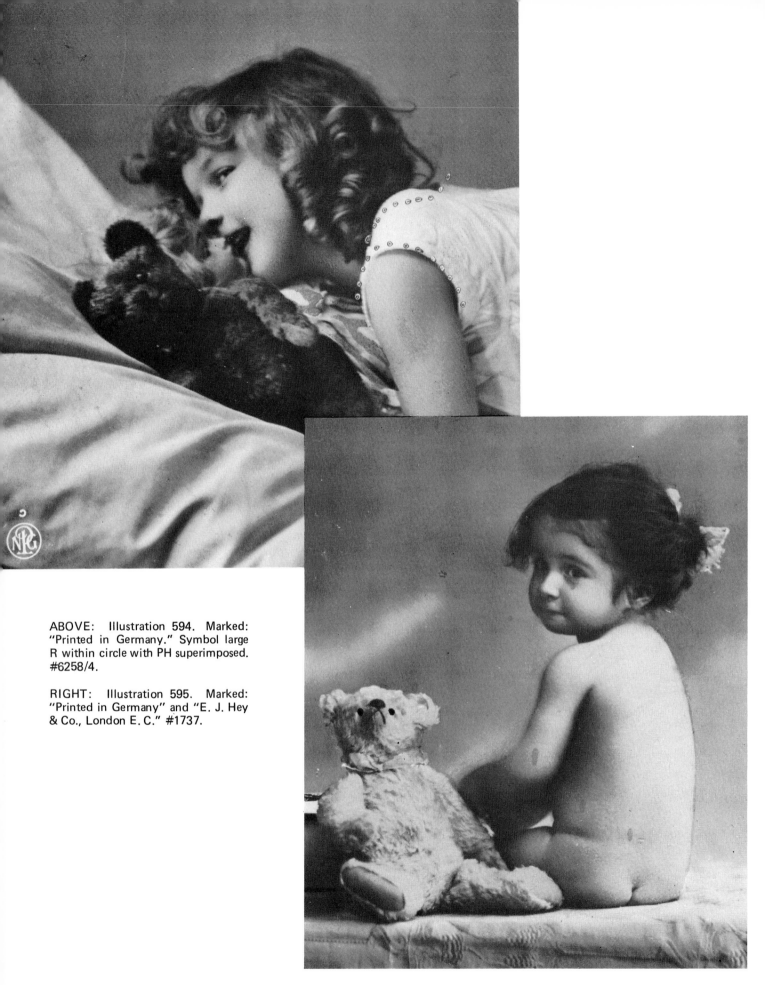

ABOVE: Illustration 594. Marked: "Printed in Germany." Symbol large R within circle with PH superimposed. #6258/4.

RIGHT: Illustration 595. Marked: "Printed in Germany" and "E. J. Hey & Co., London E. C." #1737.

Illustration 596. "Joyous Christmas." Marked: "Published by E. A. Schwerdtleger & Co. London E. C. Printed at their works in Berlin. #08363/4."

Illustration 597. Card with greeting: "Herzlichen Weihnachtsgrub." Marked: "H. B. with heart symbol. 7731/5." Small boy holds a Steiff man doll, Santa figure and Teddy.

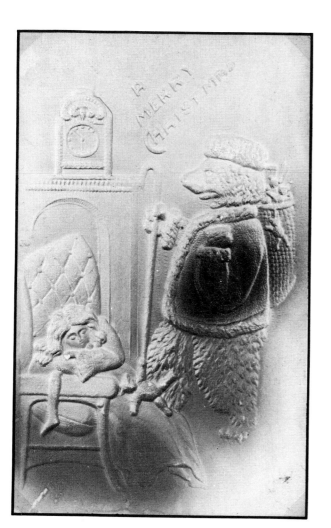

Illustration 598. Santa Claus and Teddy Bears

Almost as soon as Teddy Bear was created, he began appearing on picture post cards which were also in a great peak of popularity at the same time. To a lover of Bear-mobilia, these are some of the most delightful items for which to search. Christmas was not Christmas without a Teddy Bear, long after some writers had said the Teddy craze had passed. In an article written in 1961, Melvin Freud, President of the Toy Guidance Council, was asked what the most popular toy was. The answer was, of course, the Teddy Bear. The article was entitled "The Science of Toys" with sub-title, 'The trend is towards education and realism- -but Teddy Bear and Dolly are still King and Queen.' The holiday post cards make this very evident as the toy bear assumes his honored place among the dolls and other toys.

One of the most unique bear post cards is a heavily embossed example with simple airbrush coloring, a bit of green near the Merry Christmas message, red on Santa's jacket, and brown fur on the legs. Santa is a Bruin-Teddy! A small girl waits asleep in a chair. Santa Teddy has left a large Teddy Bear in the girl's lap. Three other smaller Teddies are seen in or on his pack. One would think the recipient would have been a cub bear rather than a child.

Illustration 600. Postcard by John Winsch of Santa Claus holding a lovely large Teddy. 1913. *Beverly Port Collection.*

TOP: Illustration 599A. Series 540C. Stecher Lith. Co. *Jean Millen Collection.*

MIDDLE: Illustration 599B. Artist signed, Ellen H. Clapsaddle, International Art Publishing Co.; 1907. *Jean Millen Collection.*

BOTTOM: Illustration 599C. Symbol of Eagle with streamer in beak. Postmarked 1910.

Illustration 601. John Winsch, 1913. *Jean Millen Collection.*

248

Illustration 602. Artist signed cards by M. Greiner, International Art Publishing Company, Series 791. Printed in Germany.

August, 1925.

IX. Teddy Bear Books

Among the most sought after books about bears are the Roosevelt Bear books about Teddy B. and Teddy G. by Seymour Eaton. Twenty leading newspapers in 1905 first carried the adventures of these famous Bruin-Teddies (*see history chapter*).

The first book was *Teddy B. and Teddy G., THE ROOSEVELT BEARS, Their Adventures and Travels* by Seymour Eaton. The illustrator was V. Floyd Campbell with 16 full color illustrations including frontispiece and cover. The large size, 8½ in. (21.5cm) x 11¼ in. (28.5cm), was hard on the book that received any rough handling whatsoever. Pages were sometimes lost. Others were taken apart by dealers to frame the illustrations. Therefore, an intact book is a treasure indeed and a top collector's item.

The second book in the series was *More about Teddy B. and Teddy G The Roosevelt Bears* by Seymour Eaton having a different illustrator, R. K. Culver. There were again 16 color illustrations.

The next in the series was *The Roosevelt Bears Abroad*, also illustrated by R. K. Culver. It is here that the bears meet King Edward, illustrated with the original comic page in the history chapter.

The last of the four books in the set published by Edward Stern and Company was *The Bear Detectives* and had still other illustrators, Francis P. Wightman and William K. Sweeney. It was only 152 pages compared to 178 of the preceding book, with eight color illustrations. With these four, one has the complete original set.

An actual review in *The Publisher's Weekly,* November 27, 1909, read:

> "Seymour Eaton, whose stories about 'Teddy-B' and 'Teddy-G' have been so vastly popular, carries on their career in a most original way. 'The Bear Detectives' tells how the two endeavor to solve the questions that have been puzzling nursery land for ages--they are engaged by Little Bo-Peep to find her sheep, they set a trap for a Fairy Queen and wish they hadn't, they explore the house that Jack built, and even arrest Little Red Riding Hood's wolf. All this is told in clever verse and fully and amusingly illustrated. The three former Roosevelt Bear Books are ready in new edition. This is book #4, $1.50."

The second series of these same adventures was published by Barse & Hopkins beginning in 1915. The size was 8½ in. (21.5cm) x 10¾ in. (27.2cm). These, when intact, contain eight color illustrations including cover and frontispiece. By 1921 there were ten books in the series which sold for $.40 each. These were not additional stories, but segments of the first four books by Edward Stern and Co., Inc.

Equally as difficult to locate is *Mother Goose's Teddy Bears* by Frederick L. Cavally, Jr., illustrated and adapted to Mother Goose, published by Bobbs-Merrill Company, Indianapolis, 1907. There are 32 full-page color illustrations as well as many black and white line drawings. This edition has often been taken apart for framing. In addition, children have loved all the Teddy Bear books literally to pieces. If you own a copy in good condition, you are surely fortunate.

One of the most appealing and desirable books in our collection of juvenile books is *The Teddy Bear That Prowled at Night.* The 9 in. (22.9cm) x 11 in. (27.9cm) size with different colored front and back pictures is very attractive. The illustrations are by Mary La Fetra Russell, story by Edna Groff Deihl; the publisher was Samuel Gabriel Sons and Co., New York, 1924. There are 22 color illustrations as well as those on the cover. A black and white bookplate is on the inside cover.

A new and revised edition of the book was issued 20 years later (1944) but entitled *The Teddy Bear that would not Sleep.* It was smaller, 8 5/8 in. (21.8cm) x 7 5/8 in. (19.3cm) with a pink background. A white bear sits beside a lighted candle. Nineteen of the color illustrations from the 1924 edition are repeated, with 21 sepia drawings added by Mary L. Russell. Another artist, Roberta Paflin, has contributed one new color illustration which is just inside the front cover as frontispiece. Two very impish Teddy Bears with enormous eyes sit together, one brown with a blue bow and the other white with a pink bow.

This one painting has been adapted to a soft cover third edition with a blue background entitled simply *Teddies.* The size is 8¼ in. (20.9cm) x 7½ in. (19cm) from Samuel Gabriel and Sons, N. Y., but no date is given. There are six pages and eleven color illustrations from the 1924 edition. They are all very collectible.

One of the most exciting surprises in the rare paper material of Loraine Burdick relating to Teddy Bears was a forgotten article in the defunct *Pictorial Review* of February, 1932. The title was "Christopher Robin's Father," A. A. Milne, author of the Winnie the Pooh stories, was making his first visit to America at this time and agreed to an interview. Best of all was a rare photograph of father, son and the original Winnie the Pooh. Christopher Robin was ten years old at the time.

The author explained that he had wanted to name his son "Billy." He humorously added that you do not go to the bishop and ask him to christen a little boy "Billy." They felt "William" was out of the question. Stating that nice initials are very important, the name 'Christopher Robin' was chosen for the sake of the initials!

> "But we never intended to call the child 'Christopher Robin.' Good gracious, no! Indeed, it was surprisingly soon that he himself thought well of 'Billy' too. He began to call himself 'Billy Moon' which is really 'Billy Milne,' although 'Moon' is easy to say, and 'Milne' is not for a baby.
>
> When it came time for 'When We Were Very Young' it turned out that Christopher Robin had its other uses for a name; yet you know it does annoy me that other people think the little boy in the book is really Christopher Robin Milne. Our boy is Billy Moon. The Christopher Robin in the book was just a little boy whom we found around; our Christopher Robin, that is, our Billy Moon, is only in three of the verses.
>
> Still, so far as the tourists were concerned, all the business about Billy and Christopher, whichever was which, made no difference. Not when they came to the house and wanted to see Christopher Robin's nursery. ...We never could have foreseen anything like that."

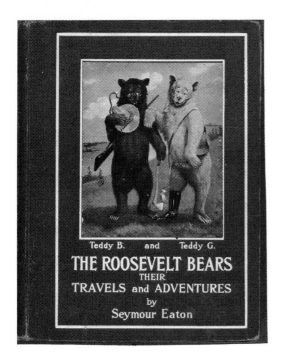

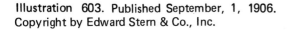

Illustration 603. Published September, 1, 1906.
Copyright by Edward Stern & Co., Inc.

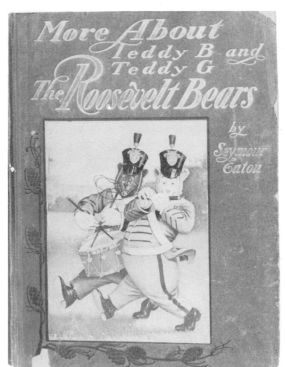

Illustration 604.
Second book in
Edward Stern and
Co., Inc. series.
*Helen Sieverling
Collection.*

Traveling Bears Series. By Seymour Eaton
  Bds. 8½x10¾. Il.........Per vol. 40
  1 The Adventures of the Traveling Bears.
  2 The Traveling Bears in the East and West
  3 The Traveling Bears in New York.
  4 The Traveling Bears in Outdoor Sports.

Illustration 605. A. C. McClurg & Co., Chicago,
1915.

Stories of Adventure
(For children from 5 to 9 years old)

———

The Traveling Bears Series

By SEYMOUR EATON

  Teddy B and Teddy G are as nearly human as it is possible for bears to be. They love children and make playmates of them wherever they go. They never have an idle moment, and their traveling adventures are amusing as well as instructive.
  Snappy, exciting tales, with plenty of action in every chapter and a laugh on every page. Books which will be read as long as there are children to read them.

 1 THE ADVENTURES OF THE TRAVELING BEARS.
 2 THE TRAVELING BEARS IN THE EAST AND WEST.
 3 THE TRAVELING BEARS IN NEW YORK.
 4 THE TRAVELING BEARS IN OUT-DOOR SPORTS.
 5 THE TRAVELING BEARS AT PLAY.
 6 THE TRAVELING BEARS IN ENGLAND.
 7 THE TRAVELING BEARS ACROSS THE SEA.
 8 THE TRAVELING BEARS IN FAIRYLAND.
 9 THE TRAVELING BEAR DETECTIVES.
10 THE TRAVELING BEAR'S BIRTHDAY

Boards, Quarto, Illustrated.

———

BARSE & HOPKINS
PUBLISHERS
NEWARK, N. J.   NEW YORK, N. Y.

Illustration 606. As shown in back of *The Traveling
Bear's Birthday.* Christmas, 1921.

Illustration 607. The "Adventures of The Traveling Bears," copyright 1905 by Seymour Eaton, tells all about the Roosevelt Bears—Teddy B. and Teddy G. Many people refer to them as Teddy "Bad" and Teddy "Good," but that this is not correct is explained in the first chapter of the book. "B" is for black or brown or brave; "G" is for grey or grizzly. "Not 'B' for bad or 'G' for good, the black bear wanted it understood!" At any rate, they have wild adventures on the train, on a farm, at school, a county fair, and on a big balloon after they leave their mountain home. The bear of metal on the bicycle in front of the book is the dark brown bear, Teddy B. *Beverly Port Collection.*

Original advertising at Christmas time, 1906 states: "Teddy-B is black and wise and brave, and makes bad boys and girls behave; while Teddy-G is gray and gay, and cuts up antics every day.

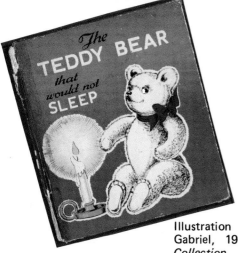

Illustration 608. Samuel Gabriel, 1944. *Jean Millen Collection.*

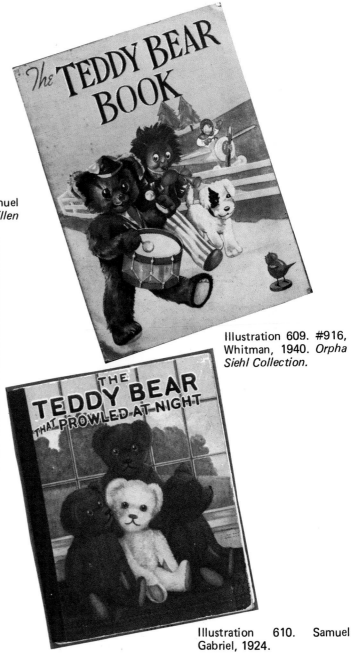

Illustration 609. #916, Whitman, 1940. *Orpha Siehl Collection.*

Denslow's Picture Books for Children.

We are pleased to offer our subscribers these Picture Books. W. W. Denslow, the artist, has revised several of the best classical fairy tales. They are new. More beautiful and striking in both text and picture than any children's books heretofore published. Each book is filled with pictures of action and fun in brilliant colors.

The twelve books are uniform in size. The titles are A B C Book; One Ring Circus; Tom Thumb; Humpty Dumpty; Old Mother Hubbard; Jack and the Bean-Stalk; Zoo; House That Jack Built; Three Bears; Little Red Riding Hood; Five Little Pigs; Mary Had a Little Lamb.

Any Four Volumes given only to **Companion** subscribers for one new subscription and 10 cents **extra**, postage and packing included. Price 25 cents each, post-paid. **See Conditions, page 501.**

Illustration 611. *The Youth's Companion,* October 22, 1903.

Illustration 610. Samuel Gabriel, 1924.

Illustration 612. Author, A. A. Milne and his son, Christopher Robin with Winnie the Pooh. Notice the long and curly mohair fur. *Loraine Burdick Collection.*

The Teddy Bears

The Greatest Children's Story Ever Written

Sales Prove It

The Teddy Bears

BY ADAH LOUISE SUTTON

Illustrated by A. J. SCHAEFER

THE Teddy Bears are not alone the quaint little stuffed creatures that at present seem to hold the world in their furry paws. They are wise, comical, half human fellows, and they fill this book with their merry and amazing pranks. At home, on the farm, in the street, they are always developing something new in the way of mischief and good times.

6 Full Pages in COLORS 36 Pen-and-Ink Drawings. Front and back covers in COLORS. Quarto, good type, fine paper, strong binding, illustrated in colors $1.00

THE author has caught the spirit of childhood, and has transmitted it to her pages. The children in her story are REAL, and their pets are LIVE ANIMALS — just such animals as one finds in a home where they are petted and caressed and become almost human.

"THE TEDDY BEARS" is the best selling juvenile of the year
Our factory is running night and day to supply the demand

Two Tremendous Editions sold **before** publication day

Order now for Fall deliveries   Liberal Discounts

The Saalfield Publishing Co., Akron, Ohio

156 Fifth Avenue, New York

Illustration 613. *Playthings,* 1907.

Illustration 614. (Front Cover) "Teddy B" and "Teddy G" (Back Cover). 5 in. (12.7cm) x 6 in. (15.2cm) Advertising booklet of Fleischmann Yeast Company. Copyright 1906-07 by Seymour Eaton and Edward Stern & Co., Inc. An adventure using nursery rhyme characters. The Roosevelt name is not used here.

F 2004—The Busy Bears.
The Hit of the season. A large size 9½x11½ fully illustrated bear book at a price within the reach of all. Book consists of 12 illustrated pages, six of which are in full colors. The text, which is bright and catchy, tells a funny bear story in simple words. The text is by Geo. W. Gunn, with illustrated by Austen. It will be a tremendous favorite. Per doz. .... .98

Illustration 615. The illustrations in this book were also issued as post cards, "The Busy Bears." G. Sommers catalog, 1907.

NOVELTY POST CARD TOY BOOKS.

The illustrations in each book are fac-similes of a complete set of popular post cards.

F 2207—The Red Line Series. A genuine novelty in juvenile books. The colors and designs of the covers are brilliant and attractive, and the pictures are bright, dashing and exceptionally pleasing to children. The stories and rhymes are by a well known writer of children's tales. Six different titles to each doz. as follows: **The Busy Bears, Sunbonnet Twins, Jolly Jingles, Bennie and Jennie, Little Susie Sunbonnet, and Polly Parson's Party.** Put up two of each title to the doz. Per doz. .... .95

Illustration 616. G. Sommers catalog, 1907.

"OH, LOOK WHO'S HERE!"

THE TEDDY BEAR
ABC
BY
Laura Rinkle Johnson
ILLUSTRATED IN COLORS
BY
Margaret L. Sanford
Square 4to, bound in cloth. Unique Cover Designs in Many Colors.

PRICE 75 CENTS
The Popular Juvenile Book of the Year. Humor with Illustrations in Color that appeal to Children of all Ages.

Ready September 1st

Send for our Illustrated Catalogue of Juvenile, Popular and Standard Books, Gift Books and Handy Volume Classics in a Variety of Original, Novel and Artistic Bindings.
Samples Sent on Request

H. M. CALDWELL CO.
PUBLISHERS
NEW YORK   BOSTON
5 and 7 East 16th Street   208 to 212 Summer Street

Illustration 617. *Playthings*, 1907.

THE TEDDY BEARS.
By Adah Louise Sutton.   Illustrated by A. J. Schaefer.

F 2015—The Teddy Bears are not alone the quaint little stuffed creatures that at present seem to hold the world in their furry paws. They are wise, comical, half human little fellows, and they fill this book with their merry and amazing pranks. At home, at the farm, or in the street, they are always developing something new in the way of mischief. The book is handsomely illustrated with many drawings of these active little Teddy Bears; illustrated in colors. Size 6x12. Each .... .75

THE BROWNS, A BOOK OF BEARS.
Fully Illustrated Text.
F 2052—Brown's Bear Book. A finely illustrated bear book within the reach of all. Each book consists of 12 entirely different bear stories, each with its own pictures, the text is also illustrated, finely printed on glazed paper, 60 pages, size 13x9¼, cloth backs, each in wrapper. Each .... .89

Illustration 618. G. Sommers catalog, 1907.

255

"*The Wonderful Story of Teddy, the Bear,* is the latest work on the ever popular Teddy. Colored illustrations abound, and the text matter tells the story in the proper style for the child reader. And right here, let it be known that the common supposition that anybody can write a child's story book is false. The art of plot structure in juvenile books is doubly hard. The story should be clean, wholesome and instructive; and still be told in a simple language that on the one hand will please the child, and, on the other hand, just faintly suggest a hidden humor or a gentle cynicism to please the child's mother who reads the book.

Animals must be made to talk, easily and naturally, and the air of mystery in the plot must never be so strong as to make the reading too heavy for young minds. The whole effect should be cheerful, buoyant, real. And this is the rare literary worth we occasionally meet. *The Wonderful Story of Teddy, the Bear,* will suit. A half dollar at retail."

Playthings, 1907.

Illustration 619. Published by Reilly and Britton Co., Chicago. G. Sommers catalog, 1907.

Illustration 620. *The Book News Monthly,* November, 1907.

JUVENILE BOOKS

"New this season is a series of bear books by John Howard Jewett. They tell of the wonderful adventures of the little Teddy bear, are illustrated in colors and sell for fifty cents the volume. They proved excellent books for the Xmas counter. The titles are: *The Three Baby Bears, The Baby Bears' Picnic, The Stories the Three Baby Bears Told, The Toy Bearkins' Christmas Tree,* and *The Little Toy Bearkins.*"

Playthings, 1907.

"These are genuine 'Teddy Bears' of the plush kind, of all ages. Their adventures with the children are told in prose, and illustrated with fourteen full-page pictures in colors, showing the Bears and the children coasting, skating, gardening, bathing, at the photographer's, at school, and in many other situations. It is one of the handsomest picture books of the season."

Playthings, 1907.

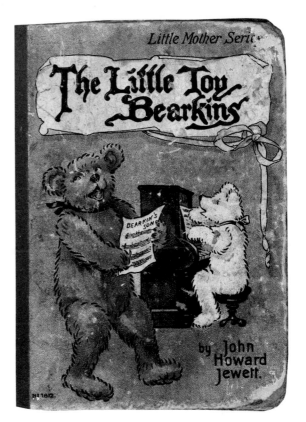

Illustration 621. The Little Toy Bearkins by John Howard Jewett.

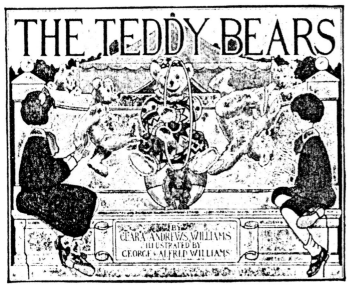

Illustration 622. Rare book by Clara Andrews Williams. *Playthings,* 1907.

Illustration 624.

"Among the delightful stories for children just reaching the reading age are *The Twinkle Tales,* by Laura Bancroft. There are six of these clever little books, each of them illustrated with sixteen illustrations in colors by Maginel Wright Enright."

Playthings, 1907.

Illustration 623. (Bear beats the drum), by L. J. Bridgman. *Playthings,* 1907.

Illustration 625. 6½ in. (16.5cm) x 11 in. (27.9cm) *MOVING PICTURE TEDDIES,* by R. H. Garman. Ideal Book Builders #604, Children's Favorite Series #1. Patented January 15, 1907, and June 25, 1907. According to original advertising by A. C. McClurg Company in 1915, this type of book was a new novelty in "shape-books." "Movable picture combinations of 120 different pictures may be made in each book. Clever verses with pictures in brilliant cols(sic)." *Loraine Burdick Collection.*

Illustration 626. 4 in. (10.2cm) x 6 in. (15.2cm), 6 pages, 12 sides. Back cover of advertising booklet. A white and gold Teddy Bear makes bread. W. W. Denslow, artist. 1908. *Mr. F. M. Gosling Collection.*

Illustration 627.
"Two very worn and well-loved Teddy Bears—the illustration by Johnny Gruelle is from a book dated 1916 by Rose Strong Hubbell. The title is *Quacky Doodles & Danny Daddles Book.* One of their friends is the 'Old Teddy Bear' and the story tells, in rhyme, how he became wobbly and wrinkly. 'He never will boast, but Old Teddy's the one that is played with the most. The children love all in the Toy Box, but still, Old Teddy's the one that they want when they're ill.' The real Teddy Bear is 'wobbly & wrinkly' just as is the one drawn by Johnny Gruelle—and probably dates from the same year; 1916. He is only 7 in. (17.8cm) tall, excelsior stuffed, and has glass eyes. The button he wears was with him when he joined our family so of course his name is 'True Blue.' "
Doll News   Beverly Port Collection

Illustration 628. From *The Bookseller,* November 15, 1911.

From "The Revel of the Toys," by H. Anabel Ingalls. Copyright, 1910, by The Ball Publishing Company.

Illustration 629. *The Bookseller, Newsdealer and Stationer* magazine, November 1910.

Illustration 630. From *Moses P. Pickles and Others* by Jane Holloway. Copyright 1910, Edward Stern and Co., Inc.

Illustration 631. *BEAR PARTY,* by William Pene Du Bois, The Viking Press, 1951; published in part in *LIFE* magazine in 1950. Story of koalas in a tree having all sorts of dress-up play. Cardboard hard cover.

Illustration 632. *The True Story of Smokey Bear,* U. S. Dept. of Agriculture//Forest Service// Designed, produced and © 1960, 1964, 1969 by Western Publishing Company, Inc.

1958

1959

1960

1967

Illustration 633. *Rupert* books, The Daily Express Annual, illustrated by A. E. Bestall. Harrison & Sons Ltd.

Best.-Nr. 1 470 gebunden
Best.-Nr. 1 300 kartoniert

Karl Rohr, Teddy

16 Seiten, Format 21 × 25 cm
Ein Bilderbuch mit Schreibschrift
(für 4- bis 6jährige)

Viele aufregende Abenteuer erlebt der kleine Teddy, als er in die Welt hinaus zieht um einen richtigen Beruf zu erlernen. Leider ist er für jede Arbeit zu tolpatschig und stellt immer wieder dumme Sachen an, bis er schließlich einsieht, daß es zu Hause doch am schönsten ist.
Eine besondere Freude werden die 4- bis 6jährigen an den lustigen Versen haben, die sie in der Schrift finden, welche sie selbst zu schreiben oder zu lesen erlernt haben.

Illustration 634. German *Teddy* book *Junior International,* Munich, Paris, London, 1968.

Illustration 636. Source and date unknown.

Illustration 635. 9½ in. (24.1cm) x 12 in. (30.5cm) Teddy - The Champion by Artcraft. Saalfield Publishing Co. #5822. *Florence Mosseri Collection.*

RIGHT: Illustration 637. 14½ in. (36.8cm) x 8¼ in. (20.9cm) Green printing, reds, blues, and browns. Copyright 1940. Samuel Lowe Company.

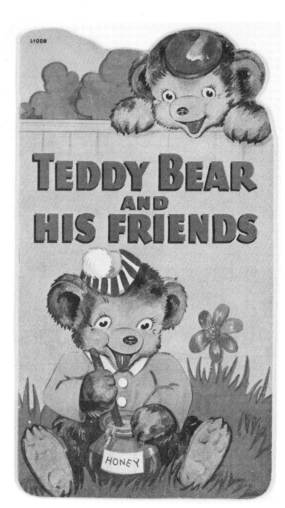

IS for Yuletide,
The grown
people's name
For the time
when my Teddy
From Santa Claus came.

ABOVE: Illustration 638. Source and date unknown.

The House at Pooh Corner

By A. A. MILNE

Illustrated by E. H. Shepard

Author of
WHEN WE WERE VERY YOUNG.

NOW WE ARE SIX.

WINNIE—THE POOH.

$2.00

Adventures of Theodore Roosevelt

By EDWIN EMERSON

It's all here—the battle of San Juan Hill—Hunting big game in Africa—Cowboys—Rough Riders. $2.50

Illustration 639A & B. *CHILD LIFE,* December, 1928.

ASK DADDY TO USE THE SANDPAPER WITH "BARNEY" IN THE TRIANGLE

QUALITY ABRASIVES

BARNEY

BEHR - MANNING   TROY, N.Y., U.S.A.

LITHO IN U.S.A.

Advertising paper doll for Behr-Manning Company, circa 1940.

X. Teddy Bear Paper Dolls

The children of 1907 were delighted with the new Teddy Bear paper dolls, as is described in the illustrated letter from Pharos to her friend, Gertrude. How fortunate that this happy moment of childhood was preserved.

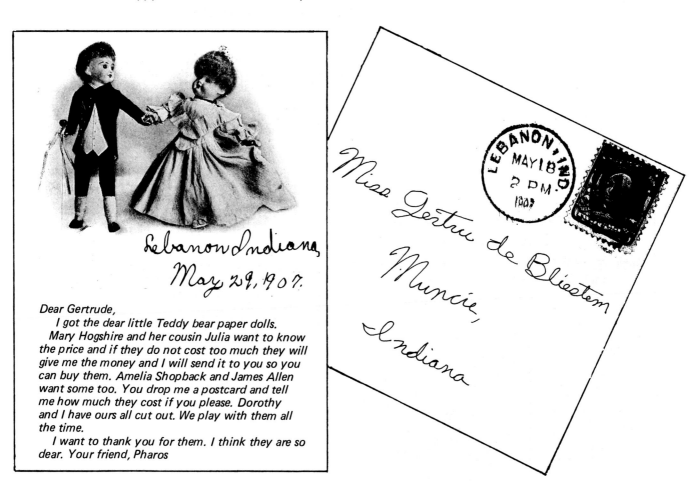

Lebanon, Indiana
May 29, 1907.

Dear Gertrude,
   I got the dear little Teddy bear paper dolls.
   Mary Hogshire and her cousin Julia want to know the price and if they do not cost too much they will give me the money and I will send it to you so you can buy them. Amelia Shopback and James Allen want some too. You drop me a postcard and tell me how much they cost if you please. Dorothy and I have ours all cut out. We play with them all the time.
   I want to thank you for them. I think they are so dear. Your friend, Pharos

Illustration 640. *Betty Brink Collection.* (Note was originally handwritten in the style as shown on the attached envelope.)

Illustration 641. The J. Ottmann Litho-graphing Company took an entire page to advertise their Teddy paper doll. One can scarcely believe that this quality item sold for only ten cents. He was used as a premium gift by some magazines seeking subscriptions. *Playthings,* 1907.

See Illustration 649 on page 272 for photo-graph of cover.

Playthings magazine made mention of the Teddy Bear paper dolls that appeared once a week in the newspaper; no doubt these were in with the Sunday comics since they do have some color. The *Boston Sunday Globe* ran "Teddy Bear" in 1907 and 1908. It is not known how many were in the complete set.

Illustration 642. Premium, 1907. *Loraine Burdick Collec-tion.*

Included here are six versions from the *Boston Sunday Globe* by the same unidentified artist. Teddy is a sailor, artist and jester by occupation; an American Indian, Chinaman and Dutchman by nationality. One can imagine the children's excitement and impatience in waiting from week to week for these to appear.

Loraine Burdick has published "Teddy Bear Paper Dolls" which includes: the golfer, yachtsman, jockey, fireman, drum major, continental soldier, blacksmith, pirate Eskimo, postman, policeman, farmer in overalls, Rough Rider, Red Riding Hood, clown, automobilist and college graduate. Teddy was a very versatile character!

Illustration 643. Boston Sunday Globe Teddy Bear paper doll series of 1907-1908, bears measure 5½ in. - 7 in. (14cm - 17.8cm) tall. All from *Loraine Burdick Collection.*

DIRECTIONS
CUT CAP ACCORDING TO PATTERN. FOLD ON DOTTED LINE 1-2. APPLY PASTE TO FLAPS A-B-C-D AND STICK BACK AND FRONT TOGETHER.

THE DUTCHMAN SUIT MAY BE CUT DOUBLE TO FORM A BACK OR WITH FLAPS AS INDICATED BY DOTTED LINES.

Illustration 643A. Brown Teddy Bear paper doll with blue cap and jacket, yellow vest and shoes and green trousers. *The Boston Sunday Globe,* January 19, 1908.

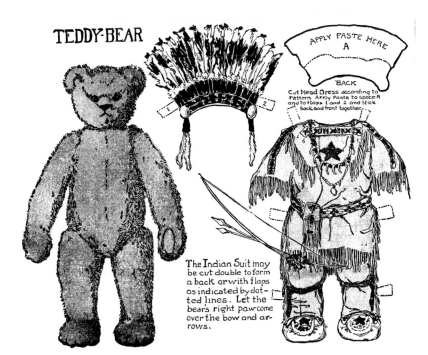

APPLY PASTE HERE A

BACK

Cut Head Dress according to Pattern. Apply Paste to space A and to flaps 1 and 2 and stick back and front together.

The Indian Suit may be cut double to form a back or with flaps as indicated by dotted lines. Let the bear's right paw come over the bow and arrows.

Illustration 643B. Teddy Bear paper doll with red and blue coloring on headdress. Yellow suit with touches of red and blue. *The Boston Sunday Globe,* January 26, 1908.

TEDDY-BEAR

BACK

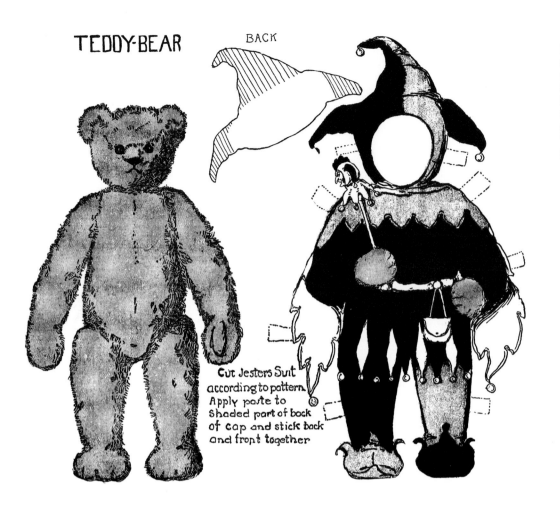

Cut Jesters Suit according to pattern. Apply paste to shaded part of back of cap and stick back and front together

Illustration 643C. Teddy Bear paper doll with red and green hood and red body. Spangles are red and yellow and shoes and socks are red and green. *The Boston Sunday Globe,* May 3, 1908.

TEDDY-BEAR

BACK

FRONT

DIRECTIONS

Cut the Beretta according to pattern. Fold back flaps A-B. Apply paste to shaded portion of back and to flaps and stick back and front together.

The Artist's Suit may be cut double to form a back or with flaps as indicated by dotted lines.

Illustration 643D. Brown Teddy Bear paper doll with blue smock, red beret and yellow trousers. *The Boston Sunday Globe,* May 10, 1908.

Illustration 643E. Brown Teddy Bear paper doll with blue cap, trousers, collar and cuffs. *The Boston Sunday Globe,* July 5, 1908.

TEDDY-BEAR

FRONT

DIRECTIONS

Cut Cap according to pattern. Fold down the flaps on back, apply paste and stick back and front together.

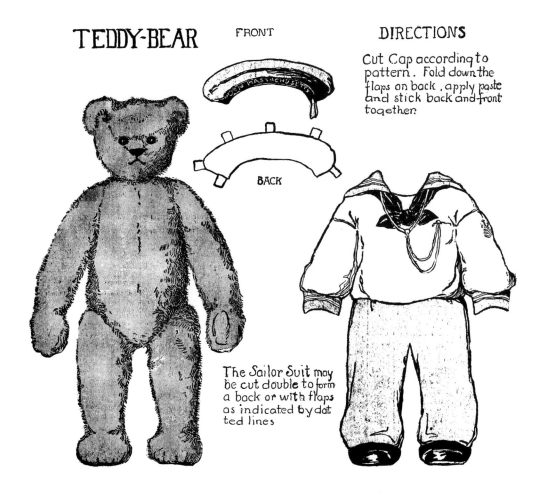

BACK

The Sailor Suit may be cut double to form a back or with flaps as indicated by dotted lines

TEDDY-BEAR

DIRECTIONS

Cut Sunshade and Cap by the pattern. Fold back flaps A-B-C-D - Apply paste to flaps and to shaded part on sunshade and fasten cap to sunshade in space so marked.

Illustration 643F. Teddy Bear paper doll with yellow, red and green sunshade. Red and blue cap. Blue and red jacket with yellow sleeves. Green trousers and red and yellow shoes. *The Boston Sunday Globe,* July 12, 1908.

It was interesting to be put in touch with Elizabeth Copeland, the niece of paper doll artist, Sheila Young. In a request to borrow negatives for this book of her Teddy Bear who had appeared in Lettie Lane and other paper doll sheets, she wrote:

"Dear Mrs. Schoonmaker, I'm delighted that you are making a Teddy Bear book. I'm glad you like my Aunt's paper dolls, too. They really are beautiful and such an accurate recording of the fashions of that period! My Teddy and monkey appeared in *Ladies' Home Journal* for December 1908 in 'Lettie Lane's Grandmother Who Brings Christmas Presents to Lettie.' I must have been given Teddy and monkey for my first Christmas so Teddy must be about 71 years old now. My Aunt was living with us at the time.

I'm much amused at Grandmother's clothes, typical of that period. Today she'd probably be clad in a bikini."

Elizabeth knit new outfits for her toys in 1974 to look just as Teddy did in 1908. Monkey originally had a green felt outfit with gold trim. They have survived beautifully.

A little known series of Teddy Bears ran in the *New York Hearld* in 1907 called "Little Nemo's Bear." The illustration shows a Rough Rider outfit and sailor suit. There was a Little Nemo cartoon drawn by Winsor McCay which may explain the derivation of this bear.

Two outstanding paper dolls of the 1930s are also included. "Teddy Bear and His Friends" by Platt and Munk is a boxed set owned by Richard Rusnock. Teddy models the clothing of the early day Pilgrim and a baseball player, as well as a fancy sailor suit, and has his own Teddy Bear. The set is not dated but was owned in 1933.

Chubby Cubby by Colorforms comes in a colorful envelope but is undated.

Illustration 644. This bear is shown in "Lettie's Grandmother Brings Christmas Presents" and "The Youngest Wedding Guest." *Elizabeth A. Copeland Collection.*

Illustration 645. From "Betty Bonnet's May Basket" by Sheila Young. *Ladies' Home Journal,* May, 1918.

Illustration 646. New blue and white sweater knit by owner in 1974. *Elizabeth A. Copeland Collection.*

Illustration 647. Teddy Bear and His Friends — one of six dolls in a boxed set by Platt and Munk. Received by original owner in 1933. *Richard Rusnock Collection.*

Illustration 648A. Outside envelope 7½ in. x 15½ in. (19.1cm x 39.4cm), American Colortype Company, Chicago, Illinois. Circa 1930.

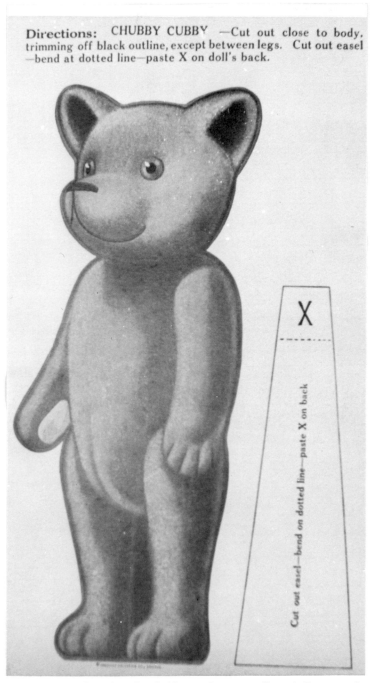

Directions: CHUBBY CUBBY —Cut out close to body, trimming off black outline, except between legs. Cut out easel —bend at dotted line—paste X on doll's back.

Illustration 648B. Chubby Cubby on heavy cardboard. Bear stands 9¾ in. (24.9cm) tall.

Illustration 648C. Chubby Cubby's Indian suit.

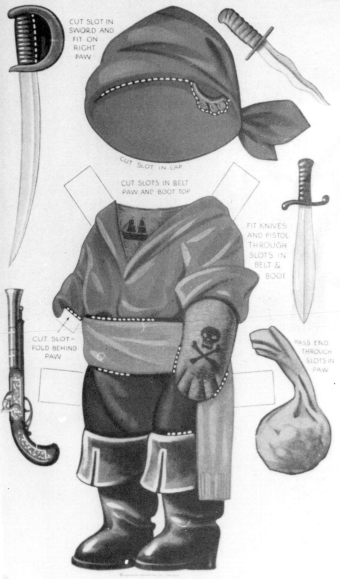

Directions: CHUBBY CUBBY SUIT—Cut out suit and hat, leaving tabs attached, and slit on dotted lines. Fold tabs over body to hold suit in place. Cut out small pieces and fit in place as indicated.

Illustration 648D. Chubby Cubby's pirate costume.

271

Illustration 649. 10½ in. (26.6cm) Teddy Bear paper doll. Heavy paperboard, golden brown with stand-up tab on back. Original envelope featured in the middle. J. Ottmann Lithographing Co., New York. Auto-outing outfit on left with hat and goggles to match. Five sets of colorful clothing. This paper bear has been reproduced in two smaller sizes, one with movable eyes. Early 1900s. *Beverly Port Collection.*

Illustration 650.

"The Teddy Bear Paper Doll, as it is called, is a very fascinating toy, and no child, whether boy or girl, would want to be without one. A Teddy Bear sheet is furnished with some of the Sunday newspapers, but it is not every child who can get these. This new toy can be purchased at retail for ten cents, and will afford the youngster a great deal of amusement. The big brown bear stands ten inches high, and has five costumes which are to be cut out. There is his baseball uniform, dressing gown, automobile suit, yachting suit and walking suit. They are printed in bright colors, and fashioned true to life. Already this article is having a heavy sale, and if merely shown in the stores will sell."

Playthings, 1907.

"The Teddy Bear Paper Doll continues to sell rapidly, and it is quite likely that if one child in a community gets one all the others will want one, too. The attractive manner in which this toy is made up appeals to the little ones, and then, besides, the mere name Teddy Bear makes it popular. The plaything that affords the child both pleasure and work, a little of the latter, is a very good thing for any child to have."

Playthings, 1907.

Illustration 651. Large white Steiff bear with button eyes, on green base. Blue sailor suit and red and blue military costume. Bear is 6¾ in. (17.2cm) tall. *Loraine Burdick Collection.*

Illustration 652. Grace Drayton child with Teddy Bear and Golliwog. Date unknown.

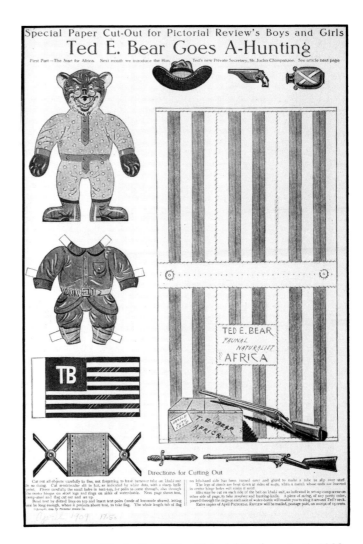

Illustration 653. *Pictorial Review,* April, 1909. The reverse side of this heavy sheet carries the story "Ted E. Bear Goes A-Hunting" with Ted E. Bear wearing above suit and hat, holding gun and canteen. Caption under the illustration is: "Dee-E-E-E-Lighted," says the Hon. Ted.

Illustration 654. "Dolly Dingle's Little Friend Joey Goes to a Carnival." *Pictorial Review,* January 1924.

Illustration 655. Teddy Bear paper doll created by Betty Grime.

Illustration 656. "The Three Bears," #2142, Saalfield Publishing Company. *Helen Sieverling Collection.*

Illustration 657. Artist, Queen Holden, Whitman #947, Stephen Slesinger, Inc., 1935. *Loraine Burdick Collection.*

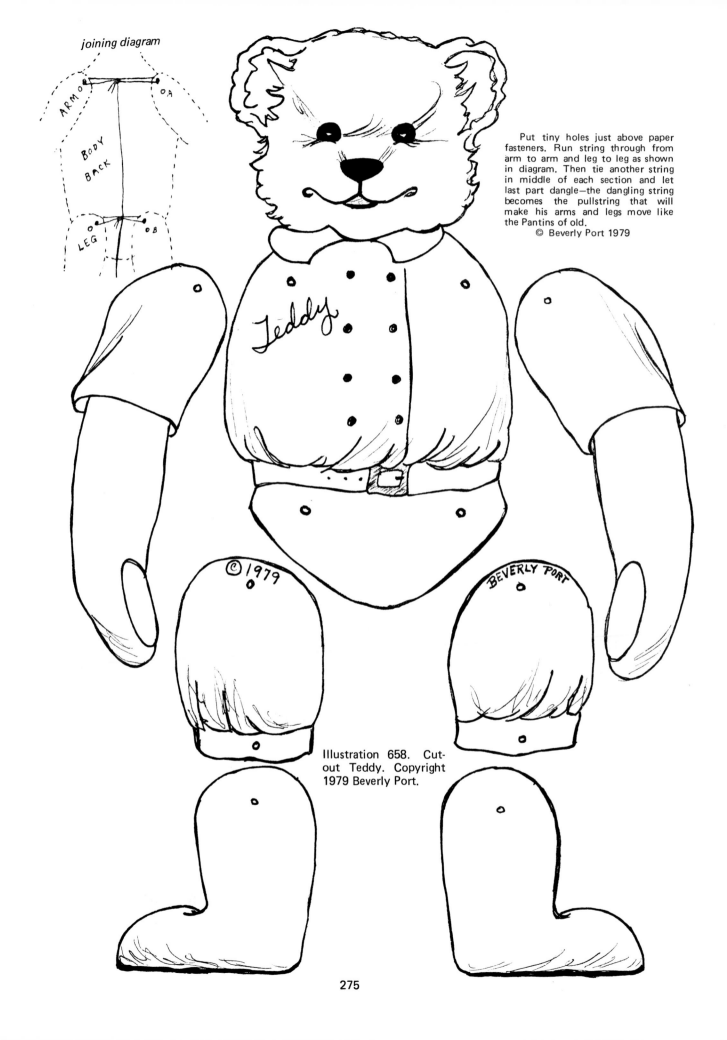

joining diagram

ARM A

O A

BODY
BACK

LEG

O B

Put tiny holes just above paper fasteners. Run string through from arm to arm and leg to leg as shown in diagram. Then tie another string in middle of each section and let last part dangle—the dangling string becomes the pullstring that will make his arms and legs move like the Pantins of old.
© Beverly Port 1979

Teddy

©1979

BEVERLY PORT

Illustration 658. Cut-out Teddy. Copyright 1979 Beverly Port.

275

DADDY USES **BARNEY'S** SANDPAPER

BEHR-MANNING, TROY, - N.Y., U.S.A.

Illustration 659. Sheet 8 in. (20.3cm) x 11 in. (27.9cm) Behr - Manning, Troy, N.Y., U.S.A. Norton Abrasives. Brown bear on green grass. Occupational costumes in reds, blues and greens. Behr - Manning used the symbol of an upright bear. *Kay Bransky Collection.*

Illustration 660. Puppen Ausschneidebogen. 16½ in. (41.9cm) tall on heavy cardboard with tri-fold of costumes. Circa 1970.

Illustration 661. "Miss Molly Munsing," blank back sheet. Compliments of The Marston Co., San Diego, California. The Munsingwear Store. One of her 11 garments on page.

276

Merry Christmas

Original Paper Doll
By
Joyce Stafford

Copyright 1978

Illustration 662. By kind permission of Joyce Stafford, NIADA artist.

277

Actual toys of Elizabeth Copeland in replacement suits knit by owner. These animals were presented in Sheila Young's Lettie Lane series, "Lettie Lane's Grandmother Brings Christmas Presents to Lettie," *Ladies' Home Journal,* December, 1908. *Elizabeth Copeland Collection. Photograph by Elizabeth Copeland.*

XI. Toys & Games

A fascinating aspect of Teddy Bear collecting is the search for the games and toys that came into being following the tremendous popularity of this animal toy. Some of them have been well known through the years but others will bring considerable surprise.

In 1907, *Playthings* magazine announced jointed celluloid Teddy Bears for the younger members of the family. They came in either cinnamon or white in a large variety of sizes. These are most likely the heavy, waxy celluloid of this period, not to be confused with the lightweight colored celluloids of the 1920s and 1930s. Another item the author has never found is an illustration in original advertising for a Teddy Bear wagon. Still another rarity is a Teddy Bear rattle which retailed at twenty-five cents in 1908. This small fur-covered stick was terminated at either end by a miniature brown Teddy Bear head with good quality eyes.

Playthings announced an excellent novelty in 1907, a hammock for bears (or dolls). The hammock swung between two iron supports making a complete little toy. It came in several colors and it was mentioned that either Bruin or Doll would find it a most comfortable article for summer.

The following is an editorial taken from *Playthings* in 1907:

MANY TEDDY BEAR NOVELTIES

"Who would have thought a year or so ago that the year 1907 would start off with such an enormous Teddy Bear craze? Manufacturers are bringing out all manner of things pertaining to bears, and are showing Teddy in all sorts of ways. We will mention a few Teddy Bear specialties that have been shown to us recently. First of all there are candy boxes, which are nothing more or less than the ordinary plush bear with a cylinder-shaped box inside of him. He looks like any other stuffed Bruin, but when his head is removed it reveals the box. These are made up in several sizes, and Bunnies are also made the same way. The manufacturer reports a pretty good demand for them. Another novelty is a bear to retail for ten cents. The foundation of the body is a flexible wire covered with a fur material, so the bear can be placed in almost any shape. This is intended more for a cotillion favor as there is a long pin on the back of the bear, by means of which it can be fastened to the coat. These, likewise, are selling very well. Teddy Bear scarf pins have been on the market for some time and retail at a popular price. Bruin can now be had in rubber, with legs of cardboard pasted to him; but he does not stay there long; as the wind goes out of him he gets thinner and thinner and finally falls over on his side. This is on the order of the dying pig, which had such a large sale a few years ago. Still another is a rubber ball with a fierce looking bear concealed inside, and when the ball is squeezed Bruin pops out. This is a ten cent seller, and should prove very popular. There are numerous other articles, such as post-cards, mechanical toys, etc. and they find much favor."

In 1908 *Playthings* announced two Jumping Jack Teddy Bears. One was a wooden 7 in. (17.8cm) imported jumping jack with a brown fur head to retail at ten cents. The second was not described but retailed for twenty-five cents.

Illustration 663A. Cover from Little Golden Locks Game. *Elayne C. Shuman Collection.*

Illustration 664. Toy automobile sold by Hamburger and Co., driven by a life-size bear.

DIRECTIONS FOR PLAYING

LITTLE GOLDEN LOCKS GAME.

Published by PARKER BROTHERS, (Inc.) Salem, Mass., U.S.A.

The Object of this game is for the Bears starting from their home, to try to catch Little Golden Locks who is in the woods near the Bear's House. If the Bears succeed in catching Golden Locks before she reaches her home they win. If, however, Golden Locks is able to reach home before the Bears catch her, she wins.

RULES FOR FOUR PLAYERS.

One player takes the large piece representing Golden Locks, and each of the other players one of the smaller pieces representing the Bears. In the beginning of the game the three Bears are placed upon the spot "Bears start here" and Golden Locks upon the spot designated for her. Players play in turn. Each spins the teetotum in turn and moves as many spaces along the tracks. Golden Locks, however, is safe upon any of the blue spots that she stops upon, the bears being obliged to catch her on a red spot only. The Bears cannot move upon any of the blue spots. In order for the Bears to catch Golden Locks they must reach the same red spot that she is occupying by exact spin. If, they are successful in doing this they win. If Golden Locks gets to the white spot marked "Golden Locks Home" she wins.

RULES FOR THREE PLAYERS.

The same as for four players except that only two Bears are used.

RULES FOR TWO PLAYERS.

When two plays one takes the three Bears and plays them exactly the same as in the four handed game, that is, each piece plays in turn.

Illustration 663B. Directions for Little Golden Locks Game that are on the inside cover of the lid. *Elayne C. Shuman Collection.*

When Bears Go Motoring.

"One of the latest fads of the day with automobilists is to have "Teddy Bears" on the side lamps of their cars, and a touring car without two brown or white bears, or a brown and a white one, is considered quite out of fashion. These bears, in sizes that correspond with the car, are attached to the lamps at the sides, so that they look as if they were driving the auto. Some of these toy animals are used without any clothing, while others are elaborately bedecked with sweaters, stockings, caps, or regulation miniature motor hats with goggles that give a decidedly sporty air."

Playthings, 1906.

Illustration 665. Newspaper advertisement.

280

THE TEDDY BEAR AUTOMOBILE

"Here is another addition to the list of Teddy Bear goods, and this time it is an automobile. It is a cute little car, painted in bright colors and substantially made. There are places in front of the hood to attach a string by means of which it is drawn along the ground. Teddy B. and Teddy G. look very comfortable and happy when seated in their up-to-date motor cars."

Playthings, 1907.

Illustration 666.
"A recent arrival which was the cause of much joy in the Bruin family is a beautiful wooden automobile built especially for bears, and it is a fine toy. Painted in bright colors it makes a splendid showing, and the bears fully appreciate it."

Playthings, 1907.

Illustration 667. American Printing Co., 1906.

DIRECTIONS — For any number of players. Pin the Teddy Bear flat on the wall. Each player has five turns and is to stand 12 feet away, take aim with forefinger extended, close eyes and walk forward until the finger hits the wall. If the bear is hit it counts 10, if within a ring count as marked therein. The highest total score wings.

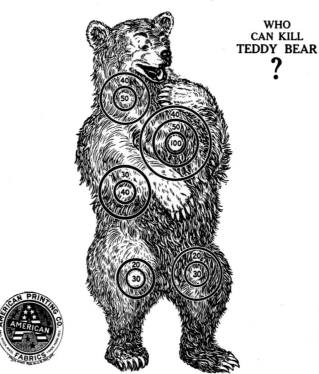

AMERICAN PRINTING COMPANY
GAME of TEDDY BEAR
(Trade-Mark Reg. in U. S. Pat. Off.)

WHO CAN KILL TEDDY BEAR **?**

Copyright 1906 by American Printing Company

Actual Size of Bear 22 x 10 inches.
An Inexpensive Parlor Game on Standard Print Cloth.
READY FOR USE. NO SEWING REQUIRED.
Two Games on Every Yard.
Directions for Playing are Printed on each Game.
For sale by Dry Goods Jobbers throughout the country.

"ROUGH-RIDER" SUIT.

Illustration 668. Child's Rough-Rider suit, *Our Wonder World*, 1907.

Illustration 669. The Teddy Bear Squeeze Ball. Bear is concealed inside ball and pops up when squeezed. Retailed at ten cents. Manufactured by the Baumann Rubber Company, New Haven, Connecticut, 1907.

Illustration 670. "The Teddy Horse," *Playthings*, 1907.

282

Illustration 671.

"An enterprising Western manufacturer has placed upon the market a line of Teddy bear carts and cages that have met with instant approval, and will make an exceptionally strong holiday line. Handsome displays can be made with these "Bruin vehicles," and it will mean the sale of the outfit, with good profit on both. The smallest cart for 16 to 20-inch bear sells to the trade at $4.50 per dozen, the next size for 20 to 30-inch bear $6.00 per dozen while the smallest cage for the smaller bears brings $11.00 per dozen, and the largest cage, to accommodate the 20 to 30-inch bears, sells at $14.50 per dozen. With these cages the children can have all sorts of fun playing circus, and to wheel a large Teddy bear in a little cart built especially for his majesty will be the height of pleasure. The goods are made in a substantial manner, and the retailer who handles them comes in for a good margin of profit."

Playthings, 1907.

RUBBER TOYS

Toys for the Tiny Tots. Made of pure red rubber.

Teddy Bear — It Squeaks!

49 E 2941 — Height, 6 inches. Shipping weight, 6 ounces   45¢

Montgomery Ward & Co.
Saint Paul

Illustration 672.

"A crying rubber Teddy bear, at ten cents, has just reached the jobber. The bear stands about five inches high, is made of a light brown rubber, and crys when squeezed. The air valve is through a hat on the bear's head; and the in-and-out pressure of the air produces two notes in the squeak. This is the first rubber Teddy bear of its kind to appear, and as it sells for ten cents it should prove a winner for the curb toy brokers.

In uniform style to this bear is a dressed rubber doll, from whose head issues a whistling sound when being blown up, and whose tender stomach gives forth two very plaintive squeaks when gently pressed. The inflated head is painted with humorous features, and bobs comically forward when the rubber baby cries."

Playthings, 1907.

Teddy Bear Leather Muzzles and Leaders No. 1, to fit 10 inch Bears	$1.50 doz.
" " " " " 2, " 12 " "	1.75 "
" " " " " 3, " 14 " "	2.00 "

HAHN & AMBERG 569-571 BROADWAY
—New York—

Illustration 673. *Playthings,* 1907.

Animals on Platforms—3 styles, 10 in. bear, tiger and elephant, on green painted platforms, red wheels.
F6807—Assorted ½ doz. in box . . . . Doz. **$2.10**

Illustration 674. G. Sommers catalog, 1907.

Illustration 675. Wooden push toy called "grotesque," meaning simply a non-realistic design. *Playthings,* 1907.

RIGHT: Illustration 676.
G. Sommers catalog, 1907.

TEDDY BEAR GAME.

Per dozen..................... $8.00

NOVELTIES IN GAMES

The Vanderbilt Cup Race Game and Teddy's Bear Hunt Game
(Copyrighted. Patents applied for.)
The Most Up=to=date, Exciting and Realistic Games on the Market

BIG SELLERS

The Vanderbilt Cup Race Game is played on a board which portrays the famous Vanderbilt Cup Course, with many interesting features, including the Hairpin Curve. Miniature racing automobiles are used.

Write for particulars

Manufactured by
Bowers & Hard
211 State Street
Bridgeport, Conn.

Selling Agent:
Henry C. Schnibbe
641 Broadway, New York City

The Game of Teddy's Bear Hunt represents the pursuit of a bear through the snowy woodland. Miniature bears and huntsmen are used. The game is an absolute innovation in the game line.

Illustration 677. *Playthings,* 1907.

285

Illustration 678.

"Teddy Bear Shoo-fly."

"The hobby-horse and the shoo-fly have long been popular nursery favorites, and many novelties have made their way into the field of recent years. This year the Teddy Bear shoo-fly was ushered in, and it immediately became a heavy seller. It is made in the form of a rocking horse, as can be seen from the accompanying illustration. It is 15x34 inches and can be sold at retail for 75 cents or $1. The seat, rockers, footboard and hand-rod are painted an attractive red."

Playthings, 1907.

Shown by Selchow & Righter.

Illustration 679.

"Those Roosevelt bears and their famous coterie are now found on the rubber stamps. Twenty-one rubber stamps of the bears and their friends and their surroundings are put up in a neatly colored box for the toy trade. Something new in rubber stamps."

Playthings, 1907.

TEDDY BEAR RUBBER STAMPS.

With these stamps a child can make his own Teddy Bears and group them to suit his own fancy. Great fun for the little folks.

S 1050—Seven stamps and an ink pad; size of box 4x4 in. Per doz. .... .78

S 1052—Large 25c. set. 15 stamps and large self-inking pad; box 5½x6½ in. Per doz. **2.00**

Illustration 680. G. Sommers catalog, 1907.

Illustration 681.

"The Teddy Bear A B C Blocks are six in number, 2x4 inches and ½ inch thick. One side of these blocks, when put together, shows a little Teddy bear carrying a parasol; on the other surface they show six interesting events in Teddy's daily life, such as Teddy going to school, Teddy at the bat, etc. On the edges, several successive letters of the alphabet and also successions of numbers are to be put together in their proper order.

★ ★ ★

The educational value of A B C blocks is one of the best reasons why they sell in such enormous quantities, but there is a new set of blocks which has a stronger pulling quality than the mere educational feature, namely, the title, for they are called "Teddy Bear A B C Blocks," and the children will be "de-lighted" with them. The blocks are beautifully lithographed, and show Bruin in many peculiar circumstances. On the edges of the blocks can be found the complete alphabet, and nothing could be better with which to start the education of an infant."

Playthings, 1907.

Illustrations 682A & B.

Teddy Bear Card Game

"It is not an altogether simple matter to devise a card game that will interest the children for any great length of time, although there are several such games on the market. The man who invented the Teddy Bear Card Game has come pretty near to striking it right, for here is a game that will delight the children, and even if they tire of playing they will still have the pleasure of looking at the funny cards, for they are indeed very comical, showing Mr. Teddy in all sorts of odd positions.

The popularity of animal toys needs but brief mention, for in a great many different kinds of toys animals hold a prominent place. They are plush animals, wooden animals, animals made of paper, rubber, tin; animal shoo-flies, games, puzzles, etc.

Among the recent parlor games is the "Teddy Bear Card Game," which retails for 50 cents. The pack consists of 132 cards, and three different games can be played with the same. One of the latest fads is "Progressive Teddy Bear"—very amusing and exciting. The game will appeal to children because of the name, if nothing more."

Playthings, 1907.

S 7088—"Teddy Bear" chime; a dancing Teddy bear in fancy costume; when toy is moved the bear dances and rings two steel bells; new this year; ½ doz. in pkg. Per doz.   2.00

Illustration 683. G. Sommers catalog, 1907.

Shown by Leo Schlesinger & Co.

Illustration 684.

Teddy Bear Pail.

"The pails come in two styles, red and white and blue and white, and each one has upon it about six different pictures of Bruin, in all sorts of positions. This is something that will surely please the little tots, who are "De-lighted" with Teddy in any way, shape or manner. The pails will retail for 10 cents each, including shovel."

Playthings, 1907.

Illustration 685. Object of this game is to feed the bear the 24 large red berries. *Playthings,* 1907.

THE ROOSEVELT STOCK FARM.
A Model Stock Farm, Complete in All Details. THIS IS THE GREATEST DOLLAR WOODEN TOY ON THE MARKET.

Illustration 686. G. Sommers catalog, 1907.

S 4056—A complete farm, with large barn, and platform leading to barn door; farm wagon, work horse, cattle, etc.; roof is detachable, and all extra pieces are packed inside; length 19½ inches; width, 13½ inches; height 20¼ inches. Each in a box. Per doz. **7·80**

S 6040X.

S 6040X—"Roosevelt" bank; 10½x 9½x3; represents "Teddy" on one of his bear hunts; when money is shot top of tree opens; bear springs out; each in wooden box. Ea. 82

Illustration 687. G. Sommers catalog, 1907.

CLOTH TEDDY BEARS.

On sheets ready to be cut out and sewed. Fine toys at small prices.

S 1962—Teddy Bears. A Teddy Bear for 10 cents; printed on best muslin in soft brown and black color; ht. 11 in.; a few stitches will complete it; 1 doz. in pgk. .72

Illustration 688. G. Sommers catalog, 1907.

ROOSEVELT BEAR MENAGERIE.

Amusing and entertaining. Endless fun for the children. Figures can be made to assume almost any conceivable position.

No.			Per Doz.
1	8 pieces in Box, 12 x12		..$9.00
2	10 pieces in Box, 16 x14½		..15.00
3	12 pieces in Box, 19½x15		..19.50

Illustration 689. G. Sommers catalog, 1907.

Illustration 690.

"The new game of "Teddy Bear," recently placed upon the market, should prove a very rapid seller, for it is an interesting game, and retails at the popular price of 25 cents. The great popularity of all toys and novelties incorporating the magic word "Teddy" is well known by the trade, and when the article is backed by individual merit there is a pretty good outlook for its success. This new game is made up in a most substantial manner, consisting of 19 pairs and 1 odd card, made of the best six-ply yellow coated cardboard, and enclosed in a neat colored box, 5x6½ inches. Each card has a pretty illustration of a Teddy bear in some comical attitude. Any number of persons, from two to six, can take part in this game, and full instructions for playing are printed on the cover of each box, and also on a separate card which is enclosed. The trade price is $1.50 per dozen."

Playthings, 1907.

Illustration 691. Inexpensive German card set, circa 1908.

F1813 – Inflates to 6½ in., bear head, 4 paws, expiring voice.
Doz. 82¢

Illustration 692. Butler Brothers catalog, 1908.

291

SEASIDE OR SAND PAILS AND SHOVELS.

Two Styles T2Z

T2Z — Ht. 3¾ in., diam. 4½ in. Famous Roosevelt Teddy Bear pail, all the rage, in different poses with sword, gun, flag, etc., wide red background with black and gold border, cooper wire bail. Each with shovel. 1 doz. in pkg.   Doz. **37¢**

Illustration 693. The rare pail at the bottom right depicts Theodore Roosevelt riding a huge Teddy Bear piggyback. Butler Brothers catalog, 1908.

TEDDY BEAR BANK.
A great favorite with the children.

F206X—6¼ x 3 in., brown enamel finish, well made, natural in appearance, hole in the head for coin. The most popular and greatest novelty bank on the market. ½ doz. in box.   Per dozen, **$1.65**

Illustration 694. Butler Brothers catalog, 1908.

Illustration 695A. Unassembled pantin bear. *Beverly Port Collection.*

Let me share your joys, my sweetheart
You must know that I adore you!
If of sorrows you have any,
Please let "Teddy Bear" them for you

Illustration 695C. Back of Pantin paper toy showing marking and verse. *Beverly Port Collection.*

Illustration 695B. 12 in. (30.5cm) Pantin paper toy by Raphael Tuck & Sons Ltd. Rich brown, embossed bear with pink mouth, red heart on chest. Marked on back, under trade mark: "TRADE MARK//RAPHAEL TUCK & SONS LTD//PUBLISHERS BY APPOINTMENT //TO THEIR MAJESTIES THE KING AND QUEEN// PRINTED IN GERMANY." Circa 1909 *Beverly Port Collection.*

Teddy Bear Hoop-La Hats

Illustration 696. Boardwalk game of chance, circa 1910.

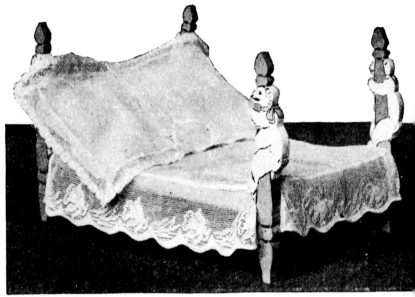

Illustration 698. Toys made by convalescent soldiers following World War I.

"This is just the kind of doll's bed that one has always wished for. Up each 10½-inch blue post climbs a playful Teddy Bear, with bright pink bow round his chuffy neck. Headpieces, 10½ by ¾ inches, are glued into slits at top, and 15-inch pieces into other slits for sides. Through tiny holes bored in the side pieces, strings are woven from side to side to hold the mattress."

"These Christmas Toys," *Ladies' Home Journal,* 1920

Illustration 697. Schoenhut Teddy Bear is a figural block of wood with reverse side showing a doll. From a set of Alfy Blocks made 1911-1934. Approximately 5 in. (12.7cm) tall and 1 in. (2.5cm) thick. *Child Life* magazine stated they could be used for building, spelling and ten pins. *Beverly Port Collection. Photograph by Beverly Port.*

Illustration 699. Card game, size 5¾ in. (14.5cm) x 4-3/8 in. (11.1cm). Milton Bradley Company. Circa 1920.

Illustration 700. Montgomery Ward catalog, 1929.

Wood Cradle $1⁹⁵

Made Special for Little Teddies

A little bear like 48 E 3161 at right just fits this bed. Strong wood enameled rose pink, blue trim. Size 14 by 8 by 7⅛ high. Colorful wood bear cutouts nailed to sides. **We Pay Postage.**
48 E 3126—
Cradle only. Bear not included.....**$1.95**

295

4770
THREE BEARS

This game comprises nine pairs of cards and one odd card.

The object is not to be left with the card Goldie Locks at the end of the game.

The two cards of a pair have pictures alike. The odd card represents Goldie Locks.

Deal all the cards with faces down, one at a time. The player on the left of the dealer draws a card from his right hand neighbor, and then if possible matches one or more pairs, which he plays face up on the table.

When the player has made all the matches possible, or if he cannot make any, the next player to the left plays in the same manner, and thus the game proceeds till all the pairs are matched, and the player then holding the odd card of Goldie Locks loses the game.

GOLDIE LOCKS

PICKING FLOWERS

BEAR'S HOUSE

FATHER BEAR

MOTHER BEAR

BABY BEAR

GOLDIE LOCKS JUMPING
THROUGH WINDOW

Illustration 701. Milton Bradley company card game, circa 1920.

296

KIRK GUILD OFFERS "WINNIE-THE-POOH" GAME

A. A. Milne's "Winnie-The-Pooh" game, coyprighted by Stephen Slesinger, New York, is being offered the trade by the Kirk Guild, Utica, New York.

The game can be played by two, three or four children. The large table top shows all the Winnie-The-Pooh characters. From the start at "Mr. Saunders" and to the finish at "My House" kiddies manipulating the little bears through the game are thrilled by this latest product of the Kirk Guild.

Toy World magazine, October, 1931.

Illustration 702. Winnie-The-Pooh game, Parker Brothers, 1962.

WINNIE-THE-POOH
Beloved A. A. Milne characters are moved on a picture-story board. No reading, no counting, youngsters play by color. $2.00

Illustration 703. *Toy World* magazine, October, 1931.

Illustration 704. This little wood and composition bear may have been inspired by earlier Schoenhuts. He was manufactured by the Twistum Toy Factory of Oakland, California. The patent date, June 29, 1920, is inscribed on the bottom of his back feet. He is jointed with long coiled springs and can be twisted into many different poses. He has five body parts and is approximately 6 in. (15.2cm) long, is black and tan with painted features. A book copyrighted 1929 by Esther M. Ames and called *Twistum Tales* shows a "Twistum" cat on the cover and there were other animals made including a giraffe, bulldog, rabbit, pig, elephant, and a dinosaur. *Beverly Port Collection. Photograph by Beverly Port.*

Musical Chair

Illustration 705. F.A.O. Schwarz catalog, 1938.

6 Styles—6¼ in., smooth white rubber, painted features and decorations, **with whistle,** cello wrapped. Japanese made.
64-7033—1 doz in box . . . . Doz .80

Illustration 706. Butler Brothers catalog, 1939.

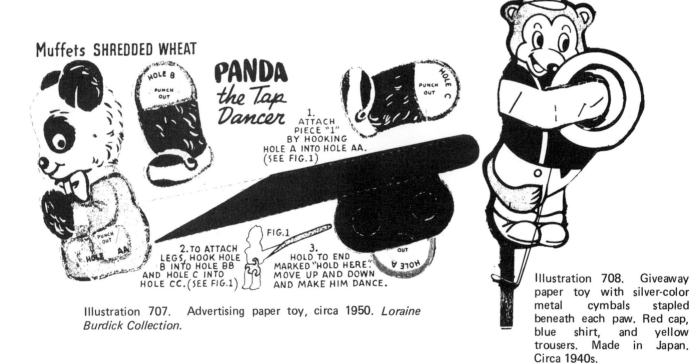

Illustration 707. Advertising paper toy, circa 1950. *Loraine Burdick Collection.*

Illustration 708. Giveaway paper toy with silver-color metal cymbals stapled beneath each paw. Red cap, blue shirt, and yellow trousers. Made in Japan. Circa 1940s.

Illustration 709. 27 in. (68.6cm) overall bear gymnasium with four 3½ in. (8.8cm) bears and a monkey priced at $9.75. F.A.O. Schwarz catalog, 1956.

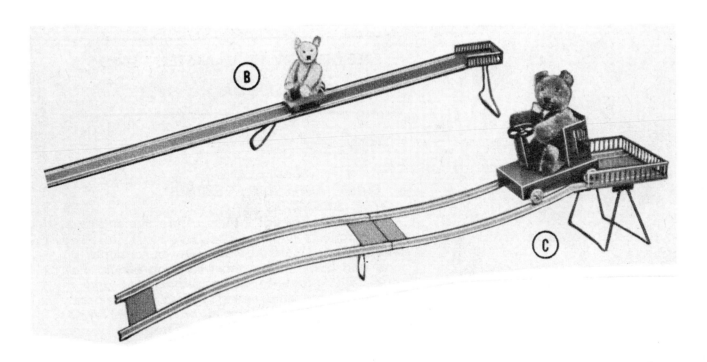

Illustration 710. 30 in. (76.2cm) overall bear roller coaster with 6 in. (15.2cm) bear priced at $4.75. F.A.O. Schwarz catalog, 1956.

Illustration 711. 9 in. (22.9cm) high Teddy Bear slide and three 3½ in. (8.8cm) bears priced at $4.75. F.A.O. Schwarz catalog, 1956.

Illustration 712. 12 in. (30.5cm) Teddy Bear merry-go-round with twin 3½ in. (8.8cm) bears priced at $4.00. F.A.O. Schwarz catalog, 1956.

300

ANIMAL PLAY EQUIPMENT (Exclusive imports) (3 to 6 yr. olds)—Big as a minute but mighty adorable are these cute little Steiff bears with an excellent conformation that is covered with a short cut mohair plush. They have arms, legs and a head that are movable. Small bears are noted for their frolics and here is play equipment for them to enjoy to their hearts content. This well made equipment is of metal and is finished in gleaming red and green enamel.

A 3-101 BEAR MERRY-GO-ROUND $4.00
Twin 3½" brother bears seated in a 12" Merry-Go-Round are excitedly awaiting a fast whirl. Ship. wt. 2 lbs.

3-104 BEAR MERRY-GO-ROUND (Not illustrated) $5.75
Same as above only 16" overall and bears are 6" tall. Ship. wt. 3 lbs.

B 3-110 BEAR ROLLER COASTER $3.00
Happily seated on his coaster is 3½" tall Johnny bear ready to zoom down his 27½" overall roller coaster. Ship. wt. 2 lbs.

C 3-130 BEAR ROLLER COASTER $4.75
This roller coaster has the additional thrill of waves as the playful little 6" bear speeds down the 30" overall roller coaster. Ship. wt. 3 lbs.

D 3-146 BEAR SLIDE $4.75
A set of three fun loving 3½" bears are included with this 9" high slide. Ship. wt. 2 lbs.

E 3-145 BEAR GYMNASIUM $9.75
An endless array of things to do for this group of four 3½" bears and a monkey friend. Gym 27" overall, has ladders, slide, two swings with rings, see-saw and climbing pole. Ship. wt. 3 lbs.

Mr. Robert Zimmerman provides the following information on items related to Theodore Roosevelt, other than Teddy Bears:

" . . . The Rooseveltian influence does not end with the Teddy Bear. Toymakers followed the exploits of T. R. until his death in 1919. An example of this is the Schoenhut "Teddy's Adventures in Africa." After serving out the remainder of McKinley's term of office, and finishing a full term of his own, Roosevelt refused re-election in 1908; thereby fulfilling a campaign promise that he would not run again. Upon turning the presidency over to his chosen heir, William Taft, Roosevelt went into self-exile in Africa with his son Kermit. Following his trek through the Dark Continent was not only the American public but also the A. Schoenhut Company of Philadelphia, Pennsylvania. In 1909 the company marketed their famous "Teddy's Adventures in Africa." This collection of toys made it possible for junior explorers to create, in fantasy, hunting trips in that far off land. The set, which consisted of some 53 pieces, included a gun bearer, a guide, a photographer, several natives and of course, a striking likeness of the former President. Some of the animals that were made for the Teddy in Africa set were undoubtedly given double duty in the Schoenhut Humpty Dumpty Circus. . ."

In 1912 . . .

"Roosevelt formed a third party, dubbing it the "Bull Moose Party." This time the E. I. Horsman Company took a chance on the marketability of T. R. and produced a plush bodied Bull Moose. This toy had the standard jointed body that was used for Puppy Pippen and the head was of the "Can't Break' em" composition. The design of the head was that of a very lifelike moose. Incised on the back of these heads was: E. I. Horsman 1912. . ."

" . . . His death should have marked the end of the Rough Riders influence on the toy world, but from time to time, T. R. toys return to immortalize the former President. Usually these toys are of a Presidential or military nature. There is even a shaving lotion bottle that bears his likeness.

Modern day doll artists are attracted to Roosevelt because of his distinct facial features. The round face, bushy moustache and pince-nez lead to a spectacular characterization found in the early political cartoons. One artist Sculptor tried to reach deeper than the comic-hero of that turn of that century age in order to unearth the real Teddy Roosevelt.

Kathy Redmond, a sculptress who uses the medium of porcelain created a Roosevelt doll that strips away the traditional T. R. image. Feeling that the characterization of the former President was "bigger than life," Ms. Redmond portrays Roosevelt as the young officer of the Rough Riders. Inspiration of this 18" figure came from photographs and prints found in Professor Frank Freidel's book *The Splendid Little War.* The uniform, a close copy of that worn by the men of the New York unit was sewn by Gladys Redmond.

Great men, it is said, are made by great times. If this is true then Theodore Roosevelt arrived at his greatness by mirroring the emotions and desires of America as an emerging world power. His popularity, then and now, stems from his dedication to the American ideals of hard work and fair play. Over the years, toy makers have realized that a man who embodies this spirit is in tune to the American buying public. For this reason it is doubtful that Teddy Roosevelt will ever disappear from the toy and doll scene."

Excerpts reprinted by permission. "A Toy Collector's Historical Perspective: Theodore Roosevelt . . . More Than a Teddy Bear," by Robert W. Zimmerman, *Doll News,* Summer 1978.

Illustration 715.
Advertisement for
Good bears of the
World.

Illustration 713. 1980 Limited
Edition Steiff Bear.

Illustration 714. 1981 Steiff
Limited Edition Mother and
Baby Teddy.

Illustration 716. Left to Right:
Jack Wilson, Chairman of House
of Nesbit, Peter Bull holding
Bully Bear (note distinctive
tag), and Timothy Atkins of
Bear Necessities, a leading teddy
bear sales organization with
shops in Boston (MA), Pitts-
burgh (PA), Boca Raton (FL)
and Providence (RI).

Appendix

SOME TEDDY BEAR MAKERS

The George Borgfeldt & Company firm was sole distributor of Steiff products for many years in the United States.

1909 in London, England, British Teddies could be bought on the spot at a factory called "The Bear Pit," 3 St. Peter's Road, Kingsland, London, N.E.

1909 A firm called Reka (run by M. D. and G. W. Baker) advertised Teeny Tiny Teddy Bear only 3/4 in. (1.8cm) in silver, gold or brown. These were apparently metal as the company also made metal soldiers.

1910 Basset-Lowke *Toys and Novelties.* Bear in brown silk plush, three sizes. Also standing bear with ring in nose.

1913 *Toys and Novelties,* April, attributes first Teddy Bears to German manufacturers. In 1912 the craze hit England, with two million sold which was more than one for each child. In 1913 the craze hit Russia and Japan.

1914 *Toys and Novelties,* May, carried advertisement for Amberg-made bears.

The firm of J. K. Farnell claimed to have made the original Teddy Bears in England which they called "Alpha Bear" designed by Miss Farnell. But there are early records of W. J. Terry of Dalston who made "Terryer Toys" and produced a 1912 Teddy, and the East London Federation (sic) Toy Factory circa 1915, made Teddies.

1915 *Toys and Novelties* contained advertising for the "Original Toy Company," Arthur Gerling being an officer. They manufactured a large variety of Teddy Bears.

1915 *Toys and Novelties,* "Gem Toy Company" made a large line of Teddy Bears, all dollar numbers.

1916 *Toys and Novelties,* February, Teddy Bear shown in Borgfeldt advertisement.

1916 *Toys and Novelties,* March, Strobel and Wilken made a new line of Teddy Bears, "equal to the best imported. No ripped seams. Bears that look like bears, not like monkeys. $3.00 dozen and up."

1918 *Toys and Novelties,* February, firm of E. A. Runnells Co., New York, made Teddy Bears.

1918 *Toys and Novelties,* March, Samuel Gabriel and Sons made Teddy Bears. Patented a "Roly Poly."

1919 American Made Toy Company, Brooklyn, New York, "Mr. Teddy," 15 in. (38.1cm) stands erect. Line of stiff Teddy Bears which stood alone.

1919 *Toys and Novelties,* February, E. Goldberger, full line of Teddy Bears.

1919 *Toys and Novelties,* March, Globe Teddy Bear Company, Brooklyn, New York, "Globe Teddies."

1919 Theodore Hess and Company, New York City. Teddy Bears with a squeak, highest grade plush.

1919 American Toys and Novelty Company, New York City.

1920 *Toys and Novelties,* February, B. Illfelder and Company.

1920 *Toys and Novelties,* Electra Toy and Novelty Co., New York.

1920 Standard Toy Company, Brooklyn, New York. Bears, popular sizes at popular prices.

1921 *The Billboard,* Tip Top Toy Company. Electric Eye Bears 22 in. (55.9cm) with ring in nose. The biggest and best quality plush electric bear on the market. All colors.

1921 *The Billboard,* Schoen Toy Mfg. Co., New York City. Electric Eye Bears. Biggest flash on the market. 24 in. (61cm) finest plush.

1921 *Toys and Novelties,* February, Ross and Ross, California. Mrs. Brown Bear and her cub each wear a leather collar. Also a cart in which Mr. Teddy reposes dressed in a red vest with pockets and a black necktie.

1921 *Toys and Novelties,* February, Meakin and Ridgeway, New York City. Importers of stuffed bears from an English manufacturer.

1921 *Toys and Novelties,* Ideal made walking Teddy Bears of long or short pile plush in 16 in. (40.6cm), 18 in. (45.7cm), 22 in. (55.9cm) and 24 in. (61cm).

1921 *Toys and Novelties,* April, Globe Teddy Bear Company, Brooklyn, New York. "The largest Teddy Bear Mfgrs. in the World, est. 1908." Brown, white, cinnamon, etc. with long and short pile plush. 16 in. - 24 in. (40.6cm - 61cm) whistling Teddies with voices in forepaw, a patented feature. "Bear whistles when you shake its hand." 10 in. - 24 in. (25.4cm - 61cm) bears with voice in body.

1922 *The Billboard,* Electric Eye Bears 22 in. (55.9cm), silk ribbon around body. Leather collar around neck. Complete with bulbs, battery and cord.

1923 Hitz, Jacobs and Kassler. Catalog on bears. U. S. Department of Commerce Report.

1924 Bureau of Foreign and Domestic Commerce, No. 267, page 4: Waltershausen Area: "The first dolls made in this center had cloth bodies and limbs of papier mache. . . .This type of doll led to the bringing out of the plush and other textile-covered stuffed animals. The German version of the Teddy bear was first made here by Robert Unger. The doll industry in Waltershausen originated over 100 years ago." (1924-100=1824).

1929 *Toys and Novelties,* Knickerbocker Toy Company, New York City. "Americas Premier Line of Stuffed Animals."

1929 *Toys and Novelties,* Mr. and Mrs. Woolnough for 21 years designers and manufacturers of Woolnough stuffed animals.

1929 *Toys and Novelties,* Gay Stuffed Toy and Novelty Co., Brooklyn, New York.

1931 *Toy World* magazine, Gund Manufacturing Company featuring the "Gee" line of stuffed animals.

1931 *Toy World* magazine, American Made Toy Co., New York. A wide range of exclusive stuffed toy specialties.

1932 *Toy World* magazine, Sam Rosenthal, New York. Musical stuffed toys. "Our toys produce a continuous loud musical sound at a jerk of a chain that is attached to jaw, or a jerk on the head; and the head moves at the same time. All sizes Teddy Bears, Elephants, Dogs, Cats, etc."

1933 The Teddy Toy Company, England, were advertising "Winnie the Pooh" at this time.

Peggy Nisbet produced Teddies based on the original Chad Valley designs. Mr. Roger Swinburne Johnson, Managing Director, was the grandson of the original Chad Valley Johnson. Information from Mary Hillier.

not be able to hold them down for the next five years. There are three times as many toys imported by Santa Claus as he ever brought in up to this date. He stores his things so as to have them handy for distrubution on Christmas eve. One store has already received five times as many toys as it imported all last year, and the papers show that more are on the way. The big feature of the toy business next season will be the Teddy bear. There are thousands here already."

One hundred great cases of toys were cleared through the custom house the other day."

Playthings, 1907.

TEDDY BEARS BURN.

"Thanksgiving Day was a sad day for the Teddy bears. Schwartz's toy store on Sixth avenue was the scene of an early morning fire, and before the flames could be checked more bears than Roosevelt ever dreamed of, besides many more valuable toys, had passed into ashes. The damage to the building will total up to about five thousand dollars, while the loss of toys and Teddy bears, which were being displayed in large quantities, will take a thousand dollars to replace."

Playthings, 1907.

CHILDREN'S PARADISE MOVES.

"Schwartz's Toy Bazaar, which has been catering to the younger element of Brooklyn for nearly forty years, was moved last month to 517-519 Fulton street, almost directly opposite the old location. They have taken a ten-year lease on the new premises, and now have a frontage of 40 feet and a depth of 100 feet. This new store is right next to the old Chapman department store, recently discontinued, but it is understood that a concern has rented the Chapman building and will open up soon a first-class department store. The new Schwartz establishment has been handsomely fitted up, and presents an even more attractive place for the children to visit. Their show windows are always filled with interesting things, which are displayed with much taste."

Playthings, 1907.

BEARS DOING STUNTS.

"In one of the Broadway show windows there are a lot of Teddy Bears up to various tricks, but most prominent of all are a couple of prize fighters. These two figures are standing in a ring, and are dressed in true pugilistic fashion, with tiny boxing gloves, etc. The other bears standing around look highly pleased with the performance, as do also the throngs that pass the window. In another window a few blocks further up the street there is a beautiful display of various plush animals dressed up in the most gorgeous costumes of velvet, lace, etc. They are arranged in such attractive positions that they gain the admiration of thousands of passers-by."

Playthings, 1907.

GETTING EVEN.

"While enjoying himself watching a trained bear recently a youngster got too close to the animal, and was suddenly seized by Bruin, who hugged him to his breast, nearly squeezing the life out of the lad. It seems only right, though, for boys have been hugging bears steadily for the past year or so. This, like many other thrilling things, happened in Belvidere, N.J."

Playthings, 1907.

THOUSANDS OF TEDDY BEARS.

"If the records of the customs houses are to be believed, Kansas City is a regular menagerie. It is none of the business of the surveyor of the port what is to be done with the things brought into the country; all that concerns him is that he gets the customs duties. Recently there were cleared through the customs house 609 bears, 5 goats, 6 cats and 8 "Toms," so the manifest read, though nobody knows what "Toms" are.

"The place won't be fit to live in," Surveyor C. W. Clarke asserted as he looked over the clearance papers.

"That is not the worst of it," said Ed. Levy, one of the customs house officers. "We have already inspected about 15,000 bears before this lot came in."

"It will be positively dangerous to spend the winter in Kansas City," was the conclusion of the surveyor.

But he did not know what he was talking about. The government knows considerable about running itself, and it employs a number of capable people, but when it comes to bears and things like that it is nonsense to have men inspect the imports. There is not a child in Kansas City that could not have told the surveyor and all his crew of customs house officers that the bears are of the Teddy variety. When Surveyor Clarke finally learned that through the medium of a little child, who heard the agitated statement of the customs house officers, he admitted that he had been fooled.

"But I will tell you," said Surveyor Clarke, "Santa Claus is overdoing it this year. He is going to spoil the children hereabouts. We will

TEDDY STUFFERS GALORE.

"Whether they had taken recent nature-faking sermons to heart, or whether some malicious person just blew a whistle, has not yet been ascertained, but a number of Teddy bear stuffers went on strike the other day and attempted to tie up a great industry. Just as the telegraph operators quit on the dot and dash, the bruin workers quit on the last stuff, left their chairs, and went away.

They left a pitiable scene behind them: Teddy bears without ears; Teddy bears without legs; sightless, noseless, jointless Teddy bears; and—greater woe!—Teddy bears without that important adjunct which Mr. Barrie has feelingly referred to as the "Little Mary," and which gives to the toy that rotundity at the belt line so endearing to the heart of childhood.

Teddy bears that looked live over-earnest devotees of the Fletcher cult; Teddy bears that seemed to have hibernated too long and fed too religiously on their paws, according to the belief of little boys and girls who know their nature-fakes; poor, emaciated Teddy bears, who yearned for sawdust and got only a taste of the "union idea."

The factory of the Bruin Manufacturing Company, at No. 497 Broome Street, was the scene of the trouble. Ordinarily, with conditions just right, one Teddy bear springs into being in that uncanny laboratory every minute through the working day. One shaggy "enemy of the maternal instinct," to quote the harsh statement of the enemy, gets stuffed, eared, legged, eyed, shaved and boxed every sixty seconds, by the clock.

First the cutter makes the preliminary form; and from that time the bear goes through twenty-one processes before it is in a shape to supplant the doll in the affections of a healthy child. Almost the last process is the stuffing. Limp, hungry-looking, and wild of eye, the Teddy bear comes to the table where the stuff of which stage Falstaffs are made is inserted. The angles are filled out with excelsior and silken floss by workmen of tender years, but of usually great earnestness. They are the stuffers—the stuffers who struck.

Stuffing, according to Mrs. Sakman, who manages the Bruin Manufacturing Company for the greater joy of childhood, and for other reasons—stuffing is unskilled labor. Anybody can stuff Teddy bears. Mrs. Sakman stuffed a bear just to show how easy it was. Then the young workman (non-union), who was at the bench, stuffed one to show how much quicker he was than Mrs. Sakman. Then the visitor stuffed one to show that he was somebody. Mrs. Sakman continued:

"You see, I can get all the stuffers I want. It isn't anything to be learned. Why, even you can stuff them. [The visitor bowed, and forgave the 'even.'] So when they struck last night I was not worried.

"They get good wages. One of them can make $12 to $14 a week on piece work by application and an ordinary amount of skill. First I had them on salary. Then they wanted to work on 'piece,' and I let them; and when I found out that they turned out three times as much in the same time, naturally I was annoyed. So I cut down the piece price, still giving them what I thought was good wages for that kind of work. The cutter there made $43 last week. That's not bad, is it?"

"Ah, but cutting Teddy bears is almost a work of genius, isn't it?"

"No; if there's any genius here, it's me. I do the designing. That's the skillful part. Besides, the lady over in Nuremberg, who invented the bear—she ought to get the credit, if there is any."

"Are there many Teddy bear factories in New York?"

"Do you mean to tell me that you don't know anything about the Teddy bear business?" was the answer. "Why, I should say there are. You've no idea of the number of people who are making bears. We have all we can possibly do to supply our customers; and we can't move into bigger quarters, because there isn't time."

Mrs. Sakman was patient, good-natured, and obliging. She was worried, though. Over the strike? Not at all. She was trying to think how in the world she was going to make her rabbits for the regular Easter rabbit trade next year. The Teddy bear is just simply driving all other toys out of the market, because there is no time to make them. It wouldn't surprise any one who knows if all the little girls and boys carried Teddy bears to the egg-rollings next Easter; and that will be a puzzling paradox, surely.

The Teddy bears are expensive, as perhaps those who have bought them know best. The fur is made of mohair, and the workmanship is excellent. And, by the way, as a finishing touch to the making of the bear, what do you suppose they do? Shave him! The "finisher," after scratching the hair with a fine tooth comb, to make it stand up, all fuzzy and belligerent, shaves the muzzle with a barber's clipper.

As Mrs. Sakman said, there is no dearth of those who are anxious to learn how to make Teddy bears. The strikers' places are filled to-day. In the queer room on Broome Street, Teddies are being cut, sewed and stuffed into existence with regular precision. And all through the morning there were plenty of applicants for places, prospective strike-breakers, "stuffers on bears," as the trade has it.

An enterprising Japanese was among the early-comers. He greeted Mrs. Sakman with one of those mystic Oriental smiles, and said, as though he was conveying a bit of pleasant information: "Lady, I am able to stuff the bears of Teddy. I am an honorable stuffer." But there was no work for the honorable stuffer."

Playthings, 1907.

THE HIT OF TOYDOM.

"The Lewis Waller Mercantile Co., who operate the toy department of the Dayton Dry Goods Co. at Minneapolis, have put into operation the scheme of schemes for a toy department. Our illustration of their Live Teddy Bear will prove that assertion with question. The Live Teddy is advertised to greet the children every afternoon at 4:30. But let us quote from the originator of this pulling attraction: "I had the suit made last July but did not put it in operation until a couple of weeks ago (about November 25th), having difficulty in getting a boy that would exactly fit it. I have now picked one up who is excellent for the purpose, being very bright and witty, which makes the bear doubly attractive. We handle it as a basement attraction, and have him meet the children every afternoon at 4:30 and every Saturday afternoon and evening, at intervals of about an hour. He also takes a trip of several blocks down Nicelet Ave. every day, though I take the precaution of having a man near him every moment, in order to protect him from newsboys, and assist him across the streets, as he cannot see on either side very distinctly. The suit is made up in a regular bear fashion, being perfect in every detail. The parts were shipped to me separately, and made up here to fit the lad, it being arranged now so that it hooks up the front clear to the nose, while a little opening around the mouth furnishes sufficient air for breathing. The eyes are merely holes cut in the proper places, as we thought it impracticable to place glass eyes on the outside. As to results I can only say that it has attracted an immense amount of attention throughout the city, and brings children and their parents into our toy basement in large numbers. It also attracts considerable attention on the streets, and we have a sign on his back reading, 'I am Teddy from Dayton's basement; come see my brothers,' and several other signs interchanging them frequently. We also have letters from children in the city, requesting us to let the bear come to lunch with them, asking what he eats, etc., which indicates a general interest among the juvenile element." Teddy got himself written up in the local press, with a picture showing him with one of his baby brothers in his arms. He saunters down the street stopping to gravely shake the hand of every guardian of the peace, looking into the shop windows, and submitting gracefully to the rather demonstrative ovations offered him by the ladies. In fact, he is said to have Hobson backed off the board when it comes to the kissing game."

Playthings, 1907.

THE BEAR MARKET.

In our issue of November, 1906, we said: "Just now bears occupy the center of the stage, and in spite of every effort on the part of domestic and foreign manufacturers, the demand cannot be met. One hears much speculation as to the future of these amusing toys—some people going so far as to assert that after Christmas they will drop with a dull thud. We think the only thud that will be heard in the trade will be the frantic knocking of these same pessimists at the doors of the importers and commission houses in their efforts to get bears. The import line is practically all sold up as far ahead as April. Perhaps that tells the story in the fewest possible words."

The other day a PLAYTHINGS representative called upon a man who had told him last November that bears would drop out of sight after the first of the present year. This same man is now of the opinion that bears will be even scarcer this Fall than they were last year, and this time he is nearer to being right. After a careful canvass of the market, it seems to be established that in spite of the enormous increase in the manufacture of bears, not only in this country, but abroad, there will be an even more serious shortage this year than last. It is a fact well known to the trade that the factory which introduced the jointed plush bear has increased its manufacturing facilities to an enormous extent. It is also reported that in addition to more than quadrupling their factory force, they have had many bears made in other places in an attempt to keep up with the demand for their product. In spite of the fact that other manufacturers abroad, and large ones, too, have taken up the manufacture of bears, it is now stated as a positive fact that deliveries on import orders will be very much behind-hand. Certain far-seeing buyers placed heavy orders in Germany for bears, buying them outright. We have been informed that three houses in this city placed orders which would aggregate a

half million dollars. Then came an avalanche of import orders which fairly swamped the manufacturer. In this country there are dozens of factories now manufacturing bears. Practically every large city in the United States contains two or more factories, while many smaller places can also boast of a place where Teddy bears are being made up for the market.

In spite of this there is still a distinct shortage for immediate delivery, and it is stated on every side that as the season progresses the shortage will become more pronounced. The difficulty lies not so much in making the bears themselves as in getting the proper variety of plush with which to make them. It will be remembered that this was the main difficulty last year, as far as the domestic manufacturer was concerned. It would be a very difficult matter to compute the total sales of bears in this country, but they will certainly run into the millions. Orders from the Pacific coast are now coming in in a way to astonish even the most optimistic manufacturers.

In view of these conditions, we would strongly advise buyers to watch their deliveries on bears carefully, and to make sure that they will not be left without an adequate supply when the season is in full swing."

Playthings, 1907.

"Just at present the trade seems to be greatly agitated as to the future of the Teddy bear; will it be a big seller this fall, or will the sales diminish or drop away to any marked degree? Inquiries have poured in on us from every side, and widely varying views have been expressed. All that we have to say can be summed up in a very few words, we stand on the Teddy bear question just exactly where we have stood for the past year, and that is firmly in the belief that bears have come to stay and that sales this year, at all seasons and at any particular season, will be better than last year. It is true that at the seaside resorts bears are not selling nearly as well as they did last year, and in certain localities the demand is almost at a stand-still, but in other places sales are so heavy as to more than make up for the slowness in some of the Eastern towns and cities where, last year, the demand could not be met. Just now the heaviest demand comes from the West, orders from Chicago showing up exceedingly well, while the Pacific coast seems unable to get enough. The explanation is easy; last year the supply was so short that sales in any quantity were confined to comparatively few localities, not because there was not a demand in other places, but because the more distant points did not begin to feel the demand until it was too late to get the goods in anything like sufficient quantities. Eastern buyers, being right on the market all the time, snapped up the goods as soon as they arrived, so that there was not much left over for distant buyers. Then again, the Teddy bear as a fad for grown-up people was doomed to a short life from the very start. Of course, women still fondle the cunning little bruins, but perhaps most of the women who are inclined this way are now supplied, and the bear is a sturdy little chap who does not "lose his head" or any other part of him very easily. But the great West has not begun to be supplied with enough bears for immediate consumption..."

Playthings, 1907.

An Apostle of the Big Family

"One of the greatest curses of this country," says the Rev. Michael G. Esper, of St. Joseph, Michigan, "is the one-child family." Father Esper holds that the avoidance of care, expense and responsibility and the love of ease and pleasure is "a common American disease, very contagious at that." In one of his speeches that has lately attracted considerable attention, he said that the Teddy bear craze was bad for little girls and tended to destroy some of that maternal instinct of which the country stands in such need. He went on to say that the mother-instinct is going out of fashion anyway, and that this was helped by the substitution of bears instead of dollies that have to be dressed and undressed and loved and kissed in the good old way.

Certainly the Teddy bears have found favor only among the little girls in America, for a German captain who recently brought over a cargo of them, made in the Fatherland for American consumption, said that the girls over there can't be persuaded to give up cuddling their dolls. So the bears come over here, where, Father Esper says, maternal instinct is dying out even so far as the poor dolls are concerned.

The Delineator, December, 1907.

LONG LIVE THE TEDDY BEAR ! ! !
THE DOLL WILL LIVE FOREVER ! ! !

"Race Suicide," declares a Michigan divine in a recent sermon, "is being fostered, developed and even encouraged by the popular but harmless Teddy Bear." This innocent toy is denounced in vigorous terms by the learned gentleman, in fact, he goes so far as to term them as "bundles of horridness," and certainly reaches the climax when he asserts that the Teddy Bear is destroying all instincts of motherhood in the little girl, who now prefers it to her doll. How much has the doll been slighted by the bear? Little, if any, as is proved by the fact that there will be more dolls imported to this country in 1907 than in any previous year.

While, of course, all the toy trade will agree that the Teddy Bear has become a craze, it is hard to see how a doll should foster the maternal instinct and the bear destroy it. The Michigan alarmist perhaps forgets that the "little mother" has a fondness for puppies, kittens and a variety of other animal toys and she cuddles and kisses them all. There is but one mother instinct and that is surely of sufficient proportion to cover each and every one of the small girl's "babies" she loves so dearly. If a child prefers the cute woolly bear, she does so because it is something new and gently lays away the favorite doll for the time being, and the bear receives that same motherly care that the doll shares and always will. (And just as soon as some now unknown stuffed animal will appear, she will be forever done with Teddy Bear, but her doll will never be forgotten.) There is indeed no difference between the care she bestows upon the doll and that which she gives the Teddy Bear; in fact it is a "square deal" all the way through, for does she not scold and love, and rock them both to sleep, and how often are not both doll and bear cuddled in one bed with the little mother. The doll is not a menace to the future of the race, and we need have but little fear for the harmful influence of Mr. Teddy Bear.

Long Live the Teddy Bear—The Doll will live forever!

ARTHUR B. MALLETT.

Boston Store, Milwaukee, Wis.

Playthings, 1907.

"Stuffed animal toys this season are unusually complete. Toy dogs, with long, shaggy coats, Pomeranians, sky terriers, Angora cats, bears, elephants, monkeys and all other stuffed toys, which in previous years were to be found only in the imported stock, are now to be seen in every size, variety and color among the domestic lines. The perfection of manufacture shown in the stuffed animal toy of to-day make it widely popular during all seasons, and unquestionably one of the leading staple toys. The bear, dog, cat and other toy pets should be fully as important a factor in the retail trade during the coming months as they have been in the past. Bears, of course, are no longer a craze; but they are proving good sellers, especially in the West and Central West and in all localities where Roosevelt is greatly admired. The wonderful run of the bear has brought into prominence all other stuffed-animal pets, instigating a strong demand for the line as a whole, which did not exist before the advent of the bear. It is now up to the makers of toys to watch carefully the trend of national sentiment towards the next President and to launch a toy upon the market that will fit as closely to some characteristic or hobby of the man as does the Teddy bear with a favorite hobby of Roosevelt."

Playthings, 1908.

"TIGE" DOGS.

"Following after the Teddy bear, and carrying further the popular idea of stuffed animals for household pets, came the "Tige" dogs. Although not associated with any political celebrity (for which fact certain mortals may well be thankful), "Tige" has many points that recommend him."

Playthings, 1908.

"Every small boy has an intense love for masquerade and make-believe, and any garment which is given him for this purpose becomes one of his most cherished possessions. Firemens' suits, policemens' uniforms and more lately Indian suits have created some thing of a furore in lines of this kind, and now that the small boy can obtain a Teddy Bear suit his delight should be without bounds. The trade is now offered these outfits in three colors of bear skin, cinnamon, brown and white. They come in three sizes for boys of 4, 6 and 8 years of age respectively. Perfectly constructed of extra quality skin in every particular, they make an ideal Christmas gift for any youngster. The trousers are full length and fasten with a draw string, while the six-button jacket has pockets for sundry articles which bears always carry around with them on foraging expeditions. These Teddy Bear suits are not only suitable for every-day play, they offer the stage manager of juvenile plays endless opportunities for the introduction of Teddy Bears into the cast of characters."

Playthings, 1908.

"RICHARD STEIFF - - The Inventor of the Teddy Bear in America"

Richard Steiff, senoir member of the famous firm of Margarete Steiff, Ltd., of Giengen-Brenz, Germany, is at present in this country for the purpose of getting better acquainted with American trade methods and to secure ideas for new toys suitable for this market.

A representative of *Playthings* found Mr. Steiff busily engaged in experimenting with a Steiff Roloplan from the roof of the Geo. Borgfeldt & Co. building. When asked as to his purpose in visiting this country Mr. Steiff stated that he wished to become more familiar with the class of toys desired by American children and also to get better acquainted with the business methods of the American toy trade. He is going over the ground very carefully and has already secured ideas for many new things, which will be brought out at a later date.

The Teddy Bear, which took the toy world by storm, was invented by Richard Steiff in 1902. It did not become popular in this country during the first few years of its existence (1903-1904-1905), but when it once took hold it did so with a vengeance. The name was given to it in this country and undoubtedly had much to do with its wonderful popularity.

Later Mr. Steiff brought out the unbreakable character doll, which has proven to be one of the biggest sellers in the market.

For many years the factory of Margarete Steiff, Ltd., was famous for its felt toys. The fundamental principle which has always been faithfully carried out by this factory is that the child should have durable and harmless playthings. This idea is applied to all of the goods they manufacture. Stuffed animals of all kinds, dolls of many descriptions and of all sizes, the Roloplan kite which flies almost perpendicular above the head of the flier and many other toys which are the product of this remarkable factory carry out the principle of the firm.

The notable new factory at Giengen-Brenz is a product of the brains of Richard Steiff. It is built almost entirely of metal and glass, in the plainest and most severe style of architecture, completely lacking those fundamental minarets and decorations which are so noticeable in German architecture. The building was erected with the idea of getting the greatest possible efficiency out of it. The floors are identical and the roof is perfectly flat. The amount of light throughout the building is the maximum which could possibly be obtained. Mr. Steiff had considerable difficulty in carrying out his ideas, as at first he was refused permission to erect a building."

Playthings, March, 1912.

MARGARETE STEIFF Born 1847 died 1909, creator of the world's first cuddly soft toy animals for children, was the founder of the present firm Margarete Steiff Ltd having the Button in the ear as trademark.

Margarete Steiff was an extremely gifted woman whose natural talents were stimulated by a great physical handicap, as she was paralyzed (victim of polio) and spent practically all of her life in a wheelchair. She was totally deprived of the use of her right arm. In spite of her tragic misfortune she courageously adapted herself to earn a living as a skilled seamstress.

Her brother's nine children were her immediate interest, and like many aunts, she enjoyed giving them little presents. Her means were limited, imagination and skill had to make up for it: Seventy years ago felt was a new material, and its special elasticity gave her an idea. She would sew a toy elephant and stuff it attractively with some elastic material. In 1880 most toys were made of wood or china, and her creations were a real new invention. Her elephant was a great success, and following the many demands for it, she found herself in an entirely new line of business.

She expanded slowly, tried new designs, carefully and lovingly worked out each toy and by 1900 she surrounded herself with a small group of skilled workers, which she herself had personally trained. All day long her wheelchair rolled from one to the other, while she supervised and explained the various processes, so that at the end each animal would be as perfect as if she had put in every stitch herself.

Meanwhile she had begun to draw her brother and his sons into the business. Many of the boys had her talents for form and construction, and in 1903 her nephew Richard Steiff, using some sketches of bear cubs he had made in art school, created the world's first Teddy Bear.

STEIFF TOYS are made by hand, each process of desigining, cutting, sewing, stuffing, painting, being parcelled out in such a manner that factory efficiency and personal care are best combined. After the designers have created the pattern, it is given to the cutting room, where skilful cutters sitting at long tables patiently snip a thousand intricate shapes from the long bolts of plush. In the sewing room, the pieces are then firmly and accurately put together and handed on to be stuffed, special care being given to the correctness of each individual form, not too hard, not too soft, so as to bring out the typical shape for each species of animal. The last touches are often the most important, and much care is exercised in painting a kitten's ear as carefully as any discriminating lady would do hers for a very important "evening out". Then the nostrils have to be set well, the eyebrows, the eyelashes, the whiskers, the claws and tails, the mottling and striping and spotting that bring out each animal's true life and charm.

Margarete Steiff's feeling for quality and workmanship has always been maintained. Steiff Toys can take it. Their seams don't give, their eyes don't fall out. The mohair plush they are made of is the finest Angora goat hair, strong, silky-smooth, and durable therefore dirt resistant. It can be cleaned with soap-foam, though dry cleaning is recommended. The stuffing is elastic but soft and hygienically absolutely safe. Every animal where the size allows it, has its own appropriate voice. All the coloring used is non-poisonous in case a toy gets too many kisses.

The riding animals are mounted on steel frames, capable of carrying even grown ups. The wheels for these animals are permanently made on and do not come off, and the rubber tires do not mar either floors or furniture. After ten years of being violently loved, a Steiff Toy may need a little re-rouging of its pink nose, but that's all.

Many of the people who work for Margarete Steiff have worked there all their lives. And they all realize what is expected of them. It is not easy to translate the flowing lines of a living creature into pieces of plush and felt which when assembled will again spring forth with grace and vigor. However the Steiff designers have solved these problems over and over again, and all their animals, cat, dog, duck, deer, horse, are astonishing by their sturdy elegance.

Excellent materials and good design, so obvious at first glance, are united by the best of craftsmanship. Seventy years of a tradition of such teamwork cannot be transplanted or imitated, because there is no substitute for it.

The toys Margarete Steiff Ltd turns out every year have all the honesty and grace that really good things have. And led by the Teddy Bear, who has already bounced to his own sure immortality, the parade of her toys is a proud one.

EXPLANATION OF NUMBERS

Each figure has its meaning: series, posture, covering, height in cm, outfit. The figure before the line means the series (kind of animal) = 12/5328,2 after the line:

Thousands	=Posture	
1 - - -	=standing	1343,2
2 - - -	=lying	2312
3 - - -	=sitting	3317
4 - - -	=begging	4322
5 - - -	=jointed	5322
6 - - -	=young	6522
7 - - -	=grotesque	7314
Hundreds	**=Covering**	
- 3 - -	=mohair plush	3317
- 4 - -	=velvet	6412
- 5 - -	=wool plush	6522
- 8 - -	=wood	895
Tens and Units	**=Height in cm**	
- - 22	=22 cm high incl. head	
	2½ cm = 1 inch	
after the comma = outfit		
- - - - ,0	=without wheels	
- - - - ,2	=good voice, automatic voice or pull voice	
- - - - ,ex	=excentric wheels	

PLEASE INDICATE:
Name of animal and number
or serie and number
Example: Teddy   5328,2
    or   12/5328,2
            (12=Teddy)

"HELEN SIEVERLING'S METHOD FOR CLEANING AND PRESERVING TEDDY BEARS"

Prepare wash water by mixing one capful of Woolite in two cups tap water. Prepare rinse water by mixing one-half cap Downey Fabric Softener in three cups regular tap water. (This is not meant to endorse products. The above mentioned are the ones I use; you may have other favorites.)

You will need a brush - - a rubber backed poodle brush from a pet store is best. Use very gently. You will also need a hair blow dryer, a soft tooth brush and a soft terry cloth towel.

Begin on Teddy's head by applying soapy mixture with soft brush in swirling motions as well as back and forth. Never do this roughly; be very gentle. After going over the entire head, take the terry cloth which has been wrung out of the rinse mixture and wipe up excess Woolite making sure the rinse cloth has touched every fiber of Teddy's coat. This insures softness.

Continue by washing and rinsing the entire torso and then do each leg in the same manner. You will notice that by using this method only the fur and backing cloth becomes wet. Teddy's stuffing remains dry and mildew will not occur.

Now you are ready to brush the fur gently as little or as much as you desire. Be careful with the poodle brush as wet cloth could tear with any rough handling. You may bring out as much fluffiness as you like.

After you finish brushing Teddy Bear he is ready to be blown dry. It is sheer joy to see Teddy restored to healthy cleanliness. You will be delighted to love and cuddle him.

He is now ready for a little sunshine for more thorough drying. Put him in a sunny, airy place for maybe two days in a row. Bring indoors before late afternoon and put out again next day. (Authors note: never leave out on a day you have called a charitable organization to pick up used clothing or furniture. A treasured Teddy was inadvertently bearnapped in this manner.) Teddy will still look old, if he is, with his worn spots from years of love, but he is clean and preserved to love for our children's children to love and enjoy.

If you prefer Teddy Bear with years of dirt and who knows what on his person, I must remind you that insects are attracted to and eat only dirty things. Watch carefully for these enemies. It would be sad to lose your wonderful Bears as well as your investment. Teddy Bear has been around for quite a while so let's preserve him forever.

Author's note: another collector uses carpet shampoo for her bear spruce-ups, following directions on can. Some bears that appear to have not too much fur appear much thicker once clean. This does not apply to threadbare cases, naturally.

STEIFF ADDENDA - - HISTORY
Steiff Production Figures
1880 - - six elephants
1885 - - 596 elephants
1886 - - 5,066 elephants
1886 - - added monkey, donkey, horse,
        pig, camel
1893 an agent sells the toys at Leipzig,
    and the first catalog is issued.
Leipzig Fair - - 1903 "Friend Petz," the
    first jointed bear is shown.
Nearly one million bears are sold in 1907.

Addenda: "HISTORY"

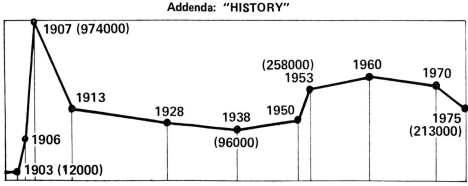

Steiff Production Curve — 1903-1975

HAVE YOU EVER PERFORMED A GROWLECTOMY?*
Robert Tynes

Unfortunately, none of the medical journals discuss growlectomies. In fact, to my knowledge there is nothing, or very little, written about this very serious and delicate operation. After having been involved in a number of these procedures I can now understand why. The answer is quite clear. How can you discuss something that is always different? Each time I perform a growlectomy I approach it with a kind of dread: "Why?" you ask. Because I never know just what to expect when the patient is opened as there seems to be an endless variety of squeakers, growlers, and so forth. Each one is an uncharted island needing new and different procedures and each bear seems to have a different type of "voice." To date, I am happy to say that all my patients are again leading normal lives and growling away. (Actually, most of them squeak. But we mustn't talk about that!) This is said not in vanity, though I am proud of my record, but rather out of thankfulness. It would pain me greatly to have to sew up a hopeful bearson without being able to put him into shape again. After all, if Teddy Bears were not meant to growl, man never would have discovered the secret of how to do it.

About repairing growlers: Basically, one has to "play it by ear." First examine the covering, which may be paper, starched fabric, or kid. If there is only a tear, often just a patch is all that is necessary to put it back into working condition again. When the covering is extremely torn or the leather is cracking and brittle you will have to replace it. Remember to make notes and sketches of the squeaker if this is the case. It is very important to measure how thick it is before removing the outer material. The cylinder or box needs to be returned to its original thickness so that there is the same tension for the inner spring as before. If you use leather, use the thin kid from ladies' gloves. With paper, one often has to try different weights. One squeaker which I mended using paper did not work. After the paper was changed several times, it worked beautifully. Which is one of the reasons that the repairs are approached with dread.

It is not until you have finished that you know if it works or not, as the cylinders must be completely sealed before they produce sound. The growler framework might be heavy cardboard or thin wood and often glued inside is a piece of reed with a sliver of embedded brass. If this is bent, it just needs to be flattened out again. For any mending I use hide glue, obtainable from an art or hardware store. It is a bit more work to use but worth the trouble since the growlers were put together with this type of adhesive. The thing that I find interesting is the endless variety of sound boxes made. In fact, I rarely find any two exactly the same.

The entire process, you will find, is mostly trial and error. Go slowly and have great patience. It is not much fun to do but it affords a great deal of pleasure and satisfaction when you successfully finish and find your bear growling again.

---

*Growlectomy—word borrowed from THE TEDDY BEAR BOOK, by Peter Bull. Random House, 1969-1970. By permission *DOLL NEWS* and author.

BEARS IN COLLECTIONS

We asked and received permission to print parts of Patricia Rowland's letter in response to a plea for help with the book in "Good Bears of the World."

Dear Pat,

It's such a pleasure to meet someone interested in the same things that can speak your language. I enjoyed our telephone conversation and hope that someday we may have a chance to meet each other in person. I have been interested in Teddy Bears for several years, and like yourself, began collecting them when it wasn't the thing to do. Unfortunately, because it is the trend old bears are becoming harder and harder to find. On the other hand, because Teddy Bears are becoming so popular again, there are some beautifully made bears on the market today and every so often I splurge on myself. Although I don't remember ever having a Teddy Bear when I was a little girl, I've always loved them. I am especially fond of old bears because they "talk" to me in a different way than all the rest. Their faces are so full of expression they look as if they could speak, they would tell you wonderful stories, and perhaps even sad stories, about who they were, where they were from and where they had been. The unhappy, grumpy looking characters might tell of neglect, being put through all sorts of indignities, or the horrible experiences of abuse and perhaps even torture. The love-worn, but happy looking ones, might tell about exciting adventures they had with the boy or girl who loved them and how they came to "find" you.

I hope I have been of some help to you already and will gladly help you in any way that I can. I have never been lucky enough to be able to help someone who is writing a book and for me it is a special honor. If you do decide to use some of my pictures, it will be a thrill to see some of my bears in print. I'm excited about your book and have been hoping for a long, long time that someone would write

a reference and study book donated entirely to Teddy Bears and related items. We've needed one for a long time and I wish you all the success for a great book.

Happy Bearing,
Patricia Rowland

P.S. I'm especially happy to know that you are a member of the Good Bears of the World. It makes me feel good to belong to an organization that does such a wonderful thing. Through our combined efforts each one of us is responsible for bringing much needed and deeply appreciated love and happiness into someone's life.

Index

Date Due

APR 2 8 1988	AUG 0 9 1994	
JUN 2 8 1988	NOV 2 0 1994	
JUL 1 9 198	NOV 0 4 2011	
DEC 2 8 1989		
NOV 6 1990		
AUG 2 1 1991		
FEB 2 0 1992		

APR 8 8